Loyalty By Design

Building Teams That Trust You, Back You, and Never Want to Leave

Yavor Aleksiev

FREILING
AGENCY

Published by Freiling Agency, LLC.

P.O. Box 1264
Warrenton, VA 20188

www.FreilingAgency.com

PB ISBN: 9978-1-963701-60-9
HB ISBN: 978-1-963701-64-7
E-book ISBN: 978-1-963701-61-6

Table of Contents

Introduction.. vii

CHAPTER 1   Loyalty Through the Ages 1

CHAPTER 2   Fostering Loyalty... 29

CHAPTER 3   Defining Loyalty 39

CHAPTER 4   Reciprocity 57

CHAPTER 5   Asabiyyah 79

CHAPTER 6   Integrity... 95

CHAPTER 7   Mutual Respect 109

CHAPTER 8   Psychological Safety 125

CHAPTER 9   Proactivity 131

CHAPTER 10   Nurturing Behavior 155

CHAPTER 11   Shared Values.. 171

CHAPTER 12   Benevolence...179

CHAPTER 13   Pride and Advocacy......................................185

CHAPTER 14   Long-Term Perspective 191

CHAPTER 15   Building Culture 199

CHAPTER 16   Conclusion.. 253

References.. 269

About the Authors 291

O, where is loyalty?
If it be banished from the frosty head,
Where shall it find a harbor in the earth?

—William Shakespeare

Introduction

IMAGINE A WORKPLACE WHERE EVERY member feels they belong—where their dedication fuels a lasting culture of mutual loyalty.

Organizations around the world are grappling with unprecedented challenges—globalization, technological disruptions, and shifting workforce demographics, to name a few. Amidst these changes, the traditional notions of employee loyalty are evolving, in part because there's no clear agreement on how to define or measure concepts like engagement and commitment. The days when loyalty was synonymous with long tenure are gone. Today, loyalty is more about a deep-rooted practical dedication to the organization's cause, an act that fuels passion and leads to long-term results.

This book responds to an urgent need to understand loyalty in ways that have been largely overlooked for the past century. It seeks to answer fundamental questions: What drives loyalty in the modern workplace? How can organizations cultivate a culture that inspires unwavering loyalty? And most importantly, how can loyalty be measured in a way that provides actionable insights for leaders and managers?

Loyalty is not just about staying with an organization; it's about being emotionally and intellectually invested in its mission and goals. It's the invisible thread that binds organizational members to their work, their teams, and their leaders through a set of practical collective characteristics. This book explores how to strengthen that thread, turning it into an unbreakable bond that benefits both the individual and the organization."

In an era where the dynamics of the workplace are continuously evolving, understanding the essence of loyalty is more crucial than ever. The purpose of this book is to provide a comprehensive framework for understanding and enhancing loyalty within organizations. By integrating the latest research with practical insights, we aim to equip leaders and managers with the tools they need to cultivate a loyal and committed workforce.

This book seeks to bridge the gap between theoretical constructs and practical applications, offering a nuanced exploration of what loyalty means in the modern organizational context. Through detailed analyses, case studies, and evidence-based strategies, we aim to demystify loyalty, making it a tangible and actionable concept for organizational leaders. By the end of this book, readers will have a clear roadmap for fostering loyalty that enhances employee retention and drives organizational performance and innovation.

As companies navigate the challenges posed by globalization, technological advancements, and demographic shifts, the need for loyal employees has never been greater. Loyalty drives productivity, reduces turnover, and fosters a positive organizational culture, making it a vital component of sustainable success. However, the complexity of loyalty has often been overlooked in favor of more tangible metrics like engagement or job satisfaction.

Loyalty is the glue that holds an organization together, especially in times of uncertainty and change. It is the invisible force that motivates employees to innovate and advocate for their organization. Yet, in many modern workplaces, loyalty is waning. Employees frequently move between jobs, driven by better offers or dissatisfaction with their current roles. This transient workforce poses a significant challenge for organizations seeking stability and long-term success.

This book underscores the importance of loyalty as the bedrock of organizational success. In a time when employees are more mobile and less bound by traditional employment norms, fostering loyalty requires a nuanced understanding of its drivers and manifestations. By delving into these aspects, this book aims to fill a significant gap in the current organizational behavior literature and provide actionable strategies for building enduring loyalty.

Unique Perspective

What sets this book apart is its integrated approach to understanding loyalty. Rather than viewing loyalty as a static trait, we explore it as a dynamic interplay of individual, relational, and organizational factors. This perspective is enriched by drawing from diverse disciplines, including insights from Aristotle, Confucius, Jim Collins, Ibn Khaldun, and Josiah Royce.

Aristotle and Confucius both emphasized the importance of virtues, including loyalty, as central to ethical behavior and social harmony. Aristotle's concept of virtue ethics underscores that loyalty, like other virtues, must be practiced consistently and in balance, ensuring it does not harm any party involved. Similarly, Confucius highlighted the importance of loyalty as a reciprocal and practical virtue, essential for maintaining social order and harmony.

Incorporating these philosophical insights, we also draw from the practical wisdom of Jim Collins' 'Level 5 Leadership,' which highlights how leaders who blend humility with fierce resolve can inspire deep-rooted loyalty within their organizations. Ibn Khaldun's concept of asabiyyah, or social cohesion, provides a historical and sociological lens to understand the collective bonds that strengthen loyalty in organizations. Josiah Royce's philosophy of loyalty offers a moral and ethical foundation, emphasizing the importance of commitment to a cause larger than oneself.

Building on these foundational ideas, our proprietary work—developed in collaboration with my father—redefines loyalty into an applicable and measurable construct. Our research has demonstrated how a well-defined approach to measuring loyalty can transform organizations into more profitable and fulfilling workplaces.

This book utilizes detailed case studies to exemplify each aspect of the definition of loyalty. By examining real-world examples, we illustrate how various organizations have either succeeded or failed in fostering loyalty, providing valuable lessons for leaders and managers.

We explore the transformation of Xerox under Anne Mulcahy's leadership, showcasing how transparent leadership can drive loyalty and organizational success. The strong organizational culture at SAS serves as a model for how social cohesion and a sense of collective identity can enhance loyalty and innovation.

The strategies employed by the TATA Group demonstrate how aligning individual values with organizational goals can lead to significant improvements in employee satisfaction and retention. Best Buy's focus on employee-centric policies highlights effective methods for building lasting loyalty.

Additionally, we analyze the leadership of Phil Jackson with the Chicago Bulls and Los Angeles Lakers, partly exemplified by Kipling's quote that the strength of the wolf is the pack, the strength of the pack is the wolf, which illustrates how fostering team loyalty can lead to exceptional performance and success. The experiences of IBM and KONE provide further insights into leveraging loyalty to boost productivity and innovation in a business context.

By identifying these successes and failures, the book creates a vivid image of what to do—and what to avoid—if you want to build a loyal, high-performing workforce. Each case study is carefully chosen to highlight specific aspects of loyalty, offering concrete examples and actionable lessons that can be applied in various organizational contexts.

Engagement vs. Loyalty Quotient to Loyalty® (LQL)

Our research defines loyalty as a willing, practical, and thorough-going dedication to a cause on the condition of reciprocity and Asabiyyah. This definition is the foundation of what we call Loyalty to Loyalty and the Loyalty Quotient to Loyalty®. This concept involves the step-by-step building of a relationship through the fostering of a culture of trust, reciprocity, and oneness supported by six behavioral determinants, further explored in the book. Loyalty is characterized by a long-term dedication to the cause of the organization rather than transitional projects and goals. This long-term process ensures the simultaneous protection of the organization's interests and one's own in times of crisis.

The main difference between engagement and loyalty is their focus and duration. Engagement focuses on active participation and effort in a task or project and can be influenced by current incentives and working conditions. Conversely, loyalty involves long-term and thoroughgoing dedication to the organization's cause, based on reciprocity and Assabiyah. The organization's cause influences loyal employees through a sense of oneness with the other members with whom they have direct contact and a two-way practical relationship with the organization.

Both concepts are related to employee retention, but stimulating engagement involves current incentives and working conditions, whereas loyalty requires building a long-term relationship and a culture of trust and reciprocity. Together with Asabiyyah, loyalty fosters community, benevolence, and long-term perspective. An employee may be highly engaged and perform well yet still lack a long-term connection to the company or a sense of shared identity, often leading them to leave the company as soon as a better offer arises. Therefore, engagement is a temporary state based on current tasks and opportunities. In times of crisis, the differences between engagement and loyalty become more apparent. Loyal employees will stay and support the company in the reciprocal manner the organization has nurtured their relationship, whereas engaged employees may withdraw if they see better opportunities elsewhere.

Gallup defines engagement as the emotional connection employees feel toward their work—fueling enthusiasm, work motivation, and extra effort to achieve its goals. Gallup's research highlights that engagement can be both short-term, related to specific projects or tasks, and influenced by job satisfaction and availability of resources, and long-term, reflecting deeper emotional investment in the organization. Employees might feel highly engaged during a particular project or under certain favorable conditions, but this engagement may not necessarily translate into a long-term commitment.

Gallup's Q12 survey tool, consisting of 12 questions related to employees' basic needs and workplace conditions, measures these aspects of engagement comprehensively. Strong engagement, Gallup argues, drives productivity, lowers turnover, and boosts employee well-being. However, engagement levels can fluctuate based on current conditions, making it essential for organizations to nurture a supportive and motivating environment continuously.

Wilmar B. Schaufeli is a noted scholar in the field of work and organizational psychology, particularly known for his work on burnout and engagement. Schaufeli and Bakker's Engagement Model (2004) underscores that engagement is a sustained state characterized by vigor (high levels of energy and mental resilience), dedication (strong sense of significance, enthusiasm, inspiration, pride, and challenge), and absorption (being fully immersed in work). It is supported by job resources (support, feedback, skill variety, autonomy) and personal resources (self-efficacy, optimism). These resources thrive in a supportive work environment.

Where burnout drains energy and breeds cynicism, engagement fuels vitality and a sense of purpose.

According to Schaufeli, the boundaries between in-role behavior (officially required behavior serving the organization's goals) and extra-role behavior (discretionary behavior that goes beyond in-role behavior) are weak at best. This suggests that 'going the extra mile' isn't a defining feature of engagement—but a separate dimension. Instead, true engagement encompasses a broader range of behaviors and attitudes that are not simply about exerting additional effort but also about bringing value and innovation to one's role.

The importance of "going the extra mile" diminishes if it is not coupled with other elements of proactive behavior. It can be seen as a dedication to the welfare of the organization and the managerial incapability of members of the organization to plan, delegate, and execute in a timely and creative manner. Schaufeli links extra-role behavior more closely to burnout and personal initiative than to true engagement. His findings are indicative of the importance of clearly defining what is being measured with its subfactors and the avoidance of overgeneralization, oversimplification, and misinterpretation of terms and concepts.

Engagement and loyalty differ in focus, duration, and what drives them. While engagement is related to current tasks and can be temporary, loyalty is a long-term dedication to the cause that is different from job satisfaction and the availability of resources. The concept of Loyalty-to-Loyalty is a process that is measured on seven levels and defined by six distinct behaviors—serving a fundamentally different purpose. Understanding these differences is key in further exploring the definition of loyalty in this book and its broad applicability.

As you embark on this journey through the pages of this book, I invite you to reflect on your own experiences with loyalty. Think about the moments when you felt a deep sense of belonging to an organization or a cause. What sparked that feeling? How did it influence your actions and dedication? Conversely, consider the times when loyalty was lacking and when it was not reciprocal. What were the consequences, and what could have been done differently?

Throughout this book, you will encounter various strategies, case studies, and practical tools designed to help you cultivate loyalty within your organization or team. I encourage you to reflect upon other people's experiences and apply the insights to your own context. Take notes, ask questions (an email is provided in the book), and consider how the principles discussed can transform your workplace into one where loyalty thrives.

By the end of this book, you will understand the complexities of loyalty in organizations and how empowering it can be for all members. Together, we can build organizations where the culture is grounded in principles and values that people truly live out in their work. Now, for the first time, a loyalty instrument has been developed, tested in multiple organizations, and proven to support all members of the organization in their development process.

CHAPTER 1

Loyalty Through the Ages

"He will win whose army is animated by the same spirit throughout all its ranks."

—Sun Tzu

LOYALTY, AS BOTH A PERSONAL virtue and social glue, has been central to human civilization since its earliest days. Across cultures and centuries, thinkers have grappled with what it means to be loyal—to a friend, a family, a community, or a state—and how that loyalty shapes the moral and political fabric of society. In this chapter, we turn to some of history's most profound minds—Aristotle in ancient Greece, Confucius in imperial China, Ibn Khaldun in the medieval Islamic world, and others—to explore how their distinct cultural contexts produced enduring insights into loyalty and the nature of human relationships.

For Aristotle, loyalty was embedded in his broader vision of philia, or friendship—a mutual bond essential not just for private happiness but for the functioning of the polis. Confucius, writing centuries earlier and thousands of miles away, emphasized loyalty as a guiding principle in hierarchical relationships, particularly within the family and state. Meanwhile, Ibn Khaldun viewed loyalty through the lens of asabiyyah, which he believed explained the rise and fall of civilizations. Each thinker reveals a different facet of how loyalty functions not only as an emotion or duty but as a pillar of human flourishing.

By tracing these perspectives, we begin to see loyalty not as a moral obligation but as a dynamic force that binds individuals into lasting communities. Whether shaped by kinship, virtue, collective survival or reciprocal behavior, loyalty emerges as a fundamental answer to the perennial human question: How should we live with one another?

Aristotle

Aristotle regarded virtues—including loyalty—as central to ethical behavior and social harmony. In his virtue ethics, loyalty is a fundamental trait of character—one that must be practiced consistently and kept in balance to avoid causing harm. This deep-rooted value was not unique to Aristotle's context; his exploration of human virtues provides a comprehensive understanding of how virtues should be integrated into daily life.

Aristotle's concept of virtue ethics is about aspiring to ideals and embodying practical wisdom, or phronesis, in the application of these virtues. Without this wisdom, virtues may become excessive, deficient, or even misplaced. Loyalty, for instance, if not balanced by other virtues such as justice and prudence, can lead to blind allegiance or detrimental favoritism. Therefore, practical wisdom ensures that loyalty is exercised in a way that upholds the well-being of all parties involved.

A key insight from Aristotle's philosophy is that virtues are not designed to stand in isolation. Instead, they exist in relation to one another, working in harmony rather than division. This harmonious existence, where each virtue complements the others, is what the ancients referred to as the "unity of virtues." In Aristotle's view, loyalty must be aligned with other virtues like honesty, courage, and justice, forming a cohesive and balanced ethical character. This interdependence of virtues ensures that loyalty contributes to the greater good and supports the stability and harmony of both individual relationships and the wider community.

Thus, Aristotle's virtue ethics provides a nuanced approach to loyalty, embedding it within a broader ethical framework that emphasizes balance, practical wisdom, and the interrelation of virtues. This holistic perspective ensures that loyalty, while crucial, is part of a larger mosaic of moral behavior aimed at achieving eudaimonia, or human flourishing.

Ibn Khaldun

Ibn Khaldun (1332-1406) was a North African Arab historian and philosopher, often recognized as one of the pioneers of the social sciences and the father of sociology. He is best known for his magnum opus, the "Muqaddimah" (translated as "Prolegomena" or "Introduction"), in which he presented an early attempt to understand the rise and fall of states and empires using an interdisciplinary approach.

Ibn Khaldun was born into an elite family in Tunis, with a lineage that traced back to Yemen. He received a comprehensive education in Islamic jurisprudence, theology, and philosophy, which was crucial for his later intellectual pursuits. His early mentors, such as Muhammad ibn Ibrahim al-Abili, significantly influenced his scholarly development.

Throughout his career, Ibn Khaldun held various political and administrative roles under different rulers, including the Hafsids, Merinids, and Nasrids. His political life was turbulent, marked by shifting allegiances and involvement in the complex tribal and dynastic politics of North Africa and Spain. Despite the instability, these experiences provided him with valuable insights into the functioning of states and societies, which he later articulated in his writings.

One of the notable episodes in Ibn Khaldun's life was his encounter with the conqueror Timur (Tamerlane) in 1401. Timur had besieged Damascus, where Ibn Khaldun was residing. Invited to meet Timur, Ibn Khaldun engaged in a series of intellectual exchanges with the conqueror, providing him with valuable insights into the political and geographical landscape of North Africa. Through his diplomatic skills and knowledge, Ibn Khaldun managed to persuade Timur to lift the siege, thereby preventing further destruction and loss of life in the city.

Ibn Khaldun's ideas have resonated through the centuries, influencing various fields and thinkers, including the administration of U.S. President Ronald Reagan. Reagan's policies, particularly those related to economic and social reforms, were reportedly inspired by Ibn Khaldun's theories. Reagan's administration cited Ibn Khaldun in support of supply-side economics, referencing his insights on taxation and state revenue.

In his later years, Ibn Khaldun settled in Egypt, where he continued his scholarly work and served as a high-ranking judge under the Mamluk Sultanate. His intellectual legacy was recognized both during his lifetime and posthumously, influencing scholars across the Islamic world and beyond. His innovative methodologies continue to be relevant in contemporary analyses of historical and social phenomena.

The "Muqaddimah"

The "Muqaddimah" is Ibn Khaldun's most celebrated work, in which he laid the foundations for several social science disciplines. He introduced key concepts such as 'asabiyyah, which he identified as a critical factor in the rise and fall of civilizations. His work is considered groundbreaking for its systematic approach to studying history, economics, sociology, and political science.

The genesis of the term 'Asabiyyah can be traced back to its pre-Islamic roots, with the term rooted in the word 'asab, meaning "finger." This is a primarily denoted lineage or descent from a shared ancestor, a foundational aspect of identity, rights, and social positioning in tribal and pre-modern societies. The elementary conception of 'Asabiyyah alluded to the loyalty an individual felt toward a group based on shared ancestry. However, in the annals of intellectual history, it was Ibn Khaldun who refined and popularized this term. In his seminal work, the "Muqaddimah", he expanded the scope of 'Asabiyyah to portray it not just as tribal loyalty but as a broader sense of social solidarity, encompassing group consciousness and mutual support, irrespective of kinship.

Asabiyyah is the collective spirit that binds individuals into a functioning group—be it a tribe, dynasty, or organization. Its significance isn't confined solely to kinship-based ties. A shared history, common objectives, and mutual adversities can all serve as crucibles for forging this potent bond. For instance, in the crucible of war, soldiers, irrespective of their familial backgrounds, might cultivate a sense of camaraderie and mutual reliance.

This social glue becomes even more palpable and vital in the face of adversity. Reflecting on the challenging desert terrains of Ibn Khaldun's world, the indispensability of tribal cohesion becomes evident. Such rugged environments necessitated unwavering solidarity for survival, both against the caprices of nature and potential external threats. In these contexts, any betrayal or weakening of the group's unity could spell collective catastrophe.

The societal advantages conferred by a strong sense of 'Asabiyyah are manifold. A community imbued with this spirit enjoys stability, collective prosperity, and security. This intangible bond engenders mutual trust, curbing internal strife and fostering efficient collaboration. However, like all societal phenomena, 'Asabiyyah is not static. As societies burgeon, enjoying the dividends of their unity, the intense social ties that 'Asabiyyah signifies can start

to attenuate. Increased prosperity may lead to heightened individualism, emergent conflicts of interest, and eventual societal
fragmentation.

The newer generation within the leader's close associates, having
inherited their forefathers' wealth, often misuses these funds,
diverting them from their original purpose of supporting the leadership. Their loyalty wanes compared to the unwavering fidelity of
their ancestors. This shift prompts the ruler to believe that he has
a greater claim to the amassed wealth, especially since it was accumulated during his predecessors' tenure and due to their influence. This unchecked self-interest becomes a contributing factor
to the decline of groups.

Injustice often signals the unraveling of civilizations. True justice
is the equilibrium established among humanity. Among the
gravest injustices that significantly expedite the erosion of civilizations are the unwarranted assignment of tasks and the coercive
conscription of citizens into forced labour.

In the broader tapestry of contemporary sociology and political science, parallels can be drawn between 'Asabiyyah and
more modern concepts like social capital, nationalistic fervor, or
communal solidarity. The underlying premise remains consistent:
societies, when undergirded by trust and mutual cooperation,
function with enhanced efficiency and harmony.

'Asabiyyah is argued to be a comprehensive term that has no
one-word translation in other languages; thus in the first translation of the book in French, 'asabiyyah was defined as collective
will. Through further research, the term could be explained as
the collective will formation and commitment to sustained action
through the sense of oneness of a group of like-minded enthusiasts and their cemented work toward a common goal.

In summary, while 'Asabiyyah's roots are ancient, its conceptual
essence remains pertinent, emphasizing the perennial importance

of societal bonds for the collective success, resilience, and well-being of communities.

Confucius

The era of the Han dynasty (206 BCE – 220CEe) is considered a golden age that lasted almost four hundred years and its mark on Chinese society has endured to this day. For the first time, China controlled the Silk Road across the middle of Asia. Confucianism was adopted as the official government orthodoxy.[1] The empire's government administration was characterized by the efficiency of its bureaucracy and the incorporation of Confucian values. The vertical movement of promotions depended on the administrative skills of the people, their social status, adherence to the elite of the empire and their knowledge of Confucian classics.

The *Lunny*, or *Analects*, is the foundational text of Confucian thought. The teachings encompass different aspects of human life, recognizing five central behaviors: benevolence, righteousness, ritual propriety, wisdom, and trustworthiness. The virtue of benevolence is the vastest one in definition, yet its compromise is deemed equivalent to death. When applied to interaction with other people, it is viewed as loyal behavior.[2] Confucius discusses loyalty separately. In Analects Book 4, Chapter 15 it is said: *Confucius said: "Shen, my way is woven into a single thread." Zengzi replied: "Indeed." After Confucius had left, the other followers asked: "What did he mean?" Zengzi said: "The way of the Master is based on loyalty and reciprocity; that and nothing more."* Followed by Analects Book 14, Chapter 7: *Confucius said: "Can you truly care for someone if you're not demanding towards them? Can you be truly loyal to someone if you refrain from admonishing them?"* () The importance of loyalty is intertwined with the benevolence and the righteousness exemplified by the leadership because Confucian teachings understood it as a reciprocal relationship. Loyalty was not to be blind or unconditional because if a ruler acted unjustly or violated the accepted principles, then loyalty belonged not to the ruler as a person, but to the agreed-upon order he was meant to uphold. The ruler and the empire were no longer the same, therefore the ruler's ministers needed to admonish their leader.

The Han dynasty fell victim to its own power and prosperity because, at the end, officials neglected the accepted Confucian values and focused on their personal ambitions and needs. Stagnation and collapse soon followed the once-powerful dynasty. Confucian teachings survived over two millennia, and its traditions have influenced the lives of Chinese intellectuals and farmers. Confucianism remains a vital part of the psycho-cultural construct of Chinese society.

Japan's Shinise Companies and Their Longevity

Rootless floating grass seems to be prospering for a while, but once it is washed away by water, it disappears without knowing its whereabouts.

In Japan, companies that have existed for at least 100 years are known as "shinise," which translates to "an old shop." According to Yoshinori Hara, dean and professor at Kyoto University's Graduate School of Management, such companies emphasize sustainability over quick profit maximization, resulting in remarkable longevity.

Makoto Kanda's research on shinise reveals their commitment to a central belief or credo that extends beyond profit generation. These companies prioritize steps that generate growth and maintain market competitiveness rather than innovation for its own sake. A prime example is the Mitsubishi Group, founded by Yataro Iwasaki in 1870. Under the leadership of Yataro's brother, son, and nephew, Mitsubishi transformed into a zaibatsu (industrial conglomerate) until 1946 and re-emerged as a single entity after a series of mergers in 1954. The enduring principles established by Koyata Iwasaki, Yataro's nephew—Corporate Responsibility to Society (Shoki Horo), Integrity and Fairness (Shoji Komei), and Global Understanding through Business (Ritsugyo Boeki)— continue to guide Mitsubishi today. Scholar U. Bandura interpreted Shoji Komei as serving the country, signifying that what benefits the country also benefits Mitsubishi.

Adapting to Change and Global Examples

Adapting to change is a critical factor in the longevity of shinise companies. These businesses demonstrate resilience by continuously evolving while maintaining their core principles. For example, Nintendo's journey from a playing card company to a global video game giant is a testament to strategic adaptation. Founded in 1889, Nintendo initially produced Hanafuda cards, a traditional Japanese card game. As the company evolved, it embraced new technologies and shifted its focus to electronic entertainment in the 1970s, introducing iconic products like the Game Boy and the Nintendo Entertainment System (NES). Despite changes in the gaming industry, Nintendo's core mission of "creating fun" has remained consistent, allowing it to adapt successfully while retaining its identity. Hara notes that sticking to the basic concept of what a company does often helps it survive even when the world around it changes.

Similarly, the kimono weaving industry in Japan has faced significant challenges due to changes in fashion and technology. Traditional kimono weavers have diversified by using their skills to produce various types of garments and textile products, incorporating modern designs and techniques such as 3-D weaving. This adaptability has allowed these artisans to stay relevant in a rapidly changing market.

Globally, Stora Enso, the world's oldest limited liability corporation, exemplifies adaptation through diversification. Originating in 1288 as a copper mining company in Finland, Stora Enso has transformed over the centuries into a leader in renewable materials. Today, it focuses on bioenergy and green construction materials, aligning with contemporary environmental concerns. This strategic shift has enabled Stora Enso to remain relevant and competitive in the modern marketplace. According to the professor's research it is not necessary for the companies to set goals to live forever, but their premature death is a tragedy and questions should be raised about what went wrong.

In Japan, Yamamotoyama, the oldest tea company established in Nihonbashi, Tokyo in 1690, exemplifies innovation within tradition. The company has continuously adapted its products while maintaining core values, it has stated that keeping tradition is to continuously change, while preserving the unchangeable fundamentals. Yamamotoyama produces traditional tea and Washi paper, which has evolved to include seaweed products since the Edo period. Despite these changes, the company upholds the Edo spirit and culture, delivering a blend of tradition and innovation to its customers.

Tradition and Innovation

Tradition in shinise companies is not static; it represents a continuous process of innovation. These businesses understand that preserving tradition involves daily renewal and adaptation. By constantly breathing new life into traditional practices, these companies ensure their offerings remain relevant and vibrant. Cherishing tradition involves a dedication to quality, community, and continuity. It requires a delicate balance between maintaining core values and embracing new ideas. For instance, Yamamotoyama's approach of integrating modern technologies and practices into its traditional tea business exemplifies this balance. By pursuing daily newness, these companies avoid stagnation and obsolescence, ensuring their traditions thrive in contemporary contexts.

Cultural Perspectives

The longevity of Japanese shinise companies is deeply rooted in cultural values. Japan's cultural orientation towards respecting tradition and ancestors plays a significant role in sustaining long-standing businesses. The country's historical isolation as an island nation has fostered a culture of making the most of available resources and preserving local enterprises.

Closing or selling a company in Japan is often viewed as a failure and a source of shame, a sentiment that has persisted for centuries. This cultural perspective encourages families to maintain and pass down their businesses through generations. Unlike the more flexible and dynamic economy of the United States, where new firms frequently emerge, Japan tends to focus on preserving and nurturing existing businesses. This tendency is evident in the commitment of shinise companies to long-term horizons and relationships, controlled growth, enduring values, risk management and a long-term view across generations. Key factors for business longevity recognized through the pioneering research of Professor Toshio Goto, Representative Director at Research Institute for Centennial Management and Research Professor at Graduate School of Management, Japan University of Economics.

Japan's shinise companies demonstrate that adherence to core principles and a balanced approach to growth and innovation are key to enduring success. These values, deeply rooted in Japanese culture, ensure that these companies continue to thrive and contribute to Japan, its economy and society. If one settles for the status quo and stagnates for even a day, tradition will surely become obsolete but pursuing daily newness, there is no time to stabilize at any time. Thus, each company should find its balance.

Loyalty and Management

The second law of thermodynamics, developed in the mid-19th century by William Thomson and Rudolf Clausius, dictates that heat cannot move from a reservoir of lower temperature to a one with higher temperature, unless an external source is supplying the energy to reverse the heat flow. Thus, all close systems experience an energy loss and require a continuous energy intake from an external source. Energy loss is called entropy. If analogically compared to corporations, large companies need a continuous input of management energy to remain in existence. However, companies should strive to nurture a long-term work relationship, and if not, self-reliance and self-centred attitude would be prevalent among employees.

Lou Gerstner, the IBM CEO who saved the company from bankruptcy in 1993, stated in an interview for McKinsey that:

> "One thing I would say, though, is that the preoccupation with short-term earnings in the public-company environment—not something private companies are so concerned with—is quite destructive of longevity. And that's a bad thing. Who says the analysts are right when they mark down a company's stock just because it makes 89 cents in the first quarter rather than the 93 forecast by the market? Are they thinking about the long-term competitiveness of the company? Are they thinking this would have been a good time to reinvest, or are they just churning out numbers and saying they want earnings per share to go up every quarter? This kind of short-term

*pressure on current earnings can lead to underinvest-
ment in the long-term competitiveness of a business."*

Profitability is what keeps companies operational in the short term. But the core concept, the cause of a company, the reason the company and its employees create a two-sided long-term relationship transcending financial gains and security, is the factor that defines companies that last through the test of time and market upheavals in the long-term.

Josiah Royce

"The willing and practical and thoroughgoing devotion of a person to a cause..." Josiah Royce's 1906 definition of loyalty marked a significant departure from the blind allegiance characteristic of the Middle Ages. Instead, Royce offered a clear definition of a person's "willing, and practical, and thoroughgoing devotion" to a cause. For loyalty to truly exist, Royce argued, a cause is essential, as its existence evokes the described devotion and its practical, sustained expression. Royce saw loyalty as marked by self-control—a disciplined devotion to a cause greater than oneself. This ensures that loyal actions are not driven by emotion or pleasure.

The aspect of self-control in Royce's definition is reminiscent of Peter Drucker's ideas in "The Practice of Management." Drucker emphasized that the application of self-control in management requires more than merely accepting the idea; it necessitates long-term changes through new tools that address a company's practices and past thinking. In business enterprises, managers often lack alignment with shared goals and objectives. Therefore, it is crucial that everyone in the hierarchical ladder has clearly defined objectives, determining the expected performance of each managerial unit.

When a person adopts a cause, they become dedicated to something larger than themselves. This dedication transcends short-term company objectives, encompassing both personal and impersonal elements. It involves the loyal individual and other people, forming a social unity. A suitable environment, augmented by a willful leader, is key to fostering loyalty. Without leadership to curb individualistic or self-interested behavior, loyalty in organizations may suffer.

Loyalty encompasses fidelity but extends beyond it. In addition to fidelity, loyalty involves decisiveness and the acceptance of a cause. The fidelity of a dog to its master is merely a fragment of the loyalty that, in humans, manifests as a fully reasonable and devoted life. The same applies to the term "faithfulness." While the loyal are absorbed in their cause, this absorption differs from the passion of an angry person. Loyalty includes trustworthiness, but unlike a watch, it reflects a conscious choice.

Royce and Ibn Khaldun

Josiah Royce and Ibn Khaldun, scholars from vastly different historical and cultural contexts, provide insights into the nature of collective identity through their respective concepts of loyalty and "Asabiyyah". At first glance, the temporal and cultural chasm between them might seem vast, yet their writings converge on the power, challenges, and imperatives inherent in the shared bonds that shape societies.

Navigating the intellectual traditions of late 19th and early 20th-century America, Josiah Royce articulated loyalty as an active, intentional devotion that extends beyond individual affiliations to encompass abstract ideals and causes. This devotion bridges the personal and communal, with individual actions gaining greater significance as they become enmeshed in a broader societal tapestry. In Royce's framework, loyalty serves as both a gyroscope and a compass, providing stability and direction amid the complex pathways of societal evolution.

Ibn Khaldun, theorizing within the crucible of the 14th-century Maghreb, described Asabiyyah as the primal bond uniting tribes or groups, frequently rooted in kinship. This inherent solidarity, originating in shared lineage, is dynamic and capable of evolving to integrate those who assimilate into the tribal ethos. Ibn Khaldun's Asabiyyah is a fundamental element in the rise and fall of civilizations, reflecting the collective strength and cohesion necessary for societal prosperity. The vitality of Asabiyyah underpins the success of tribes and dynasties, but its decline can signal societal decay, particularly when exposed to the comforts and distractions of urban existence.

A resonance emerges between the two thinkers when considering the collective as a source of strength. For Royce, societal strength springs from its collective loyalties, which harmonize individual aspirations with communal objectives, fostering unity and common purpose. In contrast, Ibn Khaldun's Asabiyyah offers a raw understanding of collective vigor. The cohesion and might of a tribe or civilization are directly tethered to the vitality of its Asabiyyah, making it the foundational bedrock of any thriving society.

Yet, both Royce and Ibn Khaldun astutely identified the fragility underpinning these bonds. Royce recognized the challenge of navigating multiple, sometimes intersecting, loyalties in complex societies. Without overarching shared commitments, these bonds risk becoming transient or diluted. Similarly, Ibn Khaldun chronicled the cyclical nature of Asabiyyah, noting that the very strength propelling a tribe or dynasty to prominence can wane, especially under the influence of luxury and complacency.

In today's globalized, interconnected world, marked by fluid identities and rapid technological evolution, the reflections of both scholars hold profound relevance. Modern democracies, with their delicate balance of individual freedoms and collective responsibilities, can draw from Royce's emphasis on the depth and nature of shared commitments. His call to introspection is crucial for maintaining societal cohesion amidst diversity.

Simultaneously, Ibn Khaldun's observations on Asabiyyah provide invaluable insights for modern nation-states, especially those forged from diverse ethnic or tribal tapestries. His cyclic perspective on societal bonds serves as a poignant reminder to contemporary superpowers of the transient nature of dominance and the importance of maintaining strong, cohesive ties within a society or an organization.

Synthesizing the thought of Royce and Ibn Khaldun unveils a rich exploration of the mechanisms that bind individuals to larger collectives. Despite their distinct epochs and cultural contexts, their insights present a timeless discourse on the interplay between personal aspirations and collective identities. Their combined wisdom underscores the importance of continually nurturing and reevaluating the ties that unite societies, especially in an ever-changing global landscape.

Jim Collins

Jim Collins, in his influential work "Good to Great," introduces the concept of "Level 5 Leadership," which emphasizes the pinnacle of leadership qualities. Level 5 leaders, as Collins describes, exhibit a combination of deep personal humility and intense professional will. They prioritize welfare and organizational success over their personal achievements. When things go well, they attribute success to their teams or external factors; when there's a setback, they look inwards and shoulder responsibility.

Collins identifies five leadership levels, Level 5 being the pinnacle. At the base, a Highly Capable Individual contributes using their skills, knowledge, and work habits. As one ascends the levels, they become a Contributing Team Member, harnessing their capabilities to help their team succeed. The next step is to become a Competent Manager, effectively organizing a group to achieve specific goals. An Effective Leader comes next, able to galvanize a department or organization towards achieving superior performance.

It is the Executive, the Level 5 leader, who truly stands out. Such leaders embody all the strengths of the previous four levels, but also possess a unique blend of humility and professional will, which is a fierce, unwavering resolve. Rather than seeking personal accolades, they are ambitious primarily for the company. Their leadership style often shuns public adulation, focusing instead on making decisions that benefit the company. Collins' research suggests that these Level 5 leaders are a primary reason why some companies leap from being good to genuinely great.

Collins' research found that companies that transitioned from good to great typically had leaders at this fifth level. They put the organization's interests above their own and have the personal humility combined with professional will to make the necessary decisions for the company to succeed. This idea of Level 5 Leadership is a shift from the traditional perception of leaders as charismatic, ego-driven individuals. Instead, it emphasizes humility, discipline, and a focus on something bigger than oneself.

Collins' Level 5 leaders blend humility with unyielding professional determination. Such leaders are self-effacing, attributing organizational successes to external factors, yet swiftly internalizing responsibility during setbacks. Their commitment transcends personal achievements; they are fervently dedicated to the organization's longevity and prosperity. This is manifested in their vision for the institution and in their meticulous preparation of successors, ensuring a seamless transition and organizational continuity.

A distinct feature of their leadership style is encapsulated in the "window and mirror" analogy, wherein successes are credited outwardly while failures prompt introspection. Their resilience and resolve, even when confronted with formidable challenges, underline their unwavering commitment to the organization's mission. In essence, Level 5 Leadership emphasizes the importance of character over charisma. It shifts the focus from personal accolades to organizational success. Level 5 leaders may have charisma—but they never rely on it. Instead, they combine their humility with a relentless drive for results, all while keeping the organization's welfare at the heart of their actions.

Collins and Royce

Josiah Royce's "The Philosophy of Loyalty" and Jim Collins' "Level 5 Leadership" concept, while originating from different disciplines, share underlying themes. At the heart of Level 5 Leadership is dedication to something greater than oneself, much like the central theme in "The Philosophy of Loyalty." Royce proposed that true personal fulfilment and moral development arise from an unwavering loyalty to a cause or community. This loyalty requires putting the chosen cause above one's personal desires, leading to a life filled with purpose and moral direction.

Royce believed that personal fulfilment and moral growth arise from loyalty to a cause. For him, loyalty was not allegiance but rather a dedicated commitment to a cause or community that gives purpose to an individual's life. Such commitment defines a person's character and provides a moral framework. Similarly, Level 5 leaders demonstrate unwavering commitment to their organization, its people and the overall success. Their personal humility, combined with an intense professional will, is focused entirely on the company's prosperity, not personal gain.

Loyalty, for Royce, requires selflessness. It involves prioritizing the chosen cause over personal desires or needs. This selflessness is mirrored in Level 5 leaders, who prioritize the company's needs over their own. They are more interested in the organization's success than in personal accolades or credit.

The highest form of moral dedication, according to Royce, is the commitment to a cause that transcends personal interest. This could be loyalty to truth, a community, or a universal ideal. Level 5 exemplifies this by committing to the long-term success and sustainability of the organization, even if it means making unpopular decisions. Their ambition is for the institution, not themselves. This long-term vision ensures that decisions are made with the future of the organization in mind, aligning with Royce's emphasis on dedication to a cause greater than oneself.

Being loyal involves recognizing a cause and taking responsibility for it. It's an active process of choosing and committing. Level 5 leaders embody this principle by not shirking responsibility. When things go wrong, they look in the mirror and take accountability. When things go right, they look out the window to attribute the success to others.

Loyalty to a cause implies present commitment and an interest in its future continuity. This extends to nurturing future custodians of the cause or community. One of the hallmarks of Level 5 leaders is ensuring that their organizations succeed beyond their tenure. They focus on setting up successors for greater success.

In essence, Jim Collins' concept of Level 5 Leadership can be interpreted as a manifestation of Royce's philosophy of loyalty within the context of organizational leadership. Both ideas champion selflessness, dedication to a cause greater than oneself, and the intrinsic moral values of such commitment. As leadership paradigms continue to evolve, these foundational principles remain timeless, emphasizing the importance of character, humility, and a cause beyond oneself.

Medieval Roots: Feudal Loyalty

Loyalty has been a cornerstone of human relationships and societal structures for millennia, but its interpretation and application have evolved, sometimes leading to detrimental misinterpretations. From the feudal bonds of the medieval era to modern corporate allegiances, the concept of loyalty has been shaped by historical contexts, often leading to blind, misplaced, and manipulated forms of loyalty. This exploration delves into how these interpretations have influenced our understanding of loyalty today, highlighting various nuanced forms of loyalty. Forms which have diluted the virtue's initial intentions.

The medieval era's feudal system epitomized a deeply personal and contractual loyalty. Lords owned vast lands and granted fiefs to vassals in exchange for military service and other obligations. This bond was formalized through ceremonies like "homage," where vassals pledged loyalty to their lords, establishing mutual obligations. This relationship wasn't merely transactional; it fostered a sense of personal allegiance.

In this hierarchical system, loyalty was a survival mechanism. Vassals relied on their lords for protection, land, and sustenance, while lords depended on their vassals for military support and governance. Though loyalty was essential to the feudal system, it differed sharply from Aristotle's virtue-driven concept.

However, the intertwining of loyalty with hierarchical feudalism and religious fervor also sowed the seeds for blind loyalty. Vassals were expected to serve their lords unquestioningly, a practice that often led to ethical and moral compromises. This medieval concept of loyalty, demanding absolute allegiance, ...still haunts modern organizations, where loyalty is sometimes demanded at the expense of personal principles.

Blind Loyalty: The Perils of Unquestioning Allegiance

Blind loyalty is the refusal to question allegiance—even when it violates one's own values. This type of loyalty often stems from societal pressures to conform, the influence of charismatic leaders, or cognitive dissonance where individuals ignore facts that challenge their loyalty.

The medieval practice of vassals pledging loyalty to lords, irrespective of the lords' actions, is a historical precursor to this phenomenon. In such a system, questioning authority was not only discouraged but severely punished. This created an environment where blind loyalty flourished, leading to the suppression of critical thinking, the reinforcement of harmful behaviors, and the entrenchment of practices that could go unchallenged for generations.

In contemporary settings, blind loyalty can lead to significant dangers such as propensity for groupthink, societal conformity, and institutionalized loyalty. For example, in corporate environments, employees might follow a leader's directives without question, even if those directives are illegal or harmful. This transformation of loyalty from a noble virtue into a tool for manipulation illustrates how blind loyalty can suppress critical thinking and moral judgment.

Misplaced Loyalty: Anchoring to the Wrong Causes

Misplaced loyalty arises when individuals devote their allegiance to unworthy or harmful entities. Driven by a desire for belonging and acceptance, people might anchor their loyalties to groups or leaders without sufficient discernment. Cognitive biases, like confirmation bias, reinforce this loyalty, leading individuals to seek out information that supports their pre-existing beliefs.

In modern times, misplaced loyalty can manifest in various forms, such as employees remaining loyal to toxic workplaces. In corporate settings, employees might stay with a company that exploits them, believing that their loyalty will eventually be rewarded. However, it is their work life balance, family, or career longevity that suffers. Misplaced loyalty dilutes the value of true loyalty and undermines both personal integrity and organizational health.

Manipulating Loyalty: Power and Control

Loyalty manipulation can be a tactic used by those in power to maintain or extend their control. By exploiting human emotions and vulnerabilities, leaders can coerce loyalty that serves their interests rather than fostering genuine mutual respect. This manipulation can be subtle, through narratives that tie personal identity to loyalty, or overt, through threats of consequences for perceived disloyalty. Like simply saying: *You are loyal to the organization, right?*

Historical examples include feudal lords who manipulated vassals' loyalty for personal gain. These lords often exploited religious and cultural norms to reinforce their power, presenting themselves as divinely appointed or morally superior. In contemporary contexts, corporate leaders might use similar tactics to ensure unwavering support, transforming loyalty into a mechanism of control rather than a mutual bond. For instance, in a corporate setting, a CEO might use fear of job loss and threat to not find another job in the industry to maintain employee loyalty, promoting a culture where questioning or dissent is seen as disloyalty.

Toxic Loyalty: Harmful Allegiance

Toxic loyalty occurs when allegiance to a person, group, or organization leads to harm or unethical behavior. It often involves suppressing personal values and morals to maintain loyalty. This type of loyalty can create a harmful environment, perpetuating abuse, fraud, or unethical practices. Recognizing and addressing toxic loyalty is crucial for maintaining personal integrity, mutual respect, and practicality for both sides.

Toxic loyalty can also foster a culture of learned helplessness, where individuals feel powerless to change their situation and continue to support wrongdoings out of a sense of inevitability. This phenomenon occurs when people, having repeatedly encountered adverse outcomes despite their efforts, come to believe that they have no control over the situation and thus resign themselves to it. In modern times, toxic loyalty is evident in scenarios where employees, feeling trapped by their circumstances and fearing retaliation, do not engage in a conversation about physical or psychological harm, a result of their work. In such cases, people could believe that this is the only reality and they have to accept it.

Loyalty in the Modern Context

Understanding the historical roots and misinterpretations of loyalty helps us navigate its complexities today. Organizations and individuals should strive to foster loyalty that upholds integrity, mutual respect, and ethical behavior. Recognizing the dangers of blind, misplaced, manipulated, and toxic loyalty and prioritizing ethical principles can transform loyalty into a powerful, positive force in personal and professional realms.

Occupational Fraud and Its Prevalence

Occupational fraud is a nuanced and challenging issue, defined as the deliberate misuse or misapplication of an organization's resources or assets for personal gain. The pervasive nature of such fraudulent activities is rooted in two fundamental issues.

Firstly, the essence of trust within organizational structures is a double-edged sword. Many organizations, by the very nature of their operational mandates, grant their employees varying degrees of access to, or control over, critical assets. These can range from financial oversight responsibilities to safeguarding stocks. However, it is this deeply ingrained trust, a foundation of corporate operational dynamics, that renders these entities susceptible. At the core of any fraud is a breach of this very trust.

Secondly, the sheer size of the global workforce offers a vast canvas for potential fraud. When the report was finalized in 2021, the labor market encompassed over 3.3 billion individuals. Though a vast majority diligently uphold their professional and ethical responsibilities, the sheer scale means that even a minuscule fraction resorting to malpractice leads to millions of occupational fraud incidents on an annual scale.

Statistical Overview and Findings

From an analytical standpoint, the Fraud Examiners Manual study covered an extensive range of cases. In total, 2,110 instances from 133 countries were analyzed. The financial implications of these cases were staggering, cumulatively amounting to $3.6 billion. Diving deeper into the financials, losses at the 25th percentile stood at $20,000. The median losses were considerably higher, recorded at $117,000, while the upper echelons, or the 75th percentile, reported losses skyrocketing to $600,000.

Furthermore, there are intricate details surrounding the nature and detection of these fraudulent activities. The average time span between the initiation and eventual discovery of a fraudulent scheme is approximately 12 months. Collaborative frauds, involving multiple perpetrators, have seen an upward trend, showing a significant 16% increase, culminating in 58% of the total cases. Interestingly, the primary mode of fraud detection is not sophisticated analytics but human intervention. A substantial 42% of these fraudulent activities are detected through individual tips, a figure that dwarfs the 16% discovered through more structured channels like internal audits.

When correlating the magnitude of losses with the size of the victimized organization, a curious pattern emerges. Small enterprises, defined as those with fewer than 100 employees, reported a median loss of $150,000. Paradoxically, major conglomerates with staffing numbers exceeding 10,000, reported median losses just slightly lower at $138,000.

The profile of a typical fraudster offers another layer of complexity. A mere 6% had any form of previous fraud convictions, a percentage that may appear reassuring at first glance. However, when juxtaposed with the fact that 42% of fraudulent incidents went unreported, it raises concerns about the potential underestimation of repeat offenders. On the organizational response front, the post-detection phase offers limited solace. An alarming 7% of identified fraudsters faced no punitive actions. An additional 11% chose voluntary resignation, and 10% reached mutual settlement agreements, thereby escaping the repercussions without a blot on their employment history.

As with any complex problem, the background of these perpetrators adds another dimension. An even split is noted when considering if fraudsters had any prior human resources-related red flags, with a 50-50 distribution. The subsequent ability of organizations to recover financial losses paints a bleak picture. Over half, precisely 52%, could not reclaim any fraud-associated financial losses. Regional analysis indicates that only the Middle East, North Africa, Southern Asia, and the Asia-Pacific regions managed to post slightly better recovery rates. However, universally, in all regions, a minimum of 40% of organizations could not recover any financial losses.

Fraud Prevention and Deterrence

The multifaceted nature of occupational fraud necessitates a multi-pronged strategy for its prevention and deterrence. Renowned behaviorist Skinner provides a compelling perspective on this matter. He posits that the most effective path to behavior modification is not through punitive measures but by replacing detrimental behaviors with constructive ones through positive reinforcement.

Close affiliations with law-abiding individuals or entities offer a predictive framework for encouraging law-abiding behavior. However, when corporate culture is juxtaposed against legal and regulatory mandates, potential areas of conflict emerge. If prevailing organizational ethos conflicts with legal stipulations, there's a discernible tendency among employees to obfuscate their wrongdoings rather than reform their actions. When opportunities within the legitimate framework appear blocked or limited, corporations, driven by various pressures, might be tempted towards illicit means.

In the realm of white-collar crimes, the principal considerations are not limited to the potential gains but are equally, if not more, influenced by liabilities and pressures. Corporations, especially large-scale ones, grapple with the challenge of enforcing consistency in rules and policies across all hierarchical levels. This disparity often results in motivation and pressure to resort to fraudulent activities to bridge perceived or real gaps.

The cyclic nature of fraud, driven by financial pressures, rationalization, and recurring opportunities, highlights the need for perpetual vigilance and a multi-dimensional approach to mitigation. To break this cycle, we must understand the inherent and residual risks—and the motives, opportunities, and rationalizations that drive fraud.

The misuse of loyalty, manifesting as blind allegiance, misplaced trust, conflicts between loyalty and personal integrity, and overt manipulation, has indubitably influenced modern societal changes. As our society grows more interconnected and informed, there's an increasing awareness of these pitfalls, prompting a shift in organizational culture and values. Modern workplaces now place emphasis on terms like work engagement, extra-role behavior, job involvement, and organizational commitment, reflecting a nuanced understanding of loyalty. However, while the intent is commendable, there's an observable blurring of lines among these terms. Conscious and unconscious attempts to consolidate the essence of these diverse concepts into a singular term have muddled their individual significance. As a result, businesses face a measurement conundrum. Tools designed to measure loyalty, organizational commitment,and engagement often face skepticism—because it's unclear what they're actually measuring. This measurement dilemma both hampers organizational growth strategies and underscores the urgent need to define, differentiate, and accurately gauge these crucial facets of modern work culture.

CHAPTER 2

Fostering Loyalty

"You are your choices."
—Seneca the Younger

INTEGRATING NEW EMPLOYEES INTO AN organization involves three key processes: identification, internalization, and socialization. These processes are crucial for fostering a sense of belonging and loyalty among new employees and are influenced by leadership and organizational culture. Although these processes don't solely determine loyalty, they significantly contribute to its development alongside six behavioral determinants, reciprocity, and the concept of Asabiyyah, or oneness. Let's explore each process in detail, starting with identification, followed by internalization and socialization.

Identification

The identification journey begins the moment a potential employee decides to apply for a position. This marks the start of aligning personal values with the organization's ethos. During this phase, individuals align their thoughts, feelings, and actions with the organization's culture, values, and mission. This alignment fosters emotional connections and encourages the adoption of behaviors and norms that resonate with the individual.

Interestingly, this identification can start even before the formal process of socialization, as new members decide whether or not to apply to join the organization. It continues through various stages, including the interview process, psychological contract, and initial onboarding. During these phases, new employees gradually recognize and align with the values and behaviors shared within the organization.

However, it's important to recognize that identification is not a static process. The failure to uphold shared values can erode the relationship between the individual and the organization, leading to potential consequences such as increased turnover. This dynamic nature of identification highlights its critical role in shaping organizational behavior.

From a dialectical materialist perspective, identification is explained by the mutual determination of individual and social functions of cognition and activation. Identification is carried out based on emotional connections and relates to reference persons and groups, transmitted through conditions of contact and communication. It involves acquiring information with programmatic content, samples, projects for actions, and regulators of behavior such as norms and value orientations.

Theoretical frameworks such as Social Identity Theory (SIT) and Symbolic Interactionism provide valuable insights into the importance of identification. SIT emphasizes how identification influences socialization and internalization, as newcomers begin to see themselves as integral parts of the organization. Symbolic Interactionism underscores the role of social interactions in constructing organizational reality, helping newcomers develop a nuanced understanding of their roles and the overall organizational culture.

Refined Egoism

Refined egoism in the context of game theory describes a sophisticated approach to decision-making in strategic situations. This
concept goes beyond the basic idea of egoism, which focuses
primarily on maximizing one's own benefits. In game theory,
refined egoism involves considering not just immediate self-interest but also the long-term consequences of actions, the impact
of decisions on relationships with other players, and the overall
context of the game. Thomas Hobbes, in his 1651 book "Leviathan"
argued that human beings are naturally selfish and that social
order arises from their considerations of self-preservation and
fear of death rather than from altruism.

In the realm of Game Theory, Robert Axelrod in his 1984 book
"The Evolution of Cooperation" discussed the iterated prisoner's
dilemma (IPD) and the "Tit for Tat" strategy which resembles to an
extent refined egoism because the idea is to win in the long-term
and not focus on the highest possible reward in the short term
in the prisoners' dilemma. Starting with cooperation and then
mirroring the opponent's previous actions, "Tit for Tat" effectively
encourages mutual cooperation and what I consider its "refined"
part is that it's not purely selfish—it retaliates against defection
but also forgives, aiming to sustain cooperation when possible.
This approach promotes a nuanced engagement where one's own
interests are pursued while also fostering a stable, cooperative
relationship. Axelrod shows how cooperation can thrive—even
among self-interested actors in competitive environments.

Applying the concept of refined egoism to the process of identification in an organizational context involves a nuanced approach
where individuals consider both their immediate self-interests
and the broader, long-term implications of their alignment with
the organization's values and goals. In the process of identification, individuals typically align their values, beliefs, and behaviors

with those of the organization or group to which they belong. This alignment is often driven by a basic form of egoism, where the immediate benefits of such alignment (like social acceptance, career advancement, or personal satisfaction) are the primary motivators.

However, when refined egoism is applied to this process, individuals take a more strategic and comprehensive approach. They consider both the short-term rewards and long-term consequences of aligning with the organization's values. For instance, an employee might align with the organizational culture not just for immediate job security or peer acceptance, but also with an understanding of how this alignment will impact their long-term career trajectory, personal growth, and professional reputation.

Refined egoism in this context also involves considering the impact of one's identification with the organization on other relationships — both within and outside the organization. This might include how such identification affects one's relationships with colleagues, superiors, or even external stakeholders. It entails a recognition that one's professional identity and reputation are shaped not just by immediate actions but also by how these actions are perceived and valued in the longer term.

Additionally, refined egoism in identification involves a degree of "strategic" empathy. Individuals consider how their alignment with the organization's values and goals will be perceived by others, and how it aligns with the broader objectives and culture of the organization. This strategic empathy ensures that the process of identification is not just a passive assimilation of values but a deliberate and thoughtful alignment that takes into consideration the dynamic nature of organizational relationships and objectives.

Internalization

Identification sparks alignment; internalization transforms it into conviction. Here, individuals integrate the organization's mission, values, and objectives into their personal belief and value systems. Internalization involves recognizing and embracing values and principles that may differ from one's own, leading to a conscious or unconscious decision to internalize these values. This transformative journey begins with hiring and continues throughout an individual's career as both the employee and the organization evolve. New values, principles, behaviors, and causes are recognized and internalized if they are perceived as beneficial, with factors such as professional development and work-life balance playing pivotal roles.

It is a deeper and more transformative process because it involves the transition and transformation of the exteriorized form of the psychic contained in the objects into the external subjective and individual form. In the organizational context, internalization refers to the deep integration of the organization's mission, values, and objectives into an individual's belief and value systems. The process involves cognitive and affective components. The cognitive aspect pertains to understanding and accepting the organization's cause, integrating it with one's cognitive framework. The affective component involves forming an emotional bond with the organization's cause, going beyond intellectual agreement to develop emotional ties.

Internalization is considered the highest level of influence, as it involves absorbing information and adapting behavior in a way that aligns with the individual's existing values and beliefs. This process is driven by the source's credibility rather than its business authority. Once internalized, these behaviors become an intrinsic part of a person's identity—not dependent on external rewards or oversight.

This is evident in behavioral manifestations congruent with the organization's values and cause, such as organizational citizenship behaviors (OCBs). Internalization is characterized by long-term stability and identity integration, where the organization's cause alters the individual's professional and sometimes personal self-concept, achieving a high level of integration where the cause and the individual's identity become intertwined.

Socialization

As employees identify with and internalize organizational values, socialization becomes the official process of integrating new members into the organization. Socialization is often outlined in standard operating procedures, serving as a roadmap to guide new employees through their roles, colleagues, work environment, and the overarching organizational culture.

The process of socialization has been extensively studied in organizational behavior and human resource management. Effective socialization yields positive organizational outcomes, including heightened job performance, increased levels of organizational identification, and reduced turnover rates. Furthermore, it facilitates the onboarding process as new employees get to know the culture, the people, and how well the organization meets its psychological contract.

Van Maanen and Schein delineate the stages of socialization, which include anticipatory socialization, encounter, and metamorphosis. These stages represent the transition from being an outsider to becoming a fully integrated insider within the organization.

Anticipatory Socialization is the initial stage which occurs before the individual joins the organization, involving the gathering of information and forming expectations about the organization and the role. In the Encounter stage, employees face the real dynamics of their role and the workplace culture, marked by learning the norms, values, and behaviors expected within the organization. The Change and Acquisition is when the individual is capable of fulfilling their job responsibilities and aligns their behaviors with organizational expectations, achieving full member status.

Importance of Organizational Socialization

The significance of socialization extends beyond knowledge acquisition. Without a structured socialization process, employees may be incapable of developing a bond with the organization. Effective socialization leads to numerous positive organizational outcomes, such as heightened job performance, higher levels of organizational identification, and reduced turnover rates.

The absence of a structured socialization process can cause role ambiguity, role conflict, and feelings of isolation. A lack of clear understanding of organizational norms and a mismatch between employee expectations and organizational reality can cause ineffective work performance and strained relationships within the workplace. Furthermore, inadequate socialization can lead to a misalignment between the employee's values and those of the organization, further exacerbating disengagement and dissatisfaction.

Example: IBM

A notable example of an effective socialization process can be found at IBM, a multinational technology company. IBM is renowned for its comprehensive and effective onboarding and socialization strategy, known as the "IBM Onboarding Experience." This approach is designed to integrate new employees into the company's culture, values, and operational practices efficiently and effectively.

From the outset, new IBMers, as they are affectionately called, are assigned a "buddy" or mentor from their department. This mentor assists them in navigating the company's vast structure and understanding their role within the organization. The buddy system is part of a larger, structured onboarding program that includes formal presentations, training sessions, and networking events aimed at immersing new employees in IBM's organizational culture and values.

IBM also leverages technology to facilitate the socialization process. New hires have access to a range of digital resources, including an onboarding portal that provides information on IBM's history, key business areas, and operational procedures. They are encouraged to engage with the company's internal social media platforms, fostering connections and deepening their understanding of the informal culture and communication styles.

The IBM Onboarding Experience extends beyond the initial weeks or months. It spans the first year of employment, ensuring that new hires feel supported as they transition into their roles. This prolonged engagement helps new employees fully internalize IBM's values and expectations, contributing to their long-term success and satisfaction within the company.

The success of IBM's socialization process is reflected in its high employee retention rates and frequent recognition as an employer of choice. By providing a comprehensive, supportive, and engaging onboarding experience, IBM ensures that new employees are well-equipped to contribute to the company's success while feeling valued and integrated within the organization.

System for Socialization

To effectively introduce new employees, organizations should conceptualize an integrative system that encompasses various components: understanding the organization's culture, comprehending the role and its scope, familiarity with processes, and clarity regarding expectations. This system should transmit organizational knowledge and foster an environment where new employees can safely explore, ask questions, and internalize the organizational values.

A structured approach involving internal mentorship programs, interactive orientations, and continuous feedback mechanisms ensures that new employees become informed and fully integrated members of the organizational community. This comprehensive system supports both the technical onboarding and the social and psychological integration of new employees into the organizational fabric. It ensures that new hires are familiar with their specific job tasks and how their roles fit into the larger organizational picture.

The system should cover the organization's cause, values, expected behaviors, and social norms, providing clear guidelines on communication, decision-making processes, and conflict (work challenges) resolution mechanisms and approaches.

Organizational socialization is a critical process that impacts both individual and organizational outcomes. By understanding and enhancing this process, organizations can create an environment where new employees feel valued, supported, and equipped to contribute to organizational success. The interplay between identification and internalization within the socialization process underscores the transformation from being an organizational outsider to becoming a committed and potentially loyal member of the organization.

The Role of Leadership and Culture

These integration processes are deeply shaped by leadership and the culture it creates. Leadership decisions and organizational culture play pivotal roles in shaping these experiences, influencing the degree of reciprocity and oneness within the organization.

The concept of Asabiyyah, or oneness, is integral to loyalty and is influenced by the culture shaped by leadership decisions at various organizational levels. The degree of reciprocity and oneness affects the proclamation and adherence to the organization's cause, fostering through dedication and commitment. This is solidified through alignment with the six behavioral determinants and the respective consequences of loyalty.

While socialization is clearly defined as a standard operating procedure, identification and internalization are dynamic processes, evolving with the individual's growth and familiarity with the organization. They represent ongoing relationships driven by reciprocal leadership and culture. Disruptions in these processes can lead to cracks in bonds created between the organization and its members, ultimately impacting the organization's most valuable asset—its people.

The processes of identification, internalization, and socialization play crucial roles in employee integration. They are dynamic and interdependent, influenced by leadership, organizational culture, and individual psychological characteristics. Through their understanding and development, organizations can create an environment where new employees feel valued, supported, and equipped to contribute to organizational success from the start.

CHAPTER 3

Defining Loyalty

*"If you want to build a ship, don't summon people to buy wood,
prepare tools, distribute jobs, and organize the work; teach
people the yearning for the wide, boundless ocean."*

—Antoine de Saint-Exupery

OUR DEFINITION OF LOYALTY, DEVELOPED through our research and practical application, is the willing, practical, and thoroughgoing dedication of a person to a cause on the condition of reciprocity and Asabiyyah. This definition breaks loyalty into essential components, revealing its full complexity and practical depth with its emphasis on the reciprocal nature of Loyalty to Loyalty.

Willingness

The aspect of willingness highlights that loyalty involves a conscious, voluntary decision. It is not an obligation imposed by external forces but a deliberate choice to dedicate oneself to a cause. This cause can pertain to an organization, a private entity, a government institution, or a group of people. When someone willingly chooses to dedicate to what an organization represents, it becomes easier for them to begin the internalization process later. Most importantly, it is easier for them to stand by their decision when faced with external challenges or inner doubts during the process. Integrity ensures this decision is made with honesty and trustworthiness.

Practicality

Practicality keeps loyalty grounded and appropriately applied. Loyalty must be practical and demonstrated through concrete actions and decisions, not theoretical or abstract commitments. Excessive or misplaced loyalty can be detrimental, which ties into the principle of reciprocity. Loyalty cannot truly exist if one party feels disadvantaged or cheated. It is a mutual exchange where both sides benefit and support each other. Practicality ensures loyalty is functional and beneficial, maintaining a balance that prevents exploitation and fosters mutual respect in a balanced manner. Psychological safety further ensures individuals feel secure to express their views and engage in a constructive dialogue.

Thoroughgoing Dedication

This involves internalizing the cause. Once internalized, the cause becomes the guiding principle or "north star" for the person, influencing their actions and decisions across various domains, whether in business or politics. The internalization process is a prerequisite for social cohesion and oneness. The person consistently acts in favor of the cause, ensuring their dedication is unwavering. Proactivity ensures individuals actively promote and sustain their dedication to the cause, while nurturing behavior fosters a supportive environment. Proactivity transforms passive loyalty into active support, while nurturing behavior strengthens the group's bonds towards their shared goals.

Historical Context of Dedication

Around the 17th century, the Latin word "dedication" involved giving oneself to a purpose deemed important. This effort and hard work for a specific purpose are rooted in the perceived significance of the cause. Over time, dedication came to reflect the intrinsic value of purposeful work. Shared values provide a common foundation that strengthens it.

Reciprocity

Inspired by Confucius's Analects, loyalty is understood as a reciprocal relationship within the context of benevolence and righteousness, exemplified by leadership. Reciprocity is a two-way street characterized by mutual trust and awareness. Each party in the relationship must fulfill their role and defend the other, provided both remain devoted to the same cause. This reciprocal nature of loyalty ensures that it is not one-sided or exploitative but built on a foundation of mutual respect and shared goals. Reciprocity enhances the stability and sustainability of loyalty by creating a balanced and equitable relationship.

Asabiyyah

Derived from Ibn Khaldun's sociological work, Asabiyyah refers to social cohesion and group solidarity. It signifies the collective will-formation and sustained action that integrate like-minded individuals into a cohesive entity working towards a common goal. The process of identifying with the values and cause (willing) and internalizing these values (thoroughgoing dedication) are necessary steps in establishing Asabiyyah. Ibn Khaldun cautioned that increased prosperity could increase individualism, leading to fragmentation and decline. Asabiyyah promotes a sense of belonging and mutual commitment, essential for the long-term success and stability of any group.

Integrating Behavioral Determinants of Loyalty

1. **Integrity** is integral to willingness, ensuring that the decision to commit to a cause is made with honesty and moral uprightness.

2. **Mutual Respect** is fundamental to practicality, fostering a supportive environment where loyalty can thrive.

3. **Psychological Safety** is essential to practicality, creating a space where individuals feel secure in their commitment.

4. **Proactivity** is crucial to thoroughgoing dedication, ensuring individuals actively promote and sustain their commitment to the cause.

5. **Nurturing Behavior** supports thoroughgoing dedication to support and empower the other members of the organization.

6. **Shared Values** underpin both the historical context of dedication and Asabiyyah, providing a common foundation that strengthens loyalty and social cohesion.

In essence, our definition of loyalty reflects a multifaceted voluntary dedication that involves practical application, thoroughgoing integration, reciprocity, and asabiyyah - oneness. This comprehensive approach ensures that loyalty is not blind or static but a dynamic, interactive relationship grounded in mutual respect, integrity, and shared values. One's loyalty level is constructed by the presence of all determinants at various rates. This nuanced understanding of loyalty is explored in greater detail through various examples and contexts throughout this book, providing a holistic view of how loyalty can be effectively fostered and maintained in modern organizations.

A Cause

A cause embodies an actionable pursuit or conviction deeply resonating with an individual or collective. Its strength is showcased in its capacity to rally individuals towards a shared vision that fills them with dedication, fervor, and a definitive sense of purpose. This intensity often comes with persistent effort, marking a clear demarcation between a genuine cause and fleeting interests. Remarkably, the universal appeal of a cause can bridge gaps across cultures, geographies, and generations, melding varied groups under a singular vision in an organization's culture.

At its core, a cause has a clear, unambiguous purpose, providing a well-defined path for individuals or groups to channel their energies and efforts. Hand-in-hand with this is the deep emotional connection it fosters, its capacity to resonate on a personal level and intertwine with one's values and beliefs, thus facilitating a strong dedication. Causes bestow empowerment, instilling the belief that one's actions, however minute, can influence the grander objective, elevating the cause to a realm beyond monetary pursuits.

A cause shares similarities with Viktor Frankl's conclusions on the importance of a purpose in one's life, as described in "Man in search of a meaning." Frankl's work emphasizes the critical nature of finding one's 'why'—a deeply rooted purpose that gives life meaning. In an organizational context, this could promote greater productivity and success and also lead to personal fulfillment and resilience in critical moments. His findings suggest that when people gravitate towards their purpose, they can look beyond mundane tasks and find joy and motivation in their contributions, no matter how small they may seem.

Joseph Campbell, an American writer and comparative mythologist credited with influencing the creation of the Star Wars saga, has remarked, "People say that what we're all seeking is a meaning for life. I don't think that's what we're really seeking. I think that what we're seeking is an experience of being alive,so that our life experiences on the purely physical plane will have resonances with our own innermost being and reality, so that we actually feel the rapture of being alive." This quote from The Power of Myth, reflects Campbell's belief that people are not simply searching for intellectual meaning or abstract purpose but rather for experiences that make them feel deeply connected to the essence of life itself. Campbell asserts that people seek not just abstract meaning, but a visceral connection to life that resonates deeply with their innermost being.

A cause, by nature, embodies this pursuit of meaning on a grander scale, offering individuals and organizations a deeply resonant purpose that they can live and breathe, providing both personal fulfillment and collective direction in following the mission and vision of the organization. Much like the personal experience of meaning that Campbell describes, a well-defined organizational cause allows individuals to feel alive in their contributions, creating that same resonance between personal values and collective action.

Ibn Khaldun, whose work was introduced earlier, stressed that a unified cause and purpose are instrumental for societies and organizations. He theorized that with collective cohesion, civilizations thrive and without it, they wane. This sentiment echoes in contemporary times, emphasizing the pivotal role of shared causes in nurturing unity and action with the creation of resilience within business organizations and communities.

When the cause (the purpose, the raison d'être) is integrated into goal-setting, performance reviews, and decision-making processes, it becomes an inherent part of the organizational fabric and its processes. This integration ensures that the cause is consistently reinforced through daily actions and decisions, making it a living part of the workplace culture rather than just a tagline.

In short, a cause represents the deeper, emotional reason for an organization's existence, rooted in its values and long-term purpose beyond profit. It provides a steady guiding force that doesn't easily change, unlike the more operational mission or vision. A mission describes the organization's current activities, who it serves, and how it operates, focusing on actionable, fairly short-term goals that help fulfill its overarching cause. A vision is future-oriented and aspirational, offering a picture of the desired outcome or change the organization strives to achieve, motivating stakeholders, and guiding long-term planning.

Phil Jackson

This was the case with the professional basketball coach Phil Jackson, who carved a legacy with both the Chicago Bulls and the Los Angeles Lakers that is rooted in a blend of Zen philosophy, Native American philosophies, unparalleled strategic acumen, and the nurturing of pivotal player relationships. At the helm of the Bulls from 1989 to 1998, Jackson masterminded a dynasty led by Michael Jordan, Scottie Pippen, and Dennis Rodman, capturing six NBA championships in the process. By incorporating Zen principles, Jackson emphasized the importance of the moment, encouraging players to be present and focused, transcending beyond the physical aspects of the game to mental and spiritual realms. This approach helped players deal with pressure, improve concentration, and work as a more unified team. Jackson's cause was to transform individual talents into a singular, collective force, reflecting the Zen concept of 'oneness'. He believed that success on the court begins with harmony and understanding off the court. His unique coaching style, emphasizing mindfulness and collective responsibility, transformed a team with undeniable talent into a cohesive, nearly unstoppable unit over the course of a decade.

When Jackson transitioned to the Lakers in 1999, skeptics wondered if he could replicate his success without the likes of Jordan. However, under his leadership, the Lakers secured five NBA titles, as Jackson adeptly managed the dynamics between stars like Kobe Bryant and Shaquille O'Neal. Here, his cause took on the challenge of harmonizing conflicting egos for a common goal. Jackson's commitment to personal growth and mutual respect among players facilitated a dynamic where individual achievements contributed to the team's success, leading to another era of dominance in the NBA. His recollection of the events alludes to a form of refined egoism. When his strategy and methodology were followed because he brought with himself Bulls' veterans and a successful track, despite not being completely understood, his loyalty has been to the principles of team basketball, personal growth, and the melding of individual talents for collective personal and professional triumph. A vision to win and a mission for the team to do it as one.

Expanding on Phil Jackson's legacy, it's clear that his cause was about the team playing the game of basketball as one and winning as a team, transforming a group of skilled individuals into a coherent, single entity with a shared vision. He applied the lessons of mindfulness and collective responsibility beyond the game, teaching players and fans alike that success is a product of internal harmony, shared goals, and a deep, collective focus.

In businesses, a cause acts as an impetus for employees and stakeholders. When the underpinnings of an employee's beliefs and values find harmony with the organization's cause, it leads to unwavering dedication, infusing their work with passion. This sense of alignment and purpose magnifies their input, as they view their endeavors as vehicles for positive change, impacting themselves, their organization, and its clientele. Such alignment, born from the intertwining of personal and organizational causes, emerges as the bedrock of organizational triumph and endurance.

Tata Group

Jamsetji Tata founded Tata Group in 1868, who was rooted in the pioneering vision of industrializing India. Since its inception, the group has been committed to improving the quality of life for the communities it serves. This foundational principle has guided the evolution of Tata's mission and vision over the years. The legacy of Jamsetji Tata, who aspired to excellence in business while contributing to society, continues to guide the group. His belief in ethical business practices and community welfare laid the groundwork for what would become the core values of the Tata Group.

The strategic objectives have been designed to transform the vision of global significance into reality. These objectives include fostering innovation, penetrating global markets, enhancing customer satisfaction, and maintaining a commitment to sustainability. The group aims to lead in various sectors by investing in research and development, thereby ensuring cutting-edge solutions and services. Tata's commitment to 'Leadership with Trust' is realized through adherence to ethical practices and contribution to economic prosperity and community welfare. Each strategic objective directly supports the group's overarching aim to not just expand its global footprint but also to ensure that such growth is ethically grounded and socially responsible.

Tata Group aspires "To be globally significant in each of our chosen businesses by 2025". This vision underscores the group's ambition to not just lead in market share or financial metrics but to set standards of excellence and innovation globally across all industries in which it operates. For example, Tata Consultancy Services (TCS) has evolved into a global IT leader, representing the group's commitment to achieving significant impacts in the technology sector worldwide.

The group's mission is to operate as "the most reliable global network for customers and suppliers, that delivers value through products and services". They aim to create value responsibly for all stakeholders involved, which is evident in initiatives like Tata Swach, an affordable water purifier addressing the critical need for clean water in underprivileged areas, and Tata Nano, which was an attempt to provide an affordable transportation solution to the masses.

In conclusion, the Tata Group's journey from its inception in 1868 to its aspirations for 2025 exemplifies the great impact of having a clear mission, a visionary outlook, and their combination into a cause. The latter is rooted in creating sustainable value not just for the business and its customers, but also for the community at large. All companies can create their mission, their vision, and set a cause, the meaning of why they do what they do. Combined with the principles in this book, a strong cause can foster loyalty and build enduring businesses.

Ralph Lauren

Ralph Lauren's journey in fashion is a powerful testament to the significance of having a cause that transcends beyond mere commercial success to touch the lives of millions around the globe. Born into a modest family, Ralph Lauren's foray into the world of fashion together with his wife and muse, Ricky, was driven not just by a passion for design but by a deeper cause — the creation of a lifestyle, an embodiment of the American dream that was inclusive yet aspirational.

Lauren's cause was embedded in the belief that fashion should not solely be about clothing but about storytelling, about crafting an identity and a narrative that people could aspire to and see themselves within. He sought to democratize fashion in a way that it became accessible to all, thereby redefining the boundaries of style and elegance. His designs were more than fabric; they were a symbol of hope, aspiration, and accessibility, echoing the possibility that anyone could achieve their own version of the American dream.

At the core of Ralph Lauren's cause was the commitment to authenticity, quality, and attention to detail. He believed in the power of dreams and the importance of staying true to one's vision, even when faced with skepticism or adversity. This conviction led him to create a brand that represented more than clothes; it represented an entire lifestyle that reflected a distinct blend of Americana, European elegance, and a hint of British nobility, creating an entirely new genre of fashion that appealed to a wide audience's aspirations and dreams.

Through his philanthropic efforts, Lauren has extended his cause beyond the runway. His dedication to cancer care and prevention, educational opportunities, and environmental sustainability highlights his commitment to societal well-being and mirrors his belief in giving back to the community that has been integral to his success. These efforts underscore the idea that a true cause encompasses not just business achievements but also the impact one has on the world. His legacy demonstrates that when you combine passion with purpose, the result is an enduring influence that extends beyond individual accolades to inspire generations to come.

Hubert Joly

A cause embodies a pursuit or conviction deeply resonating with an individual or collective, transcending goals or targets. Such a cause presents itself as an unwavering calling that demands both attention and action. More than just objectives, these causes are deeply entrenched in personal convictions and social factors. Their strength is showcased in their capacity to rally individuals towards a shared vision, turning them into impassioned advocates filled with dedication, fervor, and a definitive sense of purpose. This intensity often comes with persistent effort, marking a clear demarcation between a genuine cause and fleeting interests. Remarkably, the universal appeal of a cause can bridge gaps across cultures, geographies, and generations, melding varied groups under a singular vision. Hubert Joly illustrated this during his transformative leadership at Best Buy.

Hubert Joly, former CEO of Best Buy, embodies a cause that is deeply intertwined with personal conviction and social impact. Much like Phil Jackson's legacy in basketball, Joly's cause transcends conventional business objectives, creating a sense of purpose that has resonated across his organization. Joly's cause centers on the humanization of business, placing people at the heart of corporate strategy. His leadership philosophy emphasizes the importance of purpose and human connection, drawing inspiration from principles similar to those seen in Viktor Frankl's work on finding meaning and purpose in life.

Joly's journey at Best Buy began when the company faced significant challenges, with many predicting its imminent demise. Contrary to the conventional playbook of corporate turnarounds—characterized by drastic cost-cutting and layoffs—Joly chose a path rooted in purpose and human connection. His approach emphasized the importance of listening to employees, understanding their perspectives, and engaging them in the company's mission. By doing so, he unleashed what he called "human magic," a collective energy that drives extraordinary results.

Hubert Joly's leadership philosophy was grounded in the concept of "human magic." This idea revolves around creating an environment where employees are able to unleash their full potential. Joly believed that every individual possesses unique talents and capabilities that can be unlocked through a supportive and engaging work environment. This approach involved recognizing and nurturing employees' aspirations and dreams,and fostering a culture of autonomy, mastery, and purpose.

At Best Buy, Joly initiated the "Discover Your Purpose" program to align employees' personal dreams with the company's mission. Leaders were encouraged to have meaningful conversations with employees about their personal and professional aspirations. For instance, some employees expressed a desire to further their education, which Best Buy supported through flexible work schedules and tuition assistance. This initiative allowed employees to see their work as part of a larger, meaningful journey, significantly boosting morale and engagement.

Joly emphasized the importance of building authentic relationships within the company. He spent time visiting stores, engaging directly with employees, and listening to their concerns. For example, during his first days as CEO, he worked in a Best Buy store in St. Cloud, Minnesota, dressed in a blue shirt with a "CEO in Training" tag. This hands-on approach allowed him to understand the issues employees faced and fostered a culture of trust and collaboration. One practical outcome was the improvement of the company's website search functionality after frontline employees pointed out its flaws.

One impact of Joly's focus on fostering human connections was to foster a sense of autonomy among his employees. Regional manager Chris Schmidt's personalized approach to coaching in Denver is a prime example.. Schmidt focused on individual performance metrics rather than a one-size-fits-all approach. Sales associates received weekly one-on-one coaching sessions to review their performance and set goals, which led to a 10% increase in revenue per hour. This method empowered employees to take ownership of their development and success.

Joly championed the idea of continuous development and mastery. The "Blue Shirt Nation" initiative provided a knowledge sharing platform for employees to share best practices and learn from each other. For example, a sales associate who excelled in a specific product category would mentor others, enhancing overall team performance. This peer-to-peer learning environment encouraged continuous improvement and skill development, fostering a culture of collective growth and excellence. By investing in the growth of his employees, Joly fostered a loyal and motivated workforce that was dedicated to the company's mission. This focus on people's development is aligned with the concepts of social identity and organizational identification, where employees who feel valued and supported are more likely to identify with the organization.

Renew Blue

One of Joly's most significant initiatives was the "Renew Blue" strategy, which he implemented upon joining Best Buy in 2012. "Renew Blue" focused on building revenues and improving margins while avoiding mass layoffs and store closures as much as possible.

Joly believed that by investing in employees and focusing on customer satisfaction, the company could achieve sustainable growth. This belief was rooted in the conviction that engaged and motivated employees would drive the company's success. Under his leadership, Best Buy invested heavily in employee training and development, fostering a culture of inclusivity and respect.

During the early days of the "Renew Blue" turnaround, Joly faced a dilemma about whether to keep the plan confidential or share it within the company. He opted for transparency, gathering 150 managers to discuss the draft plan, which helped secure valuable feedback and buy-in without any leaks. This move underlined

Joly's dedication to trust, inclusivity and predictability, ensuring that employees felt part of the process and were motivated to contribute to the company's recovery.

Central to Joly's cause was his belief in the power of purpose-driven leadership. He argued that corporations are not soulless entities but human organizations with people at their center, working together in support of a common purpose. Furthermore, Joly's commitment to ethical business practices and corporate transparency reinforced his cause. He understood that a company's reputation hinges on its integrity and the trust it earns from stakeholders. By prioritizing ethical standards and open communication, Joly fostered a culture of trust and accountability within Best Buy where employees feel valued and connected to the company's mission of enriching lives through technology. This alignment of personal and organizational values both enhanced employee loyalty and strengthened customer trust and brand loyalty.

Sense of Purpose & Achievement

Joly's communications team, led by Matt Furman, was tasked with finding and sharing positive news throughout the company. The importance of celebrating small victories was emphasized so as to maintain morale and build momentum during the challenging turnaround of Best Buy. For instance, they celebrated small but meaningful wins like growth in specific markets such as Chicago and improvements in the performance of small appliances. Throughout the turnaround, Best Buy continued to share wins and positive developments. This included regular updates on new initiatives, such as the expansion of the store-within-a-store concept with brands like Samsung and Apple. These achievements were highlighted in team meetings and company town halls, sending a positive message and boosting morale across the organization and the investors.

Joly believed that maintaining a positive environment and radiating energy were crucial for motivating the team. By consistently focusing on positive developments and reinforcing an optimistic outlook, Joly helped create a culture where employees felt empowered and motivated. This positive reinforcement was a key component of the "Renew Blue" turnaround strategy.

A poignant example of celebrating small victories and maintaining a positive environment was Best Buy's response to Hurricane Maria in Puerto Rico. The company provided immediate financial support and supplies to employees affected by the hurricane, demonstrating their commitment to their workforce. The rapid reopening of stores and the substantial year-on-year sales increase post-hurricane were celebrated as major achievements, showcasing resilience and purpose.

Best Buy captured and shared stories of resilience and purpose, such as the company's efforts in Puerto Rico, during leadership meetings. For example, a video was shown at a Holiday Leadership Meeting that detailed the company's response to Hurricane Maria from the perspective of employees in Puerto Rico and those on the mainland who organized support. These stories reinforced the company's purpose and the collective effort of its employees, further building a sense of shared mission and pride.

Personal Reflections and Values

One of the defining aspects of Joly's leadership was his emphasis on authenticity and personal transformation. He believed that genuine leadership begins with personal introspection and aligning one's professional endeavors with a deeper purpose. Joly's journey was marked by a significant shift from seeking external validation to embracing a more purpose-driven approach. He learned from his experiences and mentors that leadership is not about being the smartest person in the room but about being the most connected and empathetic. His leadership at Best Buy showed that when companies focus on purpose and people, they can achieve extraordinary results, both financially and socially.

His book, "The Heart of Business: Leadership Principles for the Next Era of Capitalism," encapsulates his belief that businesses can be a force for good by focusing on human-centric principles and long-term value creation. This perspective echoes Viktor Frankl's insights on finding meaning and purpose in work, suggesting that a deep sense of purpose can drive both personal fulfillment and organizational success.

CHAPTER 4

Reciprocity

"I won't accept anything less than the best a player's capable of doing ... and he has the right to expect the best that I can do for him and the team!"

—Lou Holtz

RECIPROCITY, WITHIN BOTH THE FRAMEWORK of psychological contracts and broader organizational contexts, is a multifaceted principle that underscores the mutual exchange of benefits and loyalty between individuals and their respective organizations. Drawing upon ancient philosophies and contemporary organizational theory, the essence of reciprocity extends beyond mere transactional exchanges, embodying a deeper, relational and ethical dimension that is pivotal for fostering trust, loyalty, and mutual respect. In our view, reciprocity is the mutual exchange of respect and support through the agreed-upon psychological contract characterized by fair practices and open explanatory communication.

Aristotle's notion of civic friendship and Confucian principles highlight reciprocity as a foundational element of social harmony and ethical conduct. Aristotle perceives it as a mutual well-wishing akin to the solidarity among citizens, while Confucius emphasizes loyalty and reciprocity as the single thread weaving through the moral fabric of society. These philosophical underpinnings resonate within modern organizational settings, where reciprocity acts as the cornerstone of the psychological contract between employees and employers. This unwritten and perceived set of mutual obligations and expectations forms the bedrock of the employee-employer relationship, significantly impacting loyalty in organizations, commitment, and overall job satisfaction.

Reciprocity, as defined by Schrag, involves an expectation and actuality of mutual well-wishing between an individual and their object of loyalty, akin to mutual fellow feeling among citizens in Aristotle's notion of civic friendship. It signifies not just the individual's well-wishing towards the firm but also an anticipation that the firm reciprocates this sentiment. This mutual well-wishing might manifest in simple acknowledgments or expressions of appreciation from the firm towards the employee, highlighting the crucial link between loyalty recognition and its reward. Without reciprocity, the loyalty and well-wishing of an individual towards the corporation are unlikely to be sustained, potentially leading to a diminished sense of loyalty if the individual perceives their loyalty as unreciprocated.

In leveraging the Win/Win mentality, organizations embrace a culture where reciprocal benefits and loyalty are paramount. This approach underscores the importance of mutual respect and shared success, advocating for a collaborative environment where the success of one is seen as integral to the success of all. By prioritizing outcomes that benefit all parties, organizations can cultivate a sense of unity and collective responsibility, essential for achieving long-term objectives and sustaining a positive organizational climate.

Past research has recognized different types of reciprocity such as direct and non-direct.

Direct Reciprocity refers to actions that are directly given or received between two individuals. This form of reciprocity is straightforward and involves immediate and clear exchanges where the giver and receiver are evident, and the actions directly affect each other.

Non-Direct Reciprocity plays a crucial role in building and maintaining social cohesion (oneness) and trust within groups and communities, beyond the immediate dyadic relationships. It's particularly interesting because it extends the concept of reciprocity beyond direct exchanges, creating a more complex and interconnected web of social interactions.

In organizational contexts, non-direct reciprocity can foster a culture of collaboration and mutual support, where individuals feel encouraged to contribute to the collective well-being, even if the immediate benefits are not apparent. This can lead to a more cohesive work environment, as acts of kindness or support are undertaken not for direct reciprocation, but with the understanding that such behaviors benefit the organization as a whole.

Moreover, non-direct reciprocity can contribute to the development of social capital, as it often involves a broader network of individuals. This can enhance information flow, cooperation, and resource sharing within an organization, leading to increased innovation and productivity. However, non-direct reciprocity also relies heavily on the existing culture and norms within the organization or society. Its effectiveness can be diminished in highly individualistic or competitive environments where individuals may prioritize personal gain over collective well-being. Promoting non-direct reciprocity within organizations can lead to long-term benefits, including improved morale, stronger team dynamics, and a more positive workplace culture, as long as it is supported by clear communication, shared goals, and mutual respect among all members.

In applied terms, reciprocity in the workplace is manifested through a Win/Win mentality, advocating for outcomes that are mutually beneficial to all parties involved. This approach is rooted in mutual respect and the understanding that the collective success of an organization is inextricably linked to the well-being and success of its individual members. It calls for leaders and employees alike to recognize and act upon the understanding that each member's contribution is vital to the group's overarching objectives.

However, the sustainability of this reciprocal relationship hinges on the perception of fairness and mutual fulfillment of obligations. A breach in the psychological contract, stemming from unmet expectations or perceived inequities, can lead to disillusionment and a diminished sense of loyalty. This unwritten contract, a term coined by Denise Rousseau, encapsulates the set of mutual expectations between employees and employers. It plays a pivotal role in shaping the dynamics of the workplace, influencing employee dedication, satisfaction, and perception of organizational support.

Key aspects of the psychological contract include:

- **Expectations**: These are the beliefs held by employees about what they owe their employer and what they feel the employer owes them in return. These expectations can cover a wide range of factors, from career development opportunities to respectful treatment.

- **Perceived Promises**: Employees might believe certain promises have been made implicitly through actions, statements, or company culture. These are not always formally agreed upon but can significantly affect an employee's satisfaction and commitment.

- **Breach of Contract**: When employees perceive that their employer has failed to fulfill these unwritten obligations, they may experience a psychological contract breach. This perception can lead to decreased job satisfaction, commitment, and performance, and increased turnover intentions.

- **Reciprocity**: The psychological contract is fundamentally based on the principle of reciprocity. Employees are more likely to be motivated and committed when they believe their efforts will be reciprocated with fair treatment, opportunities for advancement, and other forms of support from their employer. Therefore, understanding reciprocity helps clarify the dynamics of how psychological contracts are formed, sustained, or violated.

Thus, organizations must be diligent in recognizing and addressing the dynamic needs and expectations of their employees, fostering an environment where reciprocity is deeply ingrained in the organizational culture. The psychological contract is dynamic and evolves over time, influenced by changes in the workplace, economic conditions, and individual circumstances. A breach of this contract, perceived when expectations are not met, can lead to a sense of betrayal, resulting in decreased morale, commitment, and productivity. Therefore, organizations must remain attuned to the expectations of their workforce and to potential new needs, actively seeking to fulfill their part of the agreement. Reciprocity starts from within. The management has to be the initiator but in a controlled genuine way.

Reciprocity within organizational settings transcends transactional exchanges and embeds itself as a cornerstone of a thriving internalized work culture. This reciprocal ethos, when effectively cultivated through leadership exemplification and the fostering of active listening among decision-makers of the organization, culminates in a cohesive culture unified by the organization's overarching objectives. By valuing employee input and demonstrating responsiveness to their needs and ideas, and not merely promising resolution without timely follow-through, organizations can foster a sense of belonging and respect, essential components of a reciprocal relationship. This two-way communication enhances problem-solving and innovation while also reinforcing employees' sense of value and belonging within the organization.

In integrating reciprocity with organizational practices such as performance evaluations, reward systems, and team dynamics, a holistic approach is required. Performance evaluations that recognize and reward collaborative efforts and contributions to team success reflect the organization's commitment to reciprocity. Similarly, reward systems that align with reciprocal behaviors, such as peer recognition programs and team-based incentives, further entrench this culture. Cultivating an internalized culture of reciprocity necessitates an organizational commitment to active listening. Communication policies that encourage open, transparent dialogues and provide platforms for employee feedback embody the essence of reciprocal exchange.

By emphasizing collective success and mutual support, organizations can dismantle silos and foster a more unified and cohesive work environment.

The integration of reciprocity extends to the development and implementation of fair and equitable policies that underscore organizational justice. Practices that ensure fair treatment, reasoning, and transparency contribute to a culture where employees feel respected and valued.

Finally, the internalized work culture of reciprocity is cemented by a shared dedication to the organization's cause. This shared dedication, galvanized by a clear and compelling organizational cause, serves as a unifying force that aligns individual and collective goals. When employees understand and identify with the organization's objectives, they are more inclined to contribute positively and support one another in achieving these goals, thereby fostering a culture of reciprocity.

The development of an internalized work culture of reciprocity is a multifaceted endeavor that necessitates intentional leadership, active listening, and the integration of reciprocal principles into organizational practices and policies. In essence, the establishment of a reciprocal work culture and leadership guided by fierce resolve and humility, represents a strategic organizational asset. It enhances the loyalty of employees and propels the organization toward sustainable success. By fostering a work environment anchored in mutual respect, shared goals, and collective well-being, organizations can unlock the full potential of their workforce, driving innovation, excellence, and a deep-seated loyalty that transcends transactional relationships.

Assumption of Universality

The assumption that reciprocity is universally valued and beneficial across all cultures and organizations overlooks the intricate variances in cultural norms and practices. Global diversity means that what constitutes reciprocity in one cultural context may not translate directly to another. For instance, in collectivist societies, reciprocity might be seen as an integral part of social harmony, deeply embedded in both personal and professional relationships. Conversely, in more individualistic cultures, the emphasis might be placed on personal achievement and autonomy, potentially clashing with collectivist notions of mutual aid and support. It would be assumed that organizations need to adopt a culturally sensitive approach to reciprocity, recognizing and adapting to the diverse expectations and interpretations held by different cultural groups. One approach to reciprocity in a multicultural setting is to create and uphold a strong company culture. One that transcends different cultures and welcomes all to the organization. It acts as an alluring aspect to all potential new hires. Through the socialization process the new organizational members can understand the culture and what reciprocity is for the organization. Clear and authentic personal examples — especially from those in leadership positions — can significantly influence new members by illustrating the tangible benefits that come from internalizing the company's cause and values.

Negative Correspondences

While the principle of reciprocity aims to foster positive relationships and collaboration within the workplace, it is essential to recognize that it can also cause negative correspondences. A workplace culture that emphasizes reciprocity without considering the balance and fairness of exchanges can lead to a tit-for-tat mentality, where employees engage in reciprocal behaviors more out of obligation or expectation of return rather than genuine goodwill. This can foster an environment of mistrust and competition rather than collaboration. Here comes the role of the psychological contract, the management and its leadership style, and the establishment of clear guidelines and expectations around reciprocal behavior which can help ensure that all employees understand what is expected and appreciated, fostering a more positive, cooperative work environment.

Neglect of Power Dynamics

Reciprocity is also intricately linked to the power dynamics within an organization. Traditional views of reciprocity often fail to consider how hierarchical relationships can skew perceptions and practices of mutual exchange. Individuals in lower power positions may feel obligated to reciprocate favors or support to those in higher positions, not out of genuine respect or willingness, but due to fear of negative consequences or a desire to advance their own positions. This coerced form of reciprocity can lead to resentment and dissatisfaction, undermining the genuine, equitable exchanges that should characterize healthy organizational relationships. Here is the key that organizational leaders have to cultivate an environment where reciprocity is based on mutual respect and support, regardless of one's position in the hierarchy. Leaders should model reciprocal behavior and utilize systems that encourage genuine exchanges, free from coercion or exploitation based on power differentials.

Universal Solution

Creating a company culture tailored specifically to the new organization is paramount. This culture should embody values that first the organization and the decision-makers agree and recognize as theirs. For fostering reciprocity, the values should promote mutual respect and understanding, transcending the constraints of cultural diversities and power imbalances.

From the initial week of employment, new hires should be seamlessly integrated into the company's established culture, which is deliberately designed to transcend typical reciprocity barriers. This culture, grounded in mutual respect, support, and fair practices, serves as the foundation for all interactions and processes within the organization. By immersing new employees in this culture from day one, companies can challenge and reshape any preconceived notions or past experiences that may not align with the organization's values. This early introduction lays the ground for the processes of identification and internalization, ensuring that employees begin their journey with a clear understanding of what is valued and expected.

As employees progress through their initial months—first week, first month, three months, and six months—their experience of the company culture deepens through structured socialization processes. These processes, which include mentorship programs, peer networking, and regular feedback mechanisms, are crucial for reinforcing the organization's reciprocal values and ensuring that new hires feel valued, understood, and integral to the company's mission. This ongoing engagement solidifies the employee's alignment with the organizational ethos and fosters a sense of belonging, essential for nurturing a productive and supportive workplace.

By systematically integrating new employees into the company's culture over these critical periods, the organization can effectively counteract previous cultural or experiential biases, fostering an environment of reciprocity. This approach leads to the gradual identification and internalization of the company's values, promoting a cohesive, supportive, and productive workplace where all members feel valued and motivated to contribute to mutual success.

Examples

Flavius Belisarius

Different types of reciprocal relationships can be found throughout history. Although one could argue that ruling over an empire is not the same as running a business organization, the similarities between the two regarding social dynamics and personal interests are not to be undermined. Flavius Belisarius (l. 505-565 CE), hailing from the modest backgrounds of Illyria in the Balkans, transcended his humble beginnings to emerge as one of Byzantium's most formidable generals. He is often celebrated as the final embodiment of Roman imperial virtues otherwise known as the title of "Last of the Romans" and later his military achievements would be compared to the ones of Alexander the Great, Julius Cesar, and Napoleon Bonaparte. His tenure under Emperor Justinian I (r. 527-565 CE) was notable not just for military achievements but also for the intricate dynamics marking their relationship.

During his teenage years as a recruit in the Byzantine military, Belisarius distinguished himself as a competent soldier, evidently leaving a strong impression on his higher-ups, as he was quickly promoted in rank under Emperor Justin I and subsequently took charge of the emperor's personal guard. The emperor, taken with the youth, elevated him to the status of an officer before further promoting him to a leadership position. Despite the potential Justin I discerned in him, Belisarius's early military endeavors were not indicative of immediate success. He faced several defeats initially until he seemingly mastered the nuances of large-scale military tactics and command. Nevertheless, following the death of Justin I, despite these earlier setbacks, Justinian I assigned him to lead the eastern battalions against the Sassanid Empire. This appointment led to his significant victory at the 530 CE Battle of Dara during the Iberian War. His subsequent battle, the 531 CE confrontation at Callinicum, however, ended in a less favorable outcome, as he suffered a defeat accompanied by substantial casualties. Subsequently, Belisarius was summoned back to Constantinople to answer for this loss under accusations of incompetence but ultimately was exonerated from all allegations and reinstated to his military duties. The taxation policies and collection methods enforced by Justinian I were deeply unpopular among the residents of Constantinople. This discontent reached a boiling point in 532 CE, culminating in the violent upheaval known as the Nika Riots.

The audience at the Hippodrome, already discontent with the sentencing and execution of athletes for murder, erupted into chaos on that day in January 532 CE. Shouting "Nika!" meaning "win," they aggressively advanced towards Emperor Justinian I's palace. Their actions were bolstered by senators disillusioned with Justinian I's governance and his neglect of their counsel in favor of his tax overseer, John the Cappadocian, known for his corrupt practices, who served from circa 532-541 CE. Facing the uprising, Justinian I contemplated abandoning the capital with his followers but was dissuaded by Empress Theodora, who argued that escape would spare his life at the cost of his honor and dignity. Heeding Theodora's advice, Justinian I commanded Belisarius to suppress the insurrection. Upon accessing the Hippodrome, Belisarius forcefully quelled the revolt, resulting in the death of an estimated 20,000 to 30,000 individuals, though some historians set it at 60 000 people.

North Africa Campaign

After quelling the revolt, Justinian I dispatched Belisarius to the African provinces in 533 CE as a reward, aiming to reclaim them for the empire and to 'rescue' the Nicene Christians suffering under the rule of the Arian Christian Vandals. The true motive behind Justinian's decision to invade North Africa—whether it was to end the persecution of Trinitarian Christians or merely a strategic move—is still a subject of scholarly debate, with some attributing the plan to Belisarius himself, as suggested by Procopius. Initially, it appears Justinian's primary ambition was the recovery of the wealthy Tripolitanian ports such as Oea, Sabratha, and Leptis Magna, which, being outside imperial control, had ceased generating revenue, especially critical given the emperor's waning popularity post-Nika Riots.

In 533 CE, Belisarius set sail with an imposing force comprising 5,000 cavalrymen, 10,000 infantrymen, 20,000 seamen aboard 500 large warships, complemented by 92 smaller vessels propelled by 2,000 slaves. Upon landing in North Africa, Belisarius led a disciplined march towards the Vandal stronghold of Carthage. He enforced rigorous discipline among his ranks, ensuring local populations were treated fairly and without harm. This honorable approach garnered the respect and support of the North African locals, who, in turn, supplied his army with provisions and valuable intelligence.

Upon receiving intelligence of an imminent Byzantine assault, Gelimer devised a strategy to ambush and annihilate the enemy forces in the valley of Ad Decium through a threefold surprise onslaught. However, as noted by historian Fuller, achieving such precise timing without the aid of clocks was highly improbable, and the likelihood of the three divisions attacking in unison was minimal. It was a complete failure and only Gelimer's forces survived as the others attacked in two early stages and were slaughtered by the Byzantines. Inadvertently this granted Belisarius the opportunity to advance unchallenged and effortlessly capture Carthage.

Gelimer advanced towards Carthage, only to be defeated at the Battle of Tricameron in December 533 CE. Overwhelmed by the Byzantine forces, Gelimer retreated from the battlefield, prompting a disorderly and panicked withdrawal among his soldiers. Following the defeat, Gelimer was pursued, apprehended, and subsequently paraded in fetters back to Constantinople. Speculation circulated that Belisarius, buoyed by his conquests, contemplated insurrection against Justinian.

In response, the Emperor offered him a pivotal decision: to either remain as the governor of the newly conquered lands or return to Constantinople to be celebrated with a triumph. Opting for the latter, Belisarius reaffirmed his allegiance to the Byzantine ruler. In recognition of his unwavering loyalty, Justinian did bestow upon him the honor of a triumphal celebration and elevated Belisarius to the position of consul, integrating him into the esteemed senatorial class of the Roman Republic. The triumph was the last Roman triumph to closely follow Roman traditions and practices.

Italian Campaign

During 535 CE, Belisarius was dispatched to combat the Ostrogoths in Italy, a country that had previously flourished under

King Theodoric the Great, contributing revenues to the Byzantine Empire. However, following Theodoric's demise, Italy descended into turmoil due to the governance of ineffectual and self-interested monarchs. By 540 CE, Belisarius successfully captured Ravenna and detained King Witigis. In response, Justinian I proposed terms to the Goths that Belisarius deemed excessively lenient: they were allowed to retain their sovereignty and were only required to relinquish half their treasury to Justinian I.

Doubting Justinian's sincerity in the agreement, and considering it excessively soft, Belisarius found himself in a moral quandary. Despite their skepticism towards Justinian and his conditions, the Goths were willing to accept the surrender terms, provided they were endorsed by Belisarius, who they respected for his fair treatment during the conflict. However, as a man of integrity and allegiance, Belisarius could not validate the terms.

Subsequently, a group within the Ostrogothic nobility proposed crowning Belisarius as their monarch as a solution. Belisarius feigned agreement to this plan while maintaining his loyalty to Justinian I and recognizing his strengths lay in military leadership rather than political rule. He proceeded with the coronation plans in Ravenna, only to arrest the conspiracy's leaders ultimately. Asserting loyalty to Justinian, he then seized the entirety of the Ostrogothic realm and its treasures in the name of the Byzantine Emperor.

Despite Belisarius's unwavering loyalty, Emperor Justinian I harbored doubts about his general's allegiance. Belisarius's widespread popularity among his troops and the territories he conquered bred suspicion within Justinian, leading him to believe that Belisarius might potentially challenge his authority. To mitigate this perceived threat, Justinian recalled Belisarius to the capital, replacing him with imperial officials in Italy. This decision backfired disastrously as these new administrators were marred by corruption, leading to widespread suffering among people in Italy and resentment from the Ostrogoths.

In Constantinople, Belisarius's popularity eclipsed that of Justinian, yet the emperor tasked him with confronting the Persian threat. Employing his characteristic strategic foresight and cunning, Belisarius cleverly deceived the Persian forces into overestimating his strength, leading to their retreat and his subsequent victory. This feat was achieved when he met Persian envoys with a large contingent, masquerading as a hunting party, which gave the impression that if a hunting party numbered so many, the army must be enormous.

Meanwhile, Italy descended into further turmoil during Belisarius's absence. The newly appointed Byzantine officials mismanaged the region, igniting an uprising spearheaded by the nationalist Ostrogoth leader Totila. Totila's leadership and magnanimity in victory attracted widespread support, swelling the ranks of his army as he successfully reclaimed Italian territories from Byzantine control.

In response to the escalating situation, Justinian dispatched Belisarius back to Italy in 545 CE to quell Totila's rebellion. However, by the end of that year, Totila had managed to capture Rome, a city of significant symbolic value to the Byzantines despite its diminished political status. This marked a pivotal moment in the Gothic Wars, underscoring the enduring strategic and symbolic significance of Rome in the ongoing conflict between the Byzantine Empire and the Ostrogoths. Totila's army and campaign's successes grew even outsmarting Belisarius who was recalled to Constantinople and later replaced by Narses who would defeat Totila in 552 CE and reconquer Italy.

Upon his return to Constantinople, Belisarius, undeterred by the injustices he faced from Emperor Justinian I, reassumed military leadership and successfully repelled a Bulgar invasion of the

Byzantine Empire in 559 CE. Demonstrating his unwavering military competence, he forced the invaders back and re-established the empire's borders. Despite his loyal service, Belisarius found himself entangled in allegations of corruption, widely regarded today as trumped-up charges, leading to his imprisonment in 562 CE. Nonetheless, Justinian I eventually granted him a pardon, reinstating his former rank and privileges within the Byzantine court. Belisarius passed away from natural causes in 565 CE, mere weeks after the death of Emperor Justinian I, at his residence on the outskirts of Constantinople.

Reciprocal Dynamics Between Belisarius and Justinian

The relationship between Belisarius and Emperor Justinian I encapsulates the essence of reciprocity within a hierarchical structure, marked by an exchange of loyalty, support, and respect. This mutual exchange, however, was fraught with complexities and conditional elements that both strengthened and tested the bonds of their relationship.

Initially, the reciprocal relationship between Justinian and Belisarius was evident through their mutual support—Belisarius, with his military acumen, significantly contributed to Justinian's imperial ambitions, while Justinian, in turn, provided Belisarius with the necessary authority and resources. Despite the political intrigues and the highs and lows in their relationship, Justinian repeatedly turned to Belisarius in times of crisis, showing a certain level of trust and reliance on his general's capabilities. This indicates that, regardless of the court politics, there was an underlying reciprocal reliance and acknowledgment of capabilities and accomplishments.

The essence of reciprocity, as characterized by mutual well-wishing, was manifest in the early stages of their relationship.

Justinian's elevation of Belisarius and the latter's successes exemplify a mutual well-wishing akin to Aristotle's notion of civic friendship, highlighting the importance of recognizing and rewarding loyalty within organizational contexts.

However, the relationship between Belisarius and Justinian also presents instances where the principles of reciprocity were strained, offering lessons on the challenges and potential pitfalls of maintaining reciprocal relationships within hierarchical settings:

Jealousy, Suspicion, and Conditional Support

The jealousy and suspicion from courtiers—and at times, from Justinian himself—toward Belisarius demonstrate the fragility of reciprocal relationships in the face of external pressures and political (corporate) intrigue. This situation reflects the challenges organizations face in sustaining reciprocal relationships amidst internal competition and external threats. Belisarius's victories and popularity made him a target for intrigue, and these factors could have led Justinian to question his loyalty, despite Belisarius's proven fidelity. The emperor's actions towards Belisarius, especially during times of dismissal and recall, suggest that the relationship was also characterized by Justinian's political and personal calculations, which did not always align with a sense of reciprocity. The emperor had to balance his trust in Belisarius with the overarching needs of his administration and the pressures from other political factions. In these instances, the relationship deviated from being purely reciprocal, as personal and political insecurities interfered.

Breach of Psychological Contract

The instances where Justinian doubted Belisarius's loyalty, leading to the general's temporary dismissal and recall, can be seen as breaches of the psychological contract. Such breaches, characterized by unmet expectations or perceived inequities, highlight the significance of maintaining clear communication and mutual respect to prevent disillusionment and a diminished sense of loyalty.

Non-Direct Reciprocity and Organizational Cohesion

Belisarius's treatment of locals in North Africa, where he ensured fair treatment and thus gained their support, illustrates non-direct reciprocity. This form of reciprocity, extending beyond direct exchanges, emphasizes the role of altruistic actions and the broader network of relationships in building social cohesion and trust within groups, akin to fostering a positive organizational culture with a vision for the long-term.

Lessons for Modern Organizations

From the story of Belisarius, modern organizations can glean several insights into cultivating and sustaining a culture of reciprocity:

- Leadership and Reciprocity: Leaders play a critical role in embodying and promoting the principles of reciprocity, demonstrating through their actions the mutual exchange of respect and support. Leadership should transcend transactional exchanges to foster a relational dimension within the organization.

- Managing the Psychological Contract: Organizations must remain attuned to the dynamics of the psychological contract, recognizing and adapting to the changing needs and expectations of their members to prevent breaches that can lead to decreased morale and productivity.

- Fostering a Culture of Mutual Support: By valuing employee contributions and ensuring perceived fairness and transparency in exchanges, organizations can cultivate a reciprocal ethos that enhances loyalty and collective responsibility toward achieving shared goals.

- Navigating Challenges to Reciprocity: Organizations should be vigilant against the internal and external factors that can strain reciprocal relationships, adopting proactive measures to address potential breaches in trust and ensure a sustained sense of mutual respect and support and direct communication.

The Cheesecake Factory

The Cheesecake Factory is known for its diverse and high-quality menu but it is also celebrated for its outstanding commitment to the well-being and satisfaction of its employees. Recognizing that happy employees lead to superior service, the organization has implemented a series of comprehensive training and recognition programs. Established by David Overton in 1978, The Cheesecake Factory has grown from a modest bakery in Los Angeles to a globally recognized brand with over two hundred locations. Despite its significant expansion, the company continues to prioritize a positive and nurturing work environment.

To enhance employee engagement and retention, The Cheesecake Factory employs a variety of strategies. Daily scheduled meetings serve as a forum for addressing operational concerns, celebrating achievements, and acknowledging personal milestones and birthdays, mirroring the practices of luxury service brands like Ritz-Carlton. Moreover, the "Wow Stories" program highlights exemplary customer service moments across the company, allowing employees to learn from each other's successes and fostering a culture of excellence and mutual appreciation.

David Overton, the CEO, emphasizes the importance of employee trust and engagement, guided by a leadership approach that treats employees with care and consideration as if they were family. This philosophy is foundational to the company's culture, aiming to create an environment of mutual respect and camaraderie among the staff. The recruitment process focuses on finding individuals whose personal values align with the company's, ensuring a cohesive and harmonious workplace culture. Overton believes that hiring passionate, caring individuals over the years has been pivotal in bringing out the best in the team.

This approach has significantly influenced the company's operations and its standing in the industry, resulting in low management turnover rates and consistent sales growth. The Cheesecake Factory's dedication to workforce training and development sets a high standard within the restaurant industry. In 2006, the company's investment in employee training surpassed many others, with programs ranging from on-the-job training for servers to comprehensive managerial courses. The company has allocated an average of $2,000 annually for the training of each hourly employee prior to 2006. The Cheesecake Factory's consistent inclusion on Fortune's list of 100 Best Companies to Work For since 2014 (the only restaurant to be on the list in 2018) underscores its commitment to employee well-being and its success in creating a workplace where employees feel valued and motivated.

Chuck Wensing, the Vice President of Performance and Development, has expressed concerns about preserving the company's essence, stating, "One of our biggest challenges is the notion of how to get big but remain small in spirit." He warns that without careful management, the quality of service that customers expect might diminish. In the nine years since Wensing joined The Cheesecake Factory, there has been a significant shift in how the Human Resources department operates, transitioning from a primarily operational role to one that's more aligned with strategic planning.

The Cheesecake Factory strongly supports the idea of career growth from within its own workforce, with a significant portion of its management positions—no less than one-fourth—being filled by employees who have risen through the ranks internally. The financial implications of this strategy are far from trivial, as a single percentage point difference in turnover rates can lead to savings of approximately $190,000 annually.

Furthermore, The Cheesecake Factory places a strong emphasis on ensuring its employees have a healthy work-life balance. It enforces policies that limit the work hours of restaurant managers to no more than 55 hours each week. The organization also offers flexible scheduling options to accommodate the personal commitments of its staff, including educational pursuits or artistic endeavors. According to Wensing, this flexibility is particularly beneficial for the many employees who are concurrently engaged in studies or creative projects, illustrating the company's understanding of its people and the commitment to supporting the varied lifestyles and ambitions of its team members.

By treating employees with care and considering them as part of a corporate family, The Cheesecake Factory fosters a culture where mutual respect and well-wishing are paramount. The company's approach to employee engagement and development is a practical application of the psychological contract theory. By setting clear expectations, recognizing achievements, and offering career growth opportunities, the company maintains a positive psychological contract with its employees. This reduces the likelihood of contract breaches, which can lead to dissatisfaction and turnover.

The Cheesecake Factory's HR practices, including comprehensive training, recognition programs, and emphasis on work-life balance, highlight the role of strategic HRM in embedding reciprocity in the organizational fabric. Strategic HRM addresses the immediate needs of employees, but most importantly, it aligns with long-term organizational goals, ensuring sustainability and growth. As organizations grow, maintaining a culture of reciprocity becomes increasingly challenging and highlights the importance of scaling reciprocal cultures. The Cheesecake Factory's concern about remaining "small in spirit" amidst expansion highlights the need for deliberate efforts to preserve core values and reciprocal practices. This lesson is crucial for organizations undergoing growth or transformation, emphasizing the importance of adaptive HR strategies and leadership models that safeguard the reciprocal ethos.

The Cheesecake Factory's experience demonstrates that investing in employees through training, recognition, and career development opportunities has both direct and indirect financial benefits, including lower turnover rates, enhanced employee satisfaction, and sustained organizational performance. This lesson underscores the multifaceted value of reciprocity, extending beyond immediate returns to long-term organizational success and employee well-being.

CHAPTER 5

Asabiyyah

"None can destroy iron, but its own rust can! Likewise, none can destroy a person, but its own mindset can!"

—Ratan Tata

ASABIYYAH, AS DETAILED, TRANSCENDS FAMILIAL or tribal loyalty to embody a broader, more profound sense of social solidarity, mutual support, and group consciousness. This principle, deeply rooted in the collective spirit and shared objectives, forms an essential underpinning for organizational cohesion and collective action which leads to collective consciousness. Compared to reciprocity, Asabiyyah is more about a collective spirit or social cohesion that binds a group beyond immediate transactions, often irrespective of direct personal gain. The current research understands Asabiyyah as the collective will-formation and commitment to sustained action through the sense of unity among a group of like-minded enthusiasts toward a common purpose – oneness.

Operational Dynamics and Business Application

Collective will-formation: In a business context, this refers to the process where all members of an organization come together to form a unified intention or decision, aligning individual desires and ideas towards a shared organizational goal. Commitment to sustained action: This emphasizes the dedication of employees to consistently contribute towards achieving long-term objectives, highlighting the importance of perseverance and ongoing effort in a business setting. Sense of unity: In the corporate environment, this pertains to employees' strong sense of togetherness and solidarity with the company and its mission, enhancing team cohesion and strengthening the overall organizational unity. Group of like-minded enthusiasts: This represents a team or workforce within a company that shares similar interests, passions, and goals, driving innovation and collaboration in pursuit of common business objectives. Common purpose: In a business setting, this refers to the overarching aim or mission that unites the company's efforts, guiding all strategic planning and activities towards achieving shared success.

Impact on Long-term Success and Challenges:

- **Inequity and Exploitation Risks**: The inherent risk in reciprocity leading to inequity, where some members may give more than they receive, threatens the foundation of trust and solidarity crucial for 'Asabiyyah. Such imbalance can foster resentment among employees, detracting from the collective spirit. To counter this, leadership plays a pivotal role. By embodying and demonstrating adherence to cultural values, pre-agreed understanding of ethical behavior, and equitable treatment, leaders set a standard for the entire organization. Furthermore, the process of socialization in the company should reinforce these shared values, ensuring all members understand and commit to equitable practices, thereby helping mitigate risks of inequity and exploitation. However, leadership's role is not a panacea. They must engage in transparent discussions about contributions and rewards and ensure that socialization processes genuinely address perceived inequities.

Implementing robust feedback mechanisms to identify and rectify grievances related to inequity and exploitation is essential.

- **Scale and Sustainability**: As organizations expand, the challenge of sustaining personal connections and reciprocal actions increases, which can dilute the strength of 'Asabiyyah. This issue is countered by establishing and consistently reinforcing shared values that transcend individual relationships. Through regular communication, team-building activities, and cultural rituals, organizations can maintain a strong sense of unity and shared purpose, ensuring that 'Asabiyyah remains robust regardless of size or time. Yet, shared values alone cannot sustain 'Asabiyyah if not actively lived. Concrete systems must be in place to integrate these values into every business decision and process. Regular assessments and realignments may be needed to ensure the expansion doesn't dilute the company's core values and that all employees remain connected to the overarching mission.

- **Misinterpretation and Manipulation**: When reciprocity is misconstrued or exploited for personal gain, it erodes the genuine community spirit essential for 'Asabiyyah. Countering this involves fostering a dedication to a common cause and nurturing an organizational culture based on shared values. By clearly defining and communicating the organization's mission and principles, leaders can minimize to an extent misunderstandings and manipulative behaviors, ensuring actions align with collective goals. Continuous education, clear policies, and a zero-tolerance stance on manipulative behaviors are crucial. Organizations must provide avenues for reporting and addressing behavior that undermines genuine community spirit.

- **Delayed Gratification**: The issue of delayed gratification, particularly in non-direct reciprocity, can lead to frustration when immediate returns are not visible. Building a culture that appreciates long-term benefits requires setting clear expectations and providing examples of sustained efforts leading to collective success. By emphasizing the importance of contribution to a common cause and exemplifying patience and persistence, organizations can foster a deeper understanding and appreciation of sustained efforts, promoting a healthier development of 'Asabiyyah. Recognizing and addressing the desire for immediate recognition can help balance immediate feedback with long-term goals, maintaining motivation and preventing disillusionment.

- **Potential Evolution into Entitlement**: Over time, the expectation of reciprocity might evolve into entitlement, undermining the spirit of sustained contribution as Ibn Haldun observed the fall of empires centuries ago. Preventing a culture of entitlement involves reinforcing shared values and creating an environment where contributions are acknowledged but entitlement attitudes are discouraged. This requires clear communication regarding expectations and rewards and discussions about the difference between earned rewards and entitled behavior to preserve the spirit of mutual contribution.

- **Idealization vs. Reality**: Addressing the gap between the idealized concept of 'Asabiyyah and the reality of fostering such oneness in diverse, competitive settings involves ensuring that hiring practices align with organizational values and setting exemplary leadership behaviors. While fostering deep social cohesion is the goal, acknowledging the practical challenges like individualism and competition is vital. Realistically, not all employees will fully embrace 'Asabiyyah, and leadership efforts may not always succeed. Acknowledging these challenges and continuously evaluating cultural initiatives can help bridge the gap between idealization and actual organizational dynamics.

- **Dynamic Nature of 'Asabiyyah**: To maintain 'Asabiyyah amidst organizational changes, adaptability to new strategic goals and clear communication of the unifying cause are essential. By keeping the organization's values and cause at the core, leaders can guide transitions and growth without losing the essence of collective spirit. Adapting to organizational changes while maintaining 'Asabiyyah involves navigating changing employee expectations, market conditions, and technological advancements. Regular revisiting and revising core values and strategic goals ensure they remain relevant and resonate with the workforce, sustaining the collective spirit amidst change.

- **Risk of Misapplication**: To counter potential misapplications of 'Asabiyyah that could foster exclusionary practices, it's vital to underscore that while diversity is encouraged, the uniqueness and unity of the organization lie in its values, culture, and cause. Clarifying the 'why' behind actions ensures that 'Asabiyyah strengthens inclusivity and solidarity, supporting the organization's broader objectives.

Examples of 'Asabiyyah

HP and Carly Fiorina

Fiorina's journey at HP can be seen as an effort to instill a new vision and strategic direction, which, while aiming to unify and propel the company forward, also encountered significant resistance and challenges that impacted the sense of unity among employees.

Fiorina's leadership was also tested by external economic factors, notably the dot-com bubble burst, which necessitated a series of tough financial and strategic decisions, including significant layoffs and cost-cutting measures. While these actions were critical for HP's survival and led to a doubling of revenue, they also resulted in a 50% decline in the company's stock price, illustrating the delicate balance between short-term financial health and long-term market confidence.

The merger with Compaq, central to Fiorina's strategy for HP, aimed to enhance the company's competitiveness and market share in the rapidly changing market. Despite initial successes, the merger faced long-term integration challenges, especially in aligning the differing cultures and work pace, values, and operational systems of HP and Compaq. The focus on rapid integration and cost efficiencies often came at the expense of building a shared vision and building employees' understanding of the merger's goals. The merger introduced a period of considerable uncertainty and disruption for employees of both HP and Compaq, who faced job insecurity and significant changes in their work environment. This uncertainty, coupled with subsequent layoffs and restructuring initiatives that saw the reduction of 30,000 jobs, led to a notable decline in employee morale and trust.

Fiorina saw the merger as a necessary transformation for survival and growth because it expanded the company's product
line and diversified its revenue streams. However, the decision
was met with significant internal and external opposition, illustrating the first major challenge to building Asabiyyah within HP.
The divisive nature of the merger highlights the difficulties in fostering a unified sense of purpose when significant factions within
the organization resist change based on differing visions for the
company's future.

A critical aspect of building Asabiyyah is effective communication and leadership that resonates with the values and aspirations of the organization's members. Fiorina's memoir reflects a
leadership style driven by conviction and a sense of urgency to
enact change. However, this approach sometimes resulted in a
perceived disconnect between HP's leadership and its employees.
Efforts to engage with and win over skeptics were overshadowed
by the sheer scale of the challenges and the pace at which changes
were implemented – the pace of the CEO and not the one of the
organization and its people.

Fiorina's leadership style—described as inspiring yet isolating—
underscored a divergence from HP's traditional engineering-
driven and consensus-oriented culture. Her efforts to redefine
HP's identity and strategic direction, though visionary, sometimes lacked the necessary groundwork in building relationships
and garnering support from the broader employee base. Critics
argue that her failure to connect with employees on a personal
level, coupled with a tendency to prioritize ambitious metrics over
realistic goals through a top-down approach, hindered the effective implementation of her vision.

Her inspiring and attractive communication backed Fiorina's
transformative strategy, almost like a rock star. However, this
was not the HP way because the values she had developed were
not corresponding to the ones at HP. Her disruptiveness was

needed but its implementation was too fast. In a way she began feeding her ego before developing rapport with her colleagues and HP employees, which distanced herself instead of gaining their support. One story says that at HP headquarters, a huge portrait of her was hung next to the company's founders, Bill Hewlett and Dave Packard, which reflected her self-perception despite the differences in work approaches.

While her approach aimed to propel HP into a new era of competitiveness, marked by rapid decision-making and an aggressive pursuit of market share, it also signaled a shift away from the collaborative and consensus-driven ethos that had previously defined the company.

The cost-cutting measures and focus on efficiency necessary for navigating the competitive market and the economic uncertainties of the time highlighted the difficult trade-offs leaders often face.

Centralized decision-making can offer efficiency and speed. It is important to consider its impact on employee morale and the potential drawbacks associated with limited stakeholder involvement and feeling of disempowerment.

Fiorina sought to change HP's culture to drive innovation and responsiveness in a competitive market. Her approach included imposing a more centralized management structure and making significant workforce reductions to cut costs and improve efficiency. Many employees, while aimed at strengthening the company, perceived these actions as a departure from HP's core values and traditions, known as the "HP Way" – a culture that emphasized employee welfare, trust, and autonomy. The tension between the need for change and the preservation of core cultural values presented another obstacle to fostering Asabiyyah, as employees struggled to reconcile the new direction with HP's historical identity.

Fiorina's leadership style and decisions at times exacerbated the sense of disunity within HP. Her focus on rapid transformation and performance metrics, while neglecting the nurturing of internal relationships and consensus-building, may have contributed to a sense of alienation and resistance among employees. The lack of Asabiyyah, or the failure to fully engage and unify employees around a shared vision and purpose, became evident in the public and contentious nature of the debates surrounding the Compaq merger and subsequent organizational changes.

In conclusion, Fiorina's memoir and tenure at HP present a case study in the complexities of leading organizational change and the critical importance of Asabiyyah in such endeavors. While her strategic vision aimed to unify and strengthen the company against external competitive pressures, the internal dynamics and cultural challenges highlight the difficulties in building a cohesive and loyal organizational community. Her approach underscored the potential pitfalls of centralized decision-making, the challenges of maintaining organizational cohesion during rapid strategic shifts, and the critical importance of balancing bold leadership with the nurturing of an inclusive, dedicated, and motivated organizational culture. The HP experience under Fiorina's leadership underscores the delicate balance required between driving strategic change and nurturing the social cohesion and solidarity essential for enduring organizational success. The HP problems of the time have been argued to be a result of both Fiorina's tenure and the board's decisions.

IBM and Lou Gerstner

Lou Gerstner's strategy diverged significantly from conventional tactics, focusing on restructuring IBM's internal culture and fostering a unified company-wide commitment to transformation. When Gerstner arrived at IBM, he found a company that was completely focused on its internal rules and conflicts. "Units competed with each other, hid things from each other. Huge staff spent countless hours debating and managing transfer pricing terms between IBM units instead of facilitating a seamless transfer of products to customers." The success in the 60s and 70s was due to a different culture, one of energy, relentlessness, and decentralization. However, the company was ready for a collective change in the 1980s and early 1990s when corporate decentralization was not maintainable.

Upon assuming leadership, Gerstner undertook a rapid evaluation of IBM's structural and operational weaknesses. Contrary to the prevailing advice from industry analysts and consultants, Gerstner chose not to dismember the company into smaller, ostensibly more manageable units. He believed that IBM's strength lay in its ability to offer integrated solutions, which smaller, disconnected units would be unable to provide. This decision underscored a key leadership principle: truly high-performing organizations are guided by core principles rather than rigid processes. He argued that effective leadership demands an understanding of the essential drivers of success within the business, allowing leaders to apply these guiding principles flexibly and wisely to suit the current circumstances. Such an approach underscores the importance of a cause or in his words: "Every business, if it is to succeed, must have a sense of direction and mission, so that no matter who you are and what you are doing, you know how you fit in and that what you are doing is important."

Gerstner's direct style was pivotal. He immersed himself in the business, meeting with employees, managers, and customers to understand their perspectives. His personal site visits broke the norm of executive detachment, allowing him to hear employee concerns directly and assure them of their key role in IBM's renewal. This approach helped in gaining insightful feedback and played a crucial role in rallying the workforce behind the transformation efforts.

By actively seeking feedback from employees and customers, Gerstner bridged the divide between leadership and the workforce, ensuring that the transformation was rooted in the real needs and capabilities of the company. This participatory strategy both garnered buy-in from across the organization and also empowered employees to be part of the change, enhancing the sense of unity and shared purpose. By realigning the company's priorities, he tackled the internal resistance to change by showing the direct benefits of his strategy in terms of market competitiveness and financial results. Gerstner modeled a leadership style that was both inclusive and decisive through the direct confrontation of challenges and by ensuring that employees felt valued and aligned with IBM's new direction. He recognized that lasting transformation required reshaping both the company's culture and structural foundations.

Echoing what my father, Ivaylo Aleksiev, described as an organization's 'collective DNA' of an organization and what Phil Jackson calls the team's DNA, Lou Gerstner emphasizes the integration of corporate values into IBM's DNA. Articulating values is only the beginning; embedding them in daily operations is what sustains a values-driven culture—particularly in team settings. Gerstner highlights that simply professing values does little if they are not actively lived out through the organization's internal processes every day. In his time at IBM, he observed that culture is not just one component of success but the core of it. He articulated that the enduring success of any organization hinges on its people's collective ability to generate value, underscoring that while vision, strategy, and management systems might set the direction, they only sustain an organization temporarily. For transformation to truly take root, these elements must be woven into the very fabric of the company's culture.

In his first meeting with the senior management team, Gerstner conveyed a clear message to focus efforts externally rather than internally, showcasing a drive towards fostering a performance-based culture. By illustrating the company's dire state through customer satisfaction and market share data, he sparked a sense of urgency and a collective aim to improve. This empowerment was not just about assigning responsibilities but also about ensuring that leaders and employees alike took ownership and active roles in the company's revival efforts. He firmly believed in the necessity of a CEO's relentless dedication over several years to personally communicate these values in clear, compelling language, fostering a deep conviction and prompting collective action throughout the organization. **8** Ultimately, he believed that the conditions for transformation have to be set by the management through objectives and incentives. Management needs to invite the workforce into the process and empower them to take ownership of cultural change.

Cultural inertia at IBM was marked by a slow, bureaucratic mentality that stifled innovation and responsiveness. Gerstner initiated cultural shifts by simplifying the company's internal processes and slashing bureaucratic layers, which enhanced decision-making speed and operational efficiency. He championed a customer-first philosophy, realigning the organization's objectives around customer satisfaction and service excellence, moving away from a product-centric approach.

Much of the cultural transformation was redefining the reward systems. Gerstner aligned incentives with performance outcomes that supported customer-centricity and collaborative success, rather than individual or product-based achievements. This shift motivated employees and helped in breaking down the silos within the company, fostering a more unified and cooperative work environment. He championed a cooperative culture over a competitive one, aligning employees across functions with IBM's strategic goals. This shift was crucial in dismantling the barriers that hindered collaboration and shared purpose among different units within IBM.

IBM created a unified corporate identity and rallied all employees to view their efforts as part of a larger collective struggle. He rebuilt trust within the workforce through consistent, transparent actions that aligned with IBM's stated values and objectives. Furthermore, he nurtured an environment that valued risk-taking and innovation, encouraging employees to support one another in pursuit of both individual and collective achievements.

Recognizing the value of a unified workforce, he worked diligently to dissolve the 'us vs. them' mentality that pervaded IBM's global offices. Through regular, transparent communications and town halls, Gerstner shared challenges and successes equally with all employees, cultivating a shared narrative and a common purpose that started the process of internalization of the practices.

He also introduced programs that encourage collaboration across different functions and geographies. This improved efficiency and knowledge sharing while reinforcing a sense of belonging among employees. Gerstner's emphasis on collective achievement over individual success helped solidify a culture of mutual support and accountability, which are fundamental to Asabiyyah.

In summary, Lou Gerstner's leadership at IBM exemplified how fostering Asabiyyah—through empowering leadership, account-ability, and creating a unified culture—can be instrumental in navigating and succeeding in transformative efforts. His actions redefined IBM's internal culture, aligning it with the strategic goals and reviving the company's fortunes. Gerstner's tenure at IBM demonstrates the pivotal role of Asabiyyah, oneness, in achieving organizational resilience and success in the face of significant challenges.

Definition of the Continuum of Loyalty and Disloyalty

Loyalty, as defined above, is measured by what The Aleksiev Group Ltd. has called the *Loyalty Quotient to Loyalty*®. The quotient is of practical application with its classification and visualization of employees' loyalty to the cause on the condition of reciprocity and Asabiyyah. Its goal is to facilitate the leadership/management of any organization in their predictions of employees' behavior and the planning of programs aimed at increasing the loyalty to loyalty within the organization. The continuum is separated into seven categories (from top to bottom): Diamond, Platinum, Gold, Silver, Bronze, Nickel, and Lead. Each is discussed separately.

The Diamond loyalty quotient is the highest one because it is indicative of a person's internalization with the cause of the organization. This is the level of selfless dedication due to the person's maximum recognition of his/her identity with the object of loyalty. Loyalty at this level does not depend so much on the amount of a reward and the person is less susceptible to negative influence than others. Such people are maximally motivated, extremely efficient and looking to increase their efficiency. A similarity can be drawn between them and Collin's Level 5 leader. Diamond loyalty implies the desire to work in the best way, the desire to respect the principles of the company, to unconditionally contribute to the achievement of its goals, to "put up" with some requirements and the ability to accept others.

The Platinum loyalty quotient is indicative of a person at the belief level. Professional motivation and performance characterize such people. Moreover, their dedication to their work to do as much as possible in a proactive manner, together with their lack of tolerance of rules violation are proof of their responsibility. They believe that it is their duty to do everything accurately, correctly, and with high quality. Their tolerance and endurance of difficult times for the organization are high, and would remain with it, driven by the very sense of loyalty and involvement. Such people trust the management and its decisions, but if the organization, for one reason or another, changes previously accepted values and beliefs, then it may have some difficulties with employees with Platinum loyalty due to their resistance. Their involvement in planning and implementing innovation is crucial.

The Gold loyalty quotient is at the action level. The respective behavior is one of observance of internal social norms adopted by the organization. Enthusiasm and a positive attitude together with desire to master the necessary professional knowledge and skills are indicative of such people. Discipline due to their attitude and not as an attempt to avoid punishment characterizes their behavior. Moreover, voluntary behavior is observed which transcends formal job duties with a touch of caring and nurturing behavior toward the people in the organization.

The Silver loyalty quotient, similarly to the Gold loyalty one, characterizes people who are motivated to transcend their formal job duties and have increased performance and job satisfaction. However, if their behavior is not recognized, their motivation will be harmed. Examples are lack of reciprocity and/or lack of a reward. The silver loyalty quotient is sufficient for most people within an organization but not sufficient to perform the functions of monitoring the activities of other employees. Although such people would align with their organization through the wearing of distinctive symbols, they are also likely to exhibit toxic behaviors directed towards their colleagues that harm them physically or mentally by making threats, making mean comments, and ignoring or undermining the person's ability to work effectively.

The Bronze loyalty quotient is characterized by relative disloyalty. A key elaboration is that lack of loyalty is not disloyalty. Therefore people within this category have no pronounced positive or negative orientation. The prime characteristic of these people is that they are less predictable than loyal or disloyal people because they are indifferent. They have a rather positive attitude towards the organization; neither they flaunt its superiority in their field, nor have a negative attitude present. They lack the desire to learn and the eagerness to do anything beyond formal job requirements or help the organization cope with a change unless it is in their own interest.

The Nickel loyalty quotient is characterized by covert disloyalty because loyal behavior is only exhibited demonstrably. Internal fraudsters tend to show a high level of loyalty. Only a deeper observation and analysis of their activity can reveal the true attitude of such people to the organization. People within this category regularly follow prescribed rules and requirements not because of their positive attitude but rather because of the fear of punishment or the expectation of a reward. They never openly challenge management's orders but instead create or provoke others to criticize and resent them while they themselves take a neutral position. Further, disloyal employees are often the ones who spread negative organizational gossip and rumors.

The Lead loyalty quotient is the one of open disloyalty - a tendency to lie, cheat, sarcasm, ridicule, neglect of values important to the object of loyalty, violation of agreements, search for personal gain, etc. The danger of the quotient is related to the people's influence on other people and groups and the undermining of the values and beliefs of their colleagues and the raise of doubts about the appropriateness of certain actions. Counterproductive behaviors are exhibited and include: workplace deviance, anti-social behavior and workplace rudeness, absenteeism/tardiness, sabotage, even theft. The latter is seen not as something extreme but rather as the delayed/postponed performance reward in a different form, thus cognitive rationalization masks any signs of guilt.

CHAPTER 6

Integrity

"If you no longer have leaves, or bark, or roots, can you go on calling yourself a tree?"

—Arthur Golden

THE INTERWOVEN QUALITIES OF INTEGRITY form the cornerstone of loyalty, particularly within a corporate context. A loyal employee is steadfast in their commitments but also unwaveringly honest, even when the truth may be challenging to convey. This synthesis of truthfulness and predictability is essential for the betterment of the company. Individuals who embody integrity ensure that both their actions and those of the organization align with its stated values and principles.

At the heart of integrity lies the courage to deliver truths that might disrupt the status quo but are essential for informed decision-making and strategic foresight. The loyal employee, armed with integrity, becomes a guardian of the company's ethos, steering it away from the pitfalls of short-term opportunism and towards sustainable success. Their reliability in consistently championing the truth solidifies their role as trusted advisors within the organization, cultivating an atmosphere where trust prevails, and a culture of openness and honesty becomes the shared language of corporate discourse. Such a culture is conducive to business practices based on principles and promotes a workspace where employees feel valued, heard, and motivated.

As a graduate of the Virginia Military Institute (VMI), the word "honor" has been with me throughout the entirety of my cadet-ship. Since I was a rat (otherwise known as a college freshman), I was told that what defines a VMI cadet is his/her honor. The VMI honor system and its honor code are one of the few in the world, which dictate that after one breach and found guilty of the said breach, a cadet is expelled from the Institute. The honor code is: A cadet will not lie, cheat, steal, or tolerate those who do. How one lives up to the honor code each moment of the cadetship is a personal choice. Integrity. The word was explained to all cadets multiple times throughout the years. To do the right thing even when no one is watching.

In many organizations, no matter if government or private, there can be found the bad practices of "do what I say, not what I do." Integrity is the opposite of this sick practice. It is about adherence to the norms, behaviors, ways of thinking, and attitudes that one has chosen to be characteristic of oneself, and others in the team, department, organization, etc. For example, if a company's leadership has chosen certain values and principles to be the ones that guide the company, they should follow them in all of their professional interactions and choices. Preferably, they exemplify them in their personal lives, or the ones they do are not the complete opposite of the professional ones.

The lack of integrity creates a workforce from top to bottom which does what suits its interests depending on the moment. This creates internal contradictions and raises questions about the organization's true identity and long-term direction.. Integrity when observed, is reminiscent of the bond between an organizational member and the organization, hence is deemed a behavioural determinant of loyalty.

In a professional atmosphere of integrity, honesty ,and integrity foster principled behaviors and encourage a sense of shared responsibility among all members of the organization. Employees develop a stronger sense of belonging and dedication to the organization. They are more likely to be loyal because of alignment with the company's values and because of a sense of being part of a trustworthy community. This, in turn, leads to higher morale, greater employee dedication, and improved productivity. The following are seven applications of integrity identified through work with various industries:

1. **Integrity and Leadership**

   Integrity is a core quality for effective leadership. Leaders with integrity are often trusted and respected by their peers and subordinates. By consistently aligning actions with the organization's values and business interests, these leaders foster a culture of trust and predictability. The impact of a leader's integrity, or its absence, resonates throughout the organizational culture and influences employee behaviors, shaping how challenges and opportunities are approached.

2. **Integrity as a Catalyst for Trust**

   Trust within an organization hinges significantly on the integrity displayed by its members. Employees who believe that their leaders and their colleagues adhere to a code of honesty are more likely to engage in open communication and be loyal to the organization. In contrast, environments lacking in integrity might breed skepticism and uncertainty, undermining the organization's cohesion and effectiveness.

3. **Integrity in Decision Making**

   The role of integrity in decision-making extends to promoting fairness and transparency. By prioritizing integrity in decisions, leaders ensure that actions consider the broader impact on all stakeholders — employees, partners, customers, investors, and the community. This approach helps in resolving conflicts and in creating solutions that are sustainable and just, bolstering the organization's reputation for fairness and reliability.

4. Integrity leads to Predictability

Integrity creates a predictable framework crucial for keeping both internal and external stakeholders informed. Our experience over the years has led us to argue for the strong necessity of predictability in the workplace. In this context, predictability is the degree to which a member of the organization can be sure of how other members of the organization behave and make decisions connected with the organization's direction. It is closely linked to the state of being informed. Akin to our observations and conclusions, Professor Howard Stevenson, Harvard Business School associate dean, has argued that managers primarily need to ensure that their organizations achieve their objectives efficiently. However, this requires involving others who cannot work effectively if they perceive a lack of order or clarity about the outcomes of their actions. He has stated that today's organizational leaders must begin with an honest evaluation of the organization's current state, the potential outcomes of any actions taken, and the implications of each outcome. Attempting to deceive employees with periodic, small-scale layoffs while falsely assuring them of the organization's health after each round undermines predictability and damages morale.

5. Integrity in Crisis Management

Integrity plays a critical role during crises, where transparent and principled conduct is crucial. How a company behaves in times of difficulty—whether it maintains transparency and sticks to its stated principles and values or not—can significantly affect its reputation and stakeholders' trust in the long term.

6. The Role of Integrity in Innovation

Integrity relates to how genuinely a company pursues innovation. A company that is honest about its capabilities and dedicated to improving its offerings is more likely to innovate in meaningful ways. This relationship between integrity and innovation showcases that a principled approach supports and enhances creative endeavors within an organization.

7. Integrity and Compliance

In regulated industries, integrity is closely tied to compliance with legal and regulatory standards. Organizations that uphold high standards of integrity are less likely to engage in unlawful practices and are better prepared to navigate legal complexities. This reduces legal risks and protects the organization from penalties and reputational damage.

The Space Shuttle Challenger

The Space Shuttle Challenger disaster is one of the most significant events in the history of American spaceflight. On January 28, 1986, the Challenger broke apart just 73 seconds after liftoff, leading to the deaths of all seven crew members on board. This tragic event marked a moment of national mourning and triggered a major reevaluation of the U.S. space program by NASA and the federal government.

On the morning of the launch, conditions were unusually cold, with temperatures at the Kennedy Space Center near freezing. The cold weather was a concern for the rubber O-ring seals used in the solid rocket boosters that helped seal the joint between the two lower segments of each booster. Engineers from Morton Thiokol, the contractor responsible for the boosters, were particularly worried that the cold could cause the O-rings to fail to seal properly. The night before the launch, engineers and NASA managers held a teleconference to discuss the risks, and despite the concerns expressed by the engineers, NASA decided to proceed with the launch.

Shortly after liftoff, at about 58 seconds into the flight, a plume of flame was seen escaping from the right solid rocket booster at the aft field joint. This was due to the failure of the O-ring seal, exacerbated by the cold temperatures. The flame escalated into a fire that caused the external fuel tank to fail structurally. Aerodynamic forces quickly broke the orbiter.

The disaster resulted in an immediate grounding of the shuttle program. President Ronald Reagan appointed a commission headed by former Secretary of State William Rogers and included physicist Richard Feynman to investigate the disaster. The Rogers Commission found that the Challenger disaster was caused by the failure of the O-ring seal in the right solid rocket booster. The commission's report also criticized NASA's decision-making processes and organizational culture. The blame was put on the poor communication between managers and engineers, who all knew of the potential of the O-rings seals to fail at launching. The lost lives of Francis Scobee, Michael Smith, Ellison Onizuka, Judith Resnik, Ronald McNair, Christa McAuliffe, and Gregory Jarvis were attributed to poor communication.

One of the objections raised by NASA during the teleconference was that "the Cape Canaveral temperatures had been below 53F and even reaching 41F." However, Thiokol never voiced any concerns about the temperature's effect on the O-ring seal, including during the various launch times of the Shuttle Columbia. The recency effect characterized by the different launch dates over the past month and the availability heuristic of the previous launch of a shuttle took precedence over the realization of new information regarding the capabilities of the O-ring seal and the recognition that for the first time ever, a contractor preferred to delay a take-off. NASA and Thiokol's management both invested themselves in the project of launching multiple shuttles over the next few years and delivering the capabilities to do so as the sole contractors for the specific parts. The two enterprises committed themselves to their objectives and had fears related to the resources available and those already used by the government and the client.

The data that Thiokol managers said have been conflicting and the job the engineers presented was not convincing, although an engineer's job is not public speaking. However, after the management decided to make a so-called managerial decision, NASA did not question it according to the provided documents and did not challenge the decision the same way it did before when it was against launching.

Four senior managers with engineering backgrounds made the Thiokol decision, excluding input from the broader engineering team. The managers took the responsibility to make the decision but assumed they had the expertise to make it without their colleagues. Therefore, one assumption is the presence of the Peter Effect because the managers, despite their engineering backgrounds, no longer possessed or exhibited the same technical vigilance and concern as the frontline engineers. Having distanced themselves from the depth of current engineering insight—or failing to grasp the recent data and warnings—they were unable to convey that caution or urgency to NASA. This disconnect between perceived expertise and actual technical awareness contributed to a decision that prioritized managerial confidence over over-engineering judgment, reflecting the idea that one cannot give what one does not genuinely possess or embody.

A key moment is what happened after the managerial decision was made and the teleconference resumed with the managers telling NASA their opinion, with no one of the Thiokol engineers raising their concerns. The engineers who were not invited to participate in the final decision, thus being mentally assessed as unqualified, behaved in a socially obedient manner to their managers during the group call. Fear of losing their job could have been present, considering that they were on a live call with a major client, but also, they lacked assertiveness as their expertise was being ignored.

The teleconference was characterized by time pressure. Although nobody would have accepted the increased risk, as later interviews with NASA revealed, the team at NASA was the one that did not transmit the new information to the astronauts, thus breaking its ethical principles. The managerial decision made by the Thiokol team, which process was not revealed to NASA, namely the lack of a unanimous decision including all on the team, was detrimental.

The Challenger disaster is a stark reminder of the importance of integrity in maintaining safety, trust, and reliability in operations. It shows that integrity is a personal choice but a practical necessity that can have real-world implications, including the safety of human lives and the success of missions.

1. **Integrity and Leadership:** In the Challenger case, leadership failed to adequately consider the safety concerns raised by engineers regarding the O-ring's performance in cold weather. Integrity aligns decision-making with the organization's fundamental values of safety and reliability.

2. **Integrity as a Catalyst for Trust:** The decision to launch Challenger, despite known risks, eroded trust within NASA and its contractors.

3. **Integrity in Decision Making:** Integrity in decision-making would have necessitated a more thorough consideration of the potential risks involved in launching the

Challenger; instead, a deviation from integral decision-making led to catastrophic results.

5. **Integrity in Crisis Management:** The Challenger disaster underscores the critical need for integrity in crisis management. Transparent and principled responses to the concerns raised could have prevented the disaster or at least mitigated its fallout by ensuring that all potential risks were adequately addressed before proceeding.

6. **The Role of Integrity in Innovation:** Innovation in space exploration relies on an honest assessment of technological capabilities and risks. Integrity ensures that innovations, such as the design and use of rocket boosters, are both safe and forward-looking, avoiding compromises that could lead to failure.

7. **Integrity and Compliance:** Adherence to safety regulations and compliance standards is crucial in the aerospace industry. The Challenger disaster illustrates the consequences of compliance failures and the importance of maintaining the agreed-on standards to meet legal and safety obligations effectively.

WorldCom and Cynthia Cooper

In the early 2000s, the business world was rocked by a series of corporate scandals that brought to light serious issues within major companies. One of the most significant of these was the accounting fraud at WorldCom, the consequences of which reverberated throughout the financial and regulatory landscapes. Central to the unraveling of this scandal was Cynthia Cooper, the Vice President of Internal Audit at WorldCom, whose courageous actions exemplified the critical role of integrity and principled leadership in corporate governance. In 2002, her investigative efforts revealed approximately $3.8 billion in fraudulent adjustments and falsified accounts, figures that would later exceed $11 billion.

WorldCom, once a telecommunications giant, began to face significant financial challenges in the late 1990s and early 2000s. Under the leadership of CEO Bernard Ebbers and CFO Scott Sullivan, the company was involved in a series of unethical accounting practices intended to mislead investors and regulatory bodies about the true financial condition of the company. These practices included the capitalization of operating costs and inflation of revenues, tactics that artificially enhanced the company's financial statements and its stability.

The process began with an examination of routine financial documents, where initial anomalies in capital expenditure accounts were discovered in 2002. The team used forensic accounting techniques to trace discrepancies and inconsistencies across various accounts. They noticed strange reactions and evasive responses from colleagues when probing certain accounting entries, including CFO Scott Sullivan, who notably discouraged her from delving deeper into the capital expenditures during an audit. The internal environment at WorldCom was fraught with fear and suppression, making the task of uncovering the truth exceedingly challenging. Undeterred by pressure to overlook the issues, Cooper led an independent investigation with her team.

Her team systematically analyzed journal entries and accounting records, identifying patterns that suggested deliberate manipulation of numbers. As they delved deeper, the complexity of the fraud became apparent, spanning several layers of financial reporting. This phase was fraught with emotional and professional stress, as highlighted by Cooper's accounts. The fear of being discovered by their superiors and the potential implications of their findings placed immense pressure on the team. They used sophisticated data analysis tools to cross-reference and validate their findings, ensuring that every piece of evidence was irrefutable before moving forward.

Cooper describes long nights of work shadowed by a sense of isolation, not just from their colleagues who were kept in the dark but also from the broader professional community to which they could not yet reach out. The investigation was a technical challenge and a test of their resilience and fortitude. As they dug deeper, the scale of the irregularities became apparent, showing systematic capitalization of line costs and falsifying financial statements to bolster the company's financial health. Their investigation revealed that WorldCom had improperly reported $3.8 billion in expenses, which later escalated to more than $11 billion in misreported funds.

Throughout the investigation, Cynthia Cooper faced numerous ethical challenges that tested her professional judgment and personal integrity. One of her most significant decisions was whether to confront senior management with the findings. Her accounts delve into this decision's mental and emotional calculus, weighing the potential risks against the imperative of truth and accountability. Cooper wrestled with the potential impact of her actions on her colleagues, many of whom might face job loss or personal repercussions due to the investigation's findings. She deliberated extensively on the potential consequences, consulting confidentially with legal and ethical advisors to gauge the ramifications of bringing the issues to light.

Cooper's upbringing and personal values played crucial roles in her decision-making process. She recounts how lessons learned from her mother about not being intimidated helped steal her resolve to pursue the investigation despite potential consequences. This moral compass was essential in deciding to move forward with the investigation and in managing the fallout, which included potential job loss, professional ostracism, and the personal safety of her team due to fear of repercussions.

Ethical decision-making went beyond management. Cooper was acutely aware of the potential impact on innocent employees and shareholders. Her decisions were guided by a responsibility to these stakeholders, ensuring that the financial truth was revealed to protect their interests and to prevent further harm caused by continued deceit. Another significant challenge was maintaining the morale and focus of her audit team amidst growing pressure and stress. Cooper had to lead her squad technically and emotionally, by fostering a sense of purpose and resilience despite the daunting obstacles they faced.

Reporting the findings to the WorldCom board represented a critical step in Cynthia Cooper's career. Her account captures the tension-filled hours leading up to the meeting with the board, where she and her team presented detailed evidence of the financial misconduct. Cooper describes meticulously preparing for the meeting, anticipating the challenges to their findings, and formulating responses.

The moment of disclosure to the board was fraught with tension. The immediate reactions of board members ranged from shock and disbelief to anger and betrayal. She navigated this critical meeting by adhering strictly to the facts and supporting each statement with clear, concise evidence. The board's response and subsequent actions taken to address the fraud underscored the significance of the findings. Cooper's courage in this moment was instrumental in catalyzing regulatory changes, including enacting the Sarbanes-Oxley Act, which aimed to prevent such fraudulent activities in the future.

Following the board meeting, making the findings public involved careful planning to manage the inevitable fallout. Cooper's team worked closely with legal teams, regulatory bodies and ultimately the media to ensure that information dissemination was controlled and accurate. The scandal resulted in WorldCom filing for bankruptcy in July 2002 and an exposure of fraud amounting to $11 billion, the largest bankruptcy in U.S. history. Cynthia Cooper stayed with the company for the next two years. Her team helped the company navigate the challenges and emerge from them. In 2006, Verizon Communications acquired WorldCom.

In her book, *"Extraordinary Circumstances: The Journey of a Corporate Whistleblower"*, Cynthia Cooper does express a deep commitment to WorldCom, highlighting her dedication to the company's well-being and her desire to address the issues she uncovered. Cooper's decision to stay with the company through its emergence from bankruptcy, helping to restructure and stabilize the company post-scandal, further underscored her dedication to the company and its future survival. Her loyalty lay not with the compromised executives but with the company's survival and the principles of good corporate governance—protecting shareholders and employees. This dedication showcases her investment in the company's future and her belief in its potential to overcome the crisis it faced. Cooper's story is a testament to the power of integrity, principled courage and dedicated individuals' impact on corporate governance and accountability.

1. **Leadership and Integrity:** Cooper, serving as Vice President of Internal Audit at WorldCom, demonstrated integrity-rooted leadership. Despite potential personal and professional repercussions, her refusal to overlook suspicious accounting entries underscores the critical importance of integrity at the leadership level. Her actions exposed the fraud and emphasized the necessity for leaders to adhere strictly to ethical standards, fostering a culture of honesty and accountability within the organization.

2. **Integrity as a Catalyst for Trust:** Cooper's dedication to principles and standards was crucial in building trust within her audit team and later among the public and stakeholders. By choosing to investigate and report the discrepancies, she reinforced the value of trust in corporate

settings. Her integrity, showcased through her actions, helped restore faith in the auditing process and highlighted the role of trust in ensuring corporate governance.

3. **Integrity in Decision Making:** Cooper's decision-making process, driven by integrity and ethical considerations, played a fundamental role in navigating the crisis. By prioritizing standards over short-term gains or personal safety, she provided a blueprint for decision-making that respects stakeholder interests and maintains corporate legitimacy.

4. **Integrity leads to Predictability:** An organization's predictability and stability greatly depend on its adherence to mutually agreed-upon practices. Cooper's integrity revealed hidden financial discrepancies, steering WorldCom towards corrective measures. Although the short-term aftermath was tumultuous, the long-term benefits of restored integrity helped pave the way for more sustainable business practices.

CHAPTER 7

Mutual Respect

"The most important figures that one needs for management are unknown or unknowable, but successful management must nevertheless take account of them."

—Lloyd S. Nelson

MUTUAL RESPECT IS A BEHAVIORAL determinant of loyalty that fosters a culture where employees feel valued and are dedicated to positively contributing towards organizational goals. Fostering a culture of respect at work transcends leniency or ignoring faults. It encompasses courteous behavior, acknowledging contributions, and inspiring excellence by recognizing commendable worth, principles, and efforts. Further, mutual respect as a behavioral determinant of loyalty manifests in accepting and valuing the diversity of contributions and perspectives. In the context of a cause for an organization, this means understanding and appreciating the varied ways in which individuals contribute and show their dedication.

Research has shown that 98% of employees experience uncivil behavior at work, significantly impacting creativity, engagement, and retention. As organizational leaders strive to create environments where respect flourishes, it becomes evident that mutual respect is not just a moral imperative but a strategic asset, directly influencing loyalty and the overall success of an organization. This chapter aims to explore the multifaceted role of mutual respect in enhancing workplace dynamics, its impact on loyalty, and the strategies for nurturing a culture where every member feels respected and included.

Geert Hofstede

Hofstede's research departs from conventional beliefs about corporate culture, which often emphasize shared values as central. Instead, his study indicates that the essence of an organization's culture lies more in the shared perceptions of daily practices. One reason for the disparity might be the corporate management literature's lack of distinction between the values held by founders and leaders versus those of the broader organization.

Often, descriptions of organizational culture rely heavily on statements from corporate figures. Hofstede's research evaluated how effectively the values communicated by leaders permeated the organization. Although the influence of founders and key leaders in shaping organizational culture is significant, it manifests more tangibly through practices among ordinary members. He concluded that departments like HR which play a crucial role in upholding these values, which is often unbeknownst to them, mediate the process. The role of values and their practical application is further discussed later in the chapter.

The socialization process within an organization, guided by the organization's culture and management's behavior, is foundational in fostering mutual respect among employees. Through this process, employees learn the organization's norms and values, including respect for one another. Leadership plays a pivotal role in modeling these values, creating a culture where mutual respect is encouraged and exemplified. Hence, the leadership's demonstration of mutual respect significantly impacts the socialization process, cultivating an environment where employees feel valued and respected. This leads them to exemplify the same towards their colleagues and the organization's management.

Depending on the organization's size and the markets it operates in, cultural competency can be of high importance to the fostering of workplace respect. Cultural competency involves recognizing and adapting to cultural differences in a way that fosters mutual respect and effective collaboration. This enables individuals to engage meaningfully across diverse cultural backgrounds because people have their own paradigms shaped by their culture and past experiences. Their influence continues to shape their professional and social behavior unless effective socialization, identification, and internalization processes occur.

Furthermore, the concepts of owed and earned respect are fundamental to nurturing a culture of mutual respect. Owed respect is a universal right of every employee, a baseline of civility and acknowledgment of each individual's inherent value within the organization. On the other hand, earned respect acknowledges and rewards individuals for their specific contributions and achievements. Striking the right balance between owed and earned respect is critical; too much emphasis on either can lead to a workplace environment that either stifles individual achievement under the guise of equality or fosters a cutthroat atmosphere where only the accomplishments matter, undermining team cohesion and solidarity. Together, these concepts form the cornerstone of a respectful workplace culture, enhancing loyalty and creating a more committed, productive, and satisfied workforce.

Navigating the balance between owed and earned respect involves understanding their distinct roles in workplace dynamics. Owed respect ensures all employees feel included and valued, fostering a positive atmosphere. However, focusing solely on owed respect without recognizing individual achievements can diminish motivation and accountability. Conversely, emphasizing earned respect can lead to excessive competition and hinder collaboration.

Leaders must strive for equilibrium, promoting a culture that honors both collective belonging and individual contributions, thereby avoiding pitfalls like incivility and abuse of power.

Leaders set the tone for the organizational culture by modeling respectful behavior, setting clear expectations for civility, and establishing norms prioritizing mutual respect. By modeling mutual respect in their interactions and decisively addressing instances of disrespect, leaders demonstrate the value of respect and set expectations for everyone in the organization to follow. This leadership approach trickles down, shaping the interactions between employees and the overall atmosphere of the workplace. Employees reflect the respect they observe in their leaders, contributing to a more harmonious and productive work environment.

Mutual respect in the workplace significantly impacts retention, collaboration, productivity, and the sense of belonging among employees. Research highlights the detrimental effects of incivility, showing that nearly half (48%) of the employees who experience disrespect intentionally reduce their work effort and time at work, with a significant number reporting a decline in performance (38%) and commitment to the organization (78%). This leads to decreased productivity and affects customer relationships, as a quarter of affected employees admit to taking out their frustration on customers. Incivility can lead to an environment where employees spend a considerable amount of time worrying about or avoiding the offender, further diminishing the workplace's collaborative and creative potential. Leaders play a crucial role in setting the tone for mutual respect by modeling appropriate behavior, underscoring the importance of respectful interactions in maintaining a positive and inclusive work culture.

Conveying respect in the workplace requires understanding your organization's unique culture and expectations. It involves recognizing how behaviors and communication styles are perceived within your particular environment. A balance must be struck by adapting your actions to align with organizational norms, while also being authentic in your interactions. People prefer to be treated the way they wish—not according to someone else's idea of respect.

Active listening and clear communication are foundational in fostering a culture of mutual respect within any organization. By engaging in active listening, leaders validate the voices and perspectives of their team members, encouraging a two-way dialogue that emphasizes asking questions and expressing gratitude. Acknowledging and valuing your team's diversity of perspectives and contributions is key. This approach fosters a respectful atmosphere and strengthens the overall cohesion and effectiveness of the team.

Creating organizational norms that uphold the dignity and worth of every individual lays the groundwork for a respectful work environment. This includes establishing clear communication channels that allow for transparent sharing of expectations and roles. Hence, the hiring process is crucial for the organization because it is about the organization to learn more about the prospective employees and for them to learn more about the organization. The expectations that are set during that process and the socialization process are the basis of the duration of your mutual work.

Leadership's role is vital in articulating and embodying these principles. By clarifying each department's and individual's importance in achieving the organization's objectives, leaders underscore the collective responsibility towards a shared goal. This reinforces the organization's mission and fosters a sense of belonging and purpose among team members.

Mutual respect could be examined through the lens of power dynamics. In hierarchical settings, those in leadership positions have a critical role in modeling respect and loyalty. Their actions and decisions set a precedent for the organization's culture. This involves not just top-down respect but also fostering an environment where feedback and dissent are respected, creating a culture of psychological safety (further discussed after the examples).

Alcibiades

Alcibiades, born in 451/450 BCE into an illustrious Athenian family, is one of the most intriguing and enigmatic figures of Classical Athens. His life was defined by brilliance, controversy, and a restless tension between personal ambition and public service. This complexity of character, alongside his shifting allegiances during the Peloponnesian War, paints a vivid picture of a man who was as admired as he was reviled.

Alcibiades was born to the Athenian politician and general Cleinias and his mother, Deinomache, who was from the ancient aristocratic Alcmaeonidae family. His early years were marked by the greatness of his uncle, the statesman Pericles, who shaped his ambitions and Athenian identity after his father died in battle. Under the mentorship of Socrates, Alcibiades developed into a charismatic yet polarizing figure known for his beauty, intelligence, and loose morals. Alcibiades and Socrates fought in the initial confrontations of the Peloponnesian War, during which they participated in the battles at Potidaea in 432 BCE, where Alcibiades was rescued by Socrates, and at Delium in 424 BCE, where Alcibiades saved Socrates. Following the death of the Athenian commander Cleon in 422 BCE, Alcibiades rose to prominence in Athens, assuming leadership of the faction advocating for continued warfare, in direct opposition to Nicias. Frustrated in 421 BCE when the Spartans selected Nicias for peace discussions, Alcibiades incited the Athenians to form an alliance with the cities of Argos, Mantinea, and Elis to launch assaults on the allies of Sparta. The alliance was projected to last a century, while Alcibiades held the general position for an unprecedented 15 consecutive years.

In 415 BCE, Alcibiades delivered an oration encouraging Athens to initiate an expedition to Sicily. This campaign was proposed after the Sicilian city-state Segesta sought Athenian support in 416/415 BCE to confront its neighbor Selinus, allied with Syracuse. Alcibiades, possibly motivated by the desire to acquire Sicilian timber crucial for the Athenian fleet and imperialist ambitions, contended that Sicily's diverse population and political turmoil would prevent a coherent defense. He further asserted that, with targeted reforms, Athens could secure strategic support from Persia. Despite skepticism from his adversary Nicias, Alcibiades successfully won the assembly's vote. Consequently, he, along with Nicias and Lamados (or Lamachus), were appointed as *strategoi autokratores* with unlimited authority, and dispatched with 6,000 soldiers and 60 ships to aid Segesta.

However, just before their departure, Athens was rocked by a scandal, possibly a conspiracy against Alcibiades, involving the vandalism of Hermai statues, which significantly dented the morale of the superstitious Athenian sailors given Hermes' role as the divine patron of travelers and messengers, whose desecration deeply unsettled the populace. This incident, believed by many to undermine Athens' democratic foundations, implicated Alcibiades, a city's elite youth member, as the main suspect. Compounded by allegations of desecrating the Eleusinian Mysteries at a feast, Alcibiades demanded an immediate trial to clear his name, perhaps due to his confidence in his innocence. Yet, Athens delayed, sending him to Sicily regardless. Soon, he was urgently summoned back to Athens to face a trial, but anticipating a death sentence, he opted to defect to Sparta, abandoning Athens at a pivotal moment.

In Sparta, he offered military counsel against Athens, significantly altering the war's course. His strategies, especially his role in the capture of Dekeleia and advice to fortify Syracuse, proved detrimental to Athens' fortunes. The Athenian campaign in Sicily turned out to be a catastrophic failure, culminating in an utter rout in 414 BCE, which resulted in the deaths of Nicias and the esteemed general Demosthenes. However, his continuous machinations and possible personal indiscretions, particularly his involvement with the Persian satrap Tissaphernes and shifting political allegiances, ultimately fractured his relationship with Sparta's ruling elite, particularly King Agis, who viewed Alcibiades' loyalties with suspicion. This eventually compelled Alcibiades to defect from Sparta and seek new alliances, ultimately aligning with Tissaphernes, a Persian Satrap, a strategic move given Persia's opposition to Athens and its aid to Sparta, an attempt to build a fleet to rival Athens.

Alcibiades advocated for Persia to maintain amicable relations with both Athens and Sparta. At the same time, he sought to portray himself as the ideal mediator for an alliance between Athens and Persia to the Athenian naval forces stationed at Samos. He knew that forging such an alliance would necessitate the establishment of an oligarchic government in Athens. Consequently, Peisandros was dispatched to Athens, where he successfully incited the elite, leading to a coup that replaced democracy with an oligarchy of 400 members and soon expanded into a broader oligarchic council of 5,000 citizens. Thus, in 412 BC, Alcibiades and Tissaphernes shifted their allegiance away from Sparta to assist Athens. Following this, Alcibiades, holding the position of strategos under the ostensibly pro-democratic navy at Samos, steered the fleet to notable victories, including against Spartan forces at Cyzicus and the Persian Satrap Pharnabazos at Abydos, as well as the capture of Byzantium.

In 407 BCE, Alcibiades made a triumphant return to Athens, where previous accusations against him were nullified and he was reinstated as *strategos autokrater*, a rank above all other generals —a rare moment in Athenian history where a previously exiled figure returned not only vindicated but elevated above his peers. Subsequently, he was involved in suppressing an uprising at Andros and undertook a campaign in northern Ionia. However, during his absence, the Athenian navy faced a significant defeat at Notium under Spartan leader Lysander due to Alcibiades leaving a mere helmsman in charge of the fleet.

Towards the end of the Peloponnesian War in 405 - 404 BC, Athens engaged in a final sea battle at Aegospotami as Sparta was gaining the upper hand. Ignoring Alcibiades' strategic counsel to avoid confrontation, Athens proceeded—and suffered a decisive and devastating defeat. Following this, Alcibiades found himself once again exiled and sought sanctuary with Pharnabazus II, a Persian military leader soon to become the satrap of Phrygia. On an ill-fated night, while preparing for a journey to meet Persian King Artaxerxes I, Alcibiades' residence was set ablaze. In a frantic escape, he was mortally wounded by a hail of arrows—possibly fired by Spartan agents or relatives of a woman tied to a romantic scandal—marking a tragic and ambiguous end to a life shaped by ambition and betrayal.

Alcibiades' life is emblematic of the interplay between personal ambition and public duty, illustrating the volatile nature of Athenian democracy and politics. His educational relationship with Socrates and his military and political exploits contributed to his lasting fame. Yet, his betrayals, real or perceived, have cemented his legacy as a symbol of treachery and the perils of excessive ambition. The life of Alcibiades, marked by dramatic reversals of fortune, exemplifies the complexities of Athenian society during one of its most tumultuous periods. His story is a testament to the classical world's intricate dynamics of power, loyalty, and personal ambition.

Alcibiades' life and his interactions with Athens and Sparta offer a compelling historical illustration of the principles of reciprocity as outlined in contemporary organizational and psychological frameworks. His life offers a vivid historical case study in the enduring value of reciprocity, mutual respect, and shared purpose—concepts that resonate powerfully within both Aristotelian ethics and modern organizational psychology.

Lessons

Alcibiades' career was marked by both brilliant successes and dramatic failures, often as a direct consequence of his relationships—rooted in mutual or lacking respect—with key political figures, his peers, and the general populace. His ability to inspire loyalty and respect and his failures in maintaining those sentiments underscores the importance of fostering and preserving mutual respect.

In organizations today, just as in the political arenas of ancient Greece, mutual respect fosters a culture where people feel valued and, therefore, are more likely to contribute positively towards organizational goals in the long term. The respect Alcibiades commanded from his peers, subordinates, and, at times, from his enemies exemplifies how respect can be a strategic asset, directly influencing loyalty and the overall success of an organization. His life story illustrates that fostering a culture of respect is not merely about leniency or ignoring faults but involves recognizing and acknowledging contributions, inspiring excellence, and appreciating how individuals contribute to the collective goals.

However, Alcibiades' eventual downfall, partially due to his perceived betrayal of Athens and his complex relationships with Sparta and Persia, highlights the fragile nature of respect and loyalty. It demonstrates that while mutual respect can be a powerful driver of loyalty, it requires consistent reinforcement and cannot be taken for granted. This lesson is particularly relevant for contemporary organizational leaders who strive to create environments where respect flourishes and not as a one time initiative.

From Alcibiades' story, organizations can learn that socialization, guided by culture and leadership behavior, is foundational in fostering mutual respect among employees. Leadership plays a pivotal role in modeling these values, which must become norms part of day-to-day activities. Hence, a culture is created where mutual respect is encouraged, exemplified , and not conveniently disregarded in emotional moments.

Zappos

Culture should drive conduct, while compliance is only a part of what constitutes conduct. Most responses to this initiative have translated themselves into "codes of conduct," legal jargon that might be useful for compliance purposes but uninspiring and restrictive regarding culture.

The journey of Zappos, from its inception to becoming a benchmark in organizational culture and customer service, is a story of bold vision, relentless perseverance, and transformative leadership. At the heart of this narrative are Nick Swinmurn, the founder, and Tony Hsieh, whose entrepreneurial acumen and dedication to a unique company ethos propelled Zappos to unparalleled success.

When Nick Swinmurn first pitched the idea of an online shoe retailer, he was met with widespread skepticism from venture capitalists who doubted consumers would abandon traditional shoe shopping for a digital platform.. They were skeptical that consumers would shift from traditional shoe buying to an online platform, despite Swinmurn's compelling argument that a significant portion of shoe sales came from mail-order catalogs. Undeterred by the initial rejections, Swinmurn's perseverance and passion eventually caught the attention of Tony Hsieh and Alfred Lin of Venture Frogs. Initially hesitant, Hsieh and Lin were soon convinced by Swinmurn's vision, marking the beginning of Zappos and setting it on a trajectory to redefine online shopping.

Tony Hsieh, born to Taiwanese immigrants and a Harvard University graduate, brought his entrepreneurial spirit and insight to Zappos, transitioning from an advisor and investor to the CEO. Under his leadership, Zappos became synonymous with exemplary customer service and a distinctive organizational culture focused on employee happiness. This culture, encapsulated in Hsieh's book "Delivering Happiness," emphasized the well-being of customers and employees as the cornerstone of business success, a philosophy that transcended corporate boundaries, most visibly in Hsieh's Downtown Project in Las Vegas, which sought to apply the same cultural principles to urban revitalization and community design

Zappos' culture is built around 10 core values, including delivering "WOW" through service, embracing and driving change, creating fun and a little weirdness, and being adventurous, creative, and open-minded. These values are not just slogans but are integrated into all aspects of the company, from hiring and onboarding new employees to day-to-day operations and customer interactions. Zappos maintains that a vibrant internal culture fuels passionate employees—who, in turn, cultivate passionate customers.

The influence of Zappos' culture on its success is multifaceted. First, its focus on customer service has led to high customer loyalty and repeat business, which is critical for any retailer but especially for an online one where competition is just a click away. *Every employee, Hsieh said, would get trained as a call center rep to start, regardless of title – so customer service would be fundamental to their job. He said these investments – instead of advertising - drive brand and word of mouth better than any advertising campaign ever could. "Everything else," he said, "can and eventually will be copied."*

Second, Zappos' culture has attracted and retained talent. By prioritizing cultural fit in its hiring process, Zappos ensures that new hires are not just capable in their roles but also contribute to and thrive in the company's unique environment. This approach reduces turnover and fosters a highly engaged workforce. Employee engagement is critical for Zappos. Engaged employees are more productive, provide better customer service, and contribute to a positive environment that further attracts talent.

The culture fosters open communication, employee empowerment, and a sense of community, all of which contribute to high customer loyalty and a productive, dedicated workforce. Despite initial resistance, Zappos' innovative management approach, such as adopting Holacracy, eliminated traditional hierarchies, further emphasizing the company's commitment to its values.

The impact of Zappos' culture led to the gradual increase of revenue from $1.6 million in 2000 to $1 billion in 2008 and this culminated in its acquisition by Amazon in 2009 for approximately $1.2 billion, a deal that underscored the e-commerce giant's recognition of Zappos' unique value proposition. Amazon's decision to allow Zappos to operate independently affirmed the significance of the culture Hsieh and Swinmurn worked so hard to establish.

Some of the key elements that have been identified in their culture are the following:

Open Communication and Transparent Decision-Making

Open communication and transparent decision-making are fundamental to fostering a trusting and inclusive workplace environment. This approach involves sharing key decisions, processes, and company updates with employees, ensuring they feel informed and valued. Transparency builds trust, as employees understand the rationale behind decisions that affect their work and the company's direction. Open communication channels encourage feedback and dialogue, enabling companies to leverage diverse perspectives for better problem-solving and innovation.

Employee Empowerment

Empowering employees means giving them the autonomy to make decisions related to their work, encouraging ownership, taking risks, and accountability. This empowerment can take various forms, such as allowing teams to set their own goals, make decisions on how to best achieve them, and solve problems independently. Empowered employees are more dedicated, motivated, and satisfied with their jobs, leading to higher productivity and innovation. Companies that prioritize employee empowerment typically support this with the necessary training, resources, and trust to make meaningful decisions.

Building Trust

Trust is the cornerstone of effective teamwork and leadership. Building trust within an organization involves consistent behavior from leaders, clear and honest communication, and actions that align with the company's values. Trust is cultivated over time by consistently meeting commitments, showing respect for employees, and fostering a safe environment where people feel they can share their thoughts and ideas without fear of retribution. A culture of trust enhances collaboration, reduces conflict, and improves morale.

Cultural Fit in Hiring

Hiring for cultural fit means assessing potential employees not just on their skills and experiences but also on how well they align with the company's values, beliefs, and behaviors. This approach can lead to higher job satisfaction, better performance, and longer tenure, as employees who fit well with the company culture are more likely to feel connected to their work and their colleagues. However, it's important to balance cultural fit with diversity, ensuring that the pursuit of fit does not exclude valuable different perspectives or lead to a homogenous workforce.

Employee Recognition and Rewards

Recognizing and rewarding employees for their contributions is crucial for maintaining high levels of engagement and motivation. Recognition can take many forms, from formal awards and promotions to informal praise and acknowledgment. Rewards can be monetary, such as bonuses or raises, or non-monetary, such as additional time off or professional development opportunities. Effective recognition is timely, specific, and aligned with the company's values, reinforcing desired behaviors and outcomes.

Professional and Personal Development

Investing in employees' professional and personal development demonstrates a commitment to their growth and well-being. This can include providing access to training, workshops, conferences, mentoring, and coaching. Encouraging continuous learning and development helps employees advance their careers, keeps their skills relevant, and can improve job satisfaction. Moreover, personal development opportunities, such as wellness programs or work-life balance initiatives, contribute to overall employee happiness and retention.

Sense of Community and Team Building Activities

Creating a sense of community within the workplace fosters a positive, supportive environment where employees feel they belong. Team building activities, both work-related and social, can strengthen relationships, improve communication, and boost team performance. Community-building can also extend beyond the immediate workplace through corporate social responsibility initiatives, volunteering, or supporting causes important to employees. A strong sense of community enhances employee dedication, loyalty and overall company culture.

These practices, when woven together into a culture, reflect a workplace where mutual respect is the norm and not an abstract idea. The sustained strength of Zappos' culture reflects not only the commitment of its leadership but also a deliberate hiring philosophy rooted in respect for each employee's individuality and their role in shaping the broader organizational identity.

CHAPTER 8

Psychological Safety

"If someone is able to show me that what I think or do is not right, I will happily change, for I seek the truth, by which no one was ever truly harmed. It is the person who continues in his self-deception and ignorance who is harmed."

—Marcus Aurelius

PSYCHOLOGICAL SAFETY, A CONCEPT EXTENSIVELY explored in organizational behavior, refers to an environment where employees can express ideas, concerns, and mistakes without fear of punishment or humiliation. First introduced by Carl Rogers in the 1950s, psychological safety has since become central to understanding team dynamics and organizational effectiveness. In environments marked by psychological safety, individuals feel empowered to engage in open communication, fostering innovative thinking and a willingness to take risks without fear of embarrassment or retribution. It functions at the group level, playing a vital role in knowledge sharing and cultivating an environment that supports risk-taking and creativity. This atmosphere is crucial for promoting a culture of learning, where mistakes are viewed as opportunities for growth rather than as failures.

Teams exhibiting high levels of psychological safety are often more creative and agile in their problem-solving approaches. They tend to engage more in brainstorming sessions, where diverse viewpoints are welcomed and encouraged. This open exchange of ideas leads to more effective and innovative solutions, driving the organization's success while reducing employee turnover.

Real-world examples of organizations that have successfully fostered psychological safety include Google and Pixar. Google, through its Project Aristotle, found that psychological safety was the most critical factor in forming successful teams. Project Aristotle was an initiative by Google to study and understand the dynamics of successful teams. Launched in 2012, the project analyzed data from hundreds of teams at Google to identify the key factors that contribute to team effectiveness. The research revealed that psychological safety was the most critical factor in forming successful teams, more so than the individual competencies of team members.

Pixar's Braintrust meetings—established by Ed Catmull—serve as a cornerstone of the company's creative process. In these meetings, Pixar team members who aren't directly involved in a project gather to watch material and provide feedback to the project's director and creative heads. These sessions rely on open, candid discussions, fostering an environment of creative risk-taking where employees feel comfortable sharing their opinions without fear of judgment or retaliation. The aim is to provide straightforward feedback to improve final products, ensuring that flaws are addressed and creative ideas are refined.

Organizations can begin promoting psychological safety by training leaders and managers in emotional and social intelligence and effective communication techniques. Those in positions of power should strive to create an environment where individuals feel safe to speak openly—free from judgment, labels, or fear of repercussions. Such a shift transforms the culture from one dominated by "yes-men" into a space where ideas flow freely and people are genuinely motivated to contribute to collective success. Team coaching programs are effective in reinforcing the principles of psychological safety because of the external mediator.

However, this ideal is often challenged by inherent power imbalances, diverse personal values, and varying perceptions of what constitutes respect. Thus, embedding mutual respect into workplace culture demands ongoing effort and adaptability. It involves institutionalizing practices that promote mutual respect, such as regular and transparent communication channels, fair and unbiased decision-making processes, and systems for recognizing and rewarding contributions that align with the organization's values and goals.

Etsy and Blameless Postmortems

An example of psychological safety in practice comes from Etsy, a technology company known for fostering a "Just Culture" through its use of blameless postmortems. This approach gained attention not just for how it handles failure, but for how it reshapes the cultural norms around accountability, learning, and trust.

At Etsy, a blameless postmortem is held after an outage or significant incident. Unlike traditional postmortems where someone is usually "held responsible" or subtly blamed for what went wrong, Etsy's approach avoids punitive responses. The goal is not to shame individuals but to understand the deeper conditions and decision-making processes that contributed to the failure. As the original article by John Allspaw explains, having a blameless process means that the engineers involved can give detailed accounts of what they did, when they did it, what they expected, and what assumptions they made - without fear of punishment or retribution.

This is not about letting people "off the hook." In fact, as Allspaw emphasizes, engineers are still deeply accountable, but they are accountable for helping the organization learn and improve. When people feel safe to speak honestly about their errors, the organization gains insight into how things actually work "on the ground," or at what Allspaw calls the *sharp end* of the system. That's where real work happens - not in Gantt charts, procedures, or theoretical workflows, but in the lived complexity of day-to-day decision-making.

Etsy's practice is based on the belief that mistakes are rarely the result of recklessness or incompetence. Instead, failures often emerge from well-intended decisions made under real constraints. As Allspaw stated, "The action made sense to the person at the time they took it, because if it hadn't made sense to them, they wouldn't have taken the action in the first place." This framing is essential. It avoids what psychologists call the *fundamental attribution error*—the tendency to blame personal flaws instead of recognizing the influence of situational factors.

Instead of asking, "Who messed up?" the team at Etsy asks, "Why did this action make sense to the person at the time?" They actively seek out what Allspaw calls the *Second Story*: a deeper understanding of the systemic vulnerabilities and contextual realities that contributed to the failure. In this view, human error is not the cause of failure but a symptom of deeper organizational issues. By uncovering these vulnerabilities, the organization can improve safety and performance.

Etsy empowers engineers to own their stories. It ensures their voices are heard and turns those voices into a force for learning and meaningful improvement. Engineers become educators and change agents, helping their peers avoid similar missteps in the future. This creates a feedback loop of trust, reflection, and improvement. It also supports the idea that psychological safety is not the absence of accountability—it's the presence of *constructive* accountability, grounded in shared purpose and mutual respect.

Ultimately, Etsy's blameless post mortem practice demonstrates that when people feel safe to speak openly, they don't hide their mistakes—they lean into them. And when an organization values learning over blame, it becomes more resilient in the face of failure and more human.

CHAPTER 9

Proactivity

*"I have been impressed with the urgency of doing so.
Knowing is not enough; we must apply. Being willing
is not enough; we must do it."*

—Leonardo da Vinci

PROACTIVITY, AS A BEHAVIORAL DETERMINANT of loyalty, manifests
in several interrelated aspects, each contributing to the efficacy
and depth of one's dedication. This dynamic approach to loyalty
is characterized by responsiveness and by a forward-thinking and
initiative-driven attitude that actively supports and enhances
the cause or organization to which one is devoted. The elements
are anticipating needs, continuously seeking and acquiring new
knowledge, preventing potential dangers, and a sense of responsibility towards the organization.

Anticipating Needs as a Proactive Determinant of Loyalty

Anticipating needs is a behavior that reflects an individual's proactive commitment to their organization. It involves predicting
and addressing the future requirements of the organization and
its stakeholders before these needs are explicitly recognized.
This forward-thinking behavior is an indicator of an individual's
loyalty, as it demonstrates a commitment to the organization's

long-term success and a willingness to invest personal effort in its continuity and growth. Individuals who consistently exhibit this behavior often display higher levels of dedication and loyalty, as they are actively involved in steering the organization towards future successes.

Environmental scanning is a critical component of anticipating needs. Individuals who excel at anticipating needs engage in several key activities that highlight their proactive approach. They keep a close eye on both external and internal dynamics that could affect their organization. By understanding market trends, regulatory changes, and technological advancements, they can foresee challenges and opportunities that might not yet be visible to others within the organization. Internally, they analyze current processes and workflows to identify potential inefficiencies or areas where improvements could be made before problems arise.

These individuals also place a high value on communication and feedback, gathering insights from a range of stakeholders including employees, customers, and industry peers. This continuous loop of feedback helps them to fine-tune their understanding of what might be needed in the future, ensuring that their initiatives are well-informed and effectively targeted.

The ability to anticipate needs can manifest in various practical applications that significantly benefit the organization. For instance, in product development, this might involve innovating new products that meet emerging customer needs before competitors recognize these trends. In customer service, it translates into personalizing experiences and resolving issues before they escalate, thereby enhancing customer satisfaction and loyalty.

In strategic human resource management, anticipating future skill requirements ensures that the organization is prepared for industry shifts, keeping it ahead of the competition and making it an attractive place for ambitious professionals who value growth and development. By foreseeing the future skills required and training employees ahead of time, organizations ensure they remain competitive and employees feel valued and prepared for future challenges.

Despite its benefits, the ability to effectively anticipate needs is not without challenges. It requires a delicate balance between taking proactive steps and the risk of overcommitting resources based on predictions that may not fully materialize. Additionally, organizational resistance can sometimes impede proactive initiatives, especially in environments that are accustomed to a more reactive, "wait-and-see" approach.

There's also a risk of over-preparing or misjudging future needs, which can lead to wasted efforts and resources if predictions do not materialize as expected. Proposing changes based on anticipated needs might face resistance from within the organization, especially if the current state is perceived as successful or stable.

Ultimately, the ability to anticipate needs is a crucial component of proactivity that can characterize an individual's loyalty to an organization. It demonstrates a deep dedication with the organization's goals and a commitment to contribute positively to its future. Cultivating this trait across the workforce can transform an organization, making it more agile, forward-thinking, and aligned with the evolving needs of its environment. By effectively anticipating needs, organizations ensure they remain resilient, adaptive, and ahead of industry curves, fostering a culture where loyalty and forward-thinking are integral to the organizational ethos. Organizations should therefore foster a culture that values and rewards this kind of proactive behavior, ensuring that it becomes a fundamental part of their strategic operations.

Continuously Seeking and Acquiring New Knowledge

The ongoing pursuit of knowledge is a critical element of proactivity that significantly contributes to an individual's loyalty to an organization. By continuously seeking and acquiring new knowledge, employees demonstrate their commitment to personal growth and their dedication to contributing positively to the organization. This behavior enhances their own capabilities and ensures that the organization remains at the cutting edge of industry developments. Employees who are constantly learning are better equipped to adapt to changes and to drive innovation, making them invaluable assets to their teams and leaders.

Individuals dedicated to lifelong learning tend to engage in several key practices that boost their professional value and align closely with the organization's long-term success. These practices include staying updated with the latest industry trends, technologies, and best practices. This proactive learning goes beyond formal education and training; it encompasses a mindset of curiosity and an eagerness to explore new ideas and skills continually. Employees who engage in continuous learning display a natural curiosity and a strong initiative to keep pace with changing business environments, internal and external.

Lifelong learners regularly expand their skill sets and deepen their expertise, which makes them more versatile and valuable to their organization. Learners often leverage a variety of resources to enhance their knowledge, such as subscribing to relevant professional journals, participating in workshops and seminars, and joining professional networks. They might also take courses to gain certifications that are beneficial for their personal career progression and bring direct benefits to their roles within the organization.

Lifelong learners bring fresh perspectives and ideas to the table. Their updated knowledge and new insights often lead to innovative solutions to complex problems, driving the organization's growth and competitive advantage.

Applying newly acquired knowledge in the workplace is where the real value of continuous learning is realized. For example, an employee who learns a new software or technology can introduce more efficient methods of working, which can lead to cost savings and productivity increases. In customer-facing roles, staying informed about the latest market trends can enable employees to offer better solutions to clients, thereby improving customer satisfaction and loyalty.

In leadership roles, continuous learning is particularly important as it equips leaders with the latest management techniques and insights into organizational behavior, which can enhance team performance and drive better decision-making processes.

For continuous learning to be effectively integrated into the workplace, organizational support is crucial. Companies can foster a culture of learning by providing access to training programs, reimbursing employees for educational expenses, and recognizing and rewarding educational achievements. Moreover, creating an environment that encourages knowledge sharing among colleagues— such as through regular 'knowledge exchange' meetings or internal seminars—can amplify the benefits of individual learning efforts.

Despite the clear benefits, promoting continuous learning in the workplace can come with challenges. There is the time and financial cost of training and development to consider, and not all employees may initially have the motivation to engage in such a process. Furthermore, measuring the direct impact of learning on performance can be complex in the long-term if the application process is vague

Organizations need to carefully design their learning and development initiatives to ensure they are relevant, accessible, and aligned with both individual career goals and organizational objectives. Encouraging a learning culture also requires leadership to actively participate in and advocate for these practices. Most importantly, continuous learning should not be for the sake of learning new information, skills, etc. which are not aligned with the strategic, tactical or operational goals of the company.

Continuously seeking and acquiring new knowledge is an indicator of an employee's loyalty and proactivity. It shows a readiness to grow and adapt in ways that align closely with the organization's needs and future challenges. By investing in continuous learning, organizations enhance their competitive edge and signal to their employees that they are valued partners in the organization's journey. This mutual investment fosters a deep sense of reciprocal loyalty, ensuring that both the organization and its employees have proactively prepared for future advancements and changes in their industry.

Preventing Potential Dangers

The proactive behavior of preventing potential dangers involves identifying, assessing, and mitigating risks before they manifest into significant problems. This element involves identifying, assessing, and mitigating risks before they become actual threats to an organization's stability or success. Employees who are adept at foreseeing potential issues and implementing preventative measures demonstrate a deep commitment to the organization's well-being, which is a strong indicator of loyalty. Vigilant guardianship is when an individual's actions are aligned with on-time identification and mitigation of potential threats before they can escalate. Such dedication reflects a protective stance toward the entity's interests, embodying a commitment that is as dynamic as it is defensive.

Vigilance in this context is closely linked to an acute awareness of the entity's operational environment. When they notice potential issues or risks, whether directly within their area of responsibility or in other parts of the organization, they take the initiative to address them. This approach ensures a comprehensive protective coverage, where risks are identified and are also effectively managed before they develop into larger problems.

Individuals who excel in preventing potential dangers possess a keen awareness of the array of risks that their organization might face. This includes everything from operational and financial risks to strategic and compliance-related risks. They maintain a vigilant approach, sometimes unconsciously, to monitoring internal processes and external changes that could pose threats, utilizing risk assessment tools and staying informed about industry trends and regulatory changes. This process often necessitates a blend of reinforcing existing measures and introducing innovative solutions.

Proactive employees use their knowledge of the industry and the organization to anticipate areas where vulnerabilities may exist. They think strategically about how external changes, like new regulations or technological advancements, might pose risks. The goal is to build resilient organizational frameworks that can withstand various uncertainties and challenges instead of undertaking actions in the short-term without evaluating the potential consequences for the organization in the long-term.

Conversely, introducing new measures is about proactively adapting to changing circumstances. This could involve adopting new technologies, diversifying strategies, or developing novel approaches to business operations. The ultimate goal in both reinforcing and introducing measures is to build resilience within the entity. This resilience acts as a buffer against potential shocks, ensuring that risks do not escalate into crises. By combining both existing strengths and new strategies, the organization is better equipped to navigate the complexities of its environment.

The ability to preemptively tackle potential dangers protects the organization from adverse outcomes and reinforces a culture of safety, preparedness, and responsiveness. This proactive approach to risk management can lead to:

- **Enhanced Organizational Resilience:** Building resilience by minimizing disruptions and ensuring the predictability of the continuity in operations.

- **Improved Trust and Reputation:** Protecting the organization from incidents that could harm its reputation, thereby maintaining stakeholder trust.

- **Cost Efficiency:** Reducing potential costs associated with managing crises or mitigating disasters after they have occurred.

While the benefits of effectively preventing potential dangers are clear, several challenges can impede these efforts. These include resistance to change, especially in established organizations where traditional practices are deeply ingrained. It requires a balance between being vigilant and being overly cautious, which might lead to unnecessary expenditures or slow down innovation. Additionally, the initial costs and resource allocation required for setting up comprehensive risk management systems can be substantial. However, the long-term benefits of preventing significant losses and enhancing organizational resilience often outweigh these challenges.

Preventing potential dangers is a crucial element of proactivity that significantly contributes to an individual's demonstration of loyalty to an organization. It involves a strategic and thoughtful approach to identifying risks and implementing measures to mitigate them before they impact the organization adversely. By fostering this proactive behavior, organizations can enhance their stability, protect their assets, and maintain a competitive edge in their respective industries.

Central to this proactive approach is a sense of responsibility towards the entity. The responsibility borne by individuals devoted to the entity involves a commitment to the entity's overall health and longevity, where every decision and action taken is weighed against its potential impact on the entity. This sense of responsibility fuels the proactive efforts to mitigate risks, driving individuals to constantly seek ways to safeguard the entity's interests.

This dedication is not passive but is an active and dynamic devotion, where individuals are consistently engaged in protecting and advancing the entity's interests. Through this lens, loyalty is seen as a protective shield, actively working to preempt challenges and fortify the entity against potential adversities.

Employees who exhibit a strong sense of responsibility adhere to their roles' expectations and also embrace the broader impact of their actions on the organization's overall health.

Ownership and Accountability

Individuals who exhibit a strong sense of responsibility view their roles through a lens of ownership. This perspective involves more than completing tasks; it includes a conscientious approach to problem-solving and decision-making that aligns with the organization's best interests. These employees are accountable for their contributions and their impact on the organization. Their dedication is visible through their efforts to optimize operations and enhance organizational capabilities, recognizing that their personal success is intertwined with the organization's success and sustainability.

Employees with a high sense of responsibility resonate strongly with the organization's values and cause. They operate in ways that reflect the organization's principles, reinforcing a culture of integrity and principled behavior. By empathizing with the organization's mission, such employees naturally advocate for practices that support sustainable business operations. This alignment enhances their ability to consistently act in the best interests of the organization.

A responsible employee does not passively wait for directions but seeks opportunities to lead and/or make meaningful contributions. Their proactive nature ensures that they do not shy away from challenges but rather embrace them as opportunities to demonstrate their value to the organization. By leading themselves this way, they encourage a culture of accountability and responsibility to their peers. Their actions inspire others to take initiative and commit fully to the organization's objectives, creating an inspired and dedicated workforce.

While fostering a sense of responsibility within the workforce is advantageous, it requires thoughtful organizational support to sustain. Without proper acknowledgment, employees who consistently take on additional responsibilities can feel undervalued and overburdened. Challenges such as role overload, unclear expectations, and lack of recognition can diminish the effectiveness of even the most responsible employees. Therefore, it is crucial for organizations to ensure clear communication of roles and expectations in a systematic way and create systems that recognize individuals' efforts to prevent burnout and maintain morale.

In conclusion, a sense of responsibility towards the organization is a vital aspect of employee loyalty. It encompasses ownership, accountability, alignment with organizational values, and a proactive approach to challenges. Organizations that foster these qualities in their employees can simultaneously enhance the individual performance and the overall organizational resilience and success. It is imperative for leaders to nurture these traits by setting clear expectations, providing necessary support, and recognizing and rewarding responsible behaviors. This will ensure a loyal workforce dedicated to the organization's long-term prosperity. Loyalty is seen as a protective shield.

The interconnection among these elements creates a cyclical reinforcement where each aspect of proactivity feeds into and enhances the others. For example, the knowledge gained from continuous learning leads to better anticipation of needs, which in turn leads to more effective risk management and a reinforced sense of responsibility to act on these anticipations and insights. This cycle continuously evolves as new knowledge is acquired, new needs are anticipated, new risks are identified, and a stronger sense of responsibility is fostered.

This dedication is active and dynamic, where individuals are consistently committed to protecting and advancing the entity's interests. Through this lens, loyalty is seen as a protective shield, actively working to preempt challenges and fortify the entity against potential adversities.

Xerox and Anne Mulcahy

Anne M. Mulcahy's ascension to the role of CEO at Xerox came during one of the company's most turbulent periods. Her direct, hardworking, and disciplined approach was precisely what Xerox needed to navigate its challenges. Mulcahy was loyal to the Xerox brand and its people and also demonstrated a unique blend of compassion and toughness that allowed her to connect with and motivate dispirited employees. Her hands-on leadership style and willingness to work closely with her team boosted her credibility and helped galvanize the workforce.

Anne Mulcahy's rise to the role of CEO at Xerox was as unexpected as it was dramatic. Despite having dedicated 24 years to Xerox, with 16 of those in sales and significant roles in human resources and as chief of staff, Mulcahy had never envisioned leading the company. Her ascent to CEO in 2001 came at a time when Xerox was facing dire financial challenges, including over $17 billion in debt and a string of annual losses that suggested the company was close to filing for Chapter 11 bankruptcy. Moreover, Xerox was embroiled in an SEC investigation concerning accounting irregularities in its Mexico operations.

From the outset of her presidency, Mulcahy emphasized the importance of transparent and direct communication. She famously noted that her role could have been aptly described as "Chief Communication Officer," highlighting her commitment to transparent and effective communication. The initial 3 months of her leadership were marked by extensive travels—covering 100,000 miles—to various Xerox locations where she engaged directly with employees and customers. Her straightforward approach in these discussions helped to reassure and re-energize employees by reinforcing her strategic vision and giving them a reason to remain hopeful.

Mulcahy's communication style was direct and honest, often stating that the success of a leader hinges on their ability to understand and meet customer requirements while fostering a motivated and proud workforce. She set clear expectations: team members were either fully dedicated to the turnaround effort, or they should leave. This forthright approach helped forge a team that was closely aligned with the recovery objectives, ensuring that everyone was pulling in the same direction.

Anne Mulcahy recognized that a series of unsuccessful reorganizations during the 1990s had left Xerox in disarray. These initiatives, while strategically intended to optimize the company, ended up creating confusion and uncertainty among employees about their roles and Xerox's direction. Mulcahy noted that the company's structure had been overly compartmentalized into various industries, product lines, and geographies—looking effective on paper but failing dramatically in practice. This segmentation led to a lack of clear accountability, making it difficult for her to make decisive business decisions without assembling a large, cumbersome team.

Further complicating matters, Xerox had attempted to centralize its administration and overhaul its sales force. These changes were theoretically sound but poorly implemented, disrupting customer relationships and damaging the trust and continuity that had been established with clients. The sales team restructuring was particularly detrimental; it was executed without sufficient consideration of the impacts on customer service and employee morale. This misstep was widely recognized within the company as a flawed move, yet there was a noticeable lack of communication from the field personnel to the management about these concerns.

Upon assuming leadership, Mulcahy implemented a "back to basics" strategy that focused sharply on operational efficiency. This involved cutting capital expenditures by 50 percent, reducing sales, general, and administrative expenses by a third, and halving the company's overwhelming debt. This disciplined approach to cost management was crucial in stabilizing the company's financial health.

Recognizing that Xerox had lost touch with its market base, Mulcahy leveraged her sales background to realign the company's focus towards customer needs and market demands. This shift was crucial as Xerox had previously maintained a cost model that was increasingly disconnected from market realities. Under her leadership, Xerox recommitted to its core business operations with an enhanced emphasis on sales and operational efficiency.

The restructuring efforts under Mulcahy's leadership were both for the company's immediate survival and for setting the stage for future growth. She recognized that simply cutting costs and managing debt was insufficient. To rejuvenate Xerox, she aimed to redefine the company's core focus and invest in areas that offered sustainable growth opportunities. This forward-thinking approach was vital for Xerox's recovery and subsequent success, enabling the company to emerge as a stronger competitor in the global market.

One of the critical financial maneuvers executed by Mulcahy involved securing the company's liquidity. She was tasked with convincing 58 banks to renew Xerox's revolving line of credit to avoid bankruptcy. All but two banks agreed, and she turned to Sandy Weill of Citigroup, a leading figure in banking, who helped sway the remaining banks. This move was pivotal in stabilizing Xerox's financial standing.

Mulcahy also made tough decisions regarding the company's operational strategy. Recognizing areas where Xerox could not compete effectively, she discontinued the ink-jet printer division, acknowledging that Xerox was a follower rather than a leader in this technology segment. This decision highlighted her strategic focus on investing in areas where Xerox could genuinely differentiate itself and lead the market.

Despite skepticism from industry analysts, Mulcahy boldly reinvested in innovation and research, dedicating $1 billion annually to these areas. She also expanded Xerox's services into consulting, helping businesses improve their document management processes and set up more efficient computer networks. The focus on core business strengths, coupled with stringent financial controls and a reinvigorated innovation drive, slowly restored profitability and market confidence.

Anne Mulcahy openly criticized the intense pressure for short-term performance from Wall Street, which she believed was one of the most problematic trends in the marketplace. Despite these challenges, her tenure at Xerox demonstrated that she could deliver impressive results swiftly. Under her leadership, the company reversed a loss of $273 million in 2000 to generate a profit of $91 million in 2003, eventually reaching profits of $859 million on sales of $15.7 billion by the last recorded year. During this period, Xerox's stock performance significantly outstripped the market, with a 75% return over five years, contrasting sharply with a 6% loss in the Dow Jones Total Stock Market Index.

Anne Mulcahy's tenure at Xerox is a masterclass in crisis management and leadership. Her unexpected rise to CEO brought a fresh perspective that was desperately needed. Through a combination of stringent financial management, strategic clarity, and honest communication, she steered Xerox away from the precipice of bankruptcy towards renewed viability and competitiveness. Her story remains a compelling narrative of how visionary and proactive leadership can completely transform a company.

Anticipating Needs

Mulcahy's proactive approach was evident in her ability to foresee the company's requirements to avoid bankruptcy. Recognizing the need to stabilize the company financially, she quickly addressed Xerox's liquidity issues, negotiated with banks to secure a line of credit, and made tough decisions on cost-cutting measures.

Continuously Seeking and Acquiring New Knowledge

Mulcahy spent her initial months as CEO traveling extensively to understand the ground realities within Xerox, gathering insights that were crucial for formulating an effective turnaround strategy. This demonstrates her commitment to continuous learning and understanding complex challenges, which enabled her to make informed decisions that aligned with the company's operational needs and market demands.

Preventing Potential Dangers

By taking decisive actions to restructure the company's debt and overhaul its operational framework, Mulcahy mitigated immediate financial risks and preempted further organizational dysfunction. Her proactive measures in streamlining operations, cutting unnecessary costs, informing all employees of the new direction (predictability), and refocusing on core business strengths were crucial in setting the company in a new direction.

Sense of Responsibility Towards the Organization

Mulcahy's deep dedication and loyalty to Xerox is reflected in her hands-on leadership and her no-nonsense approach to management. Her efforts to maintain high morale among employees, ensuring their alignment with the company's recovery goals, and her open communication style all highlight her responsibility towards fostering a resilient organizational culture.

AMD and Jerry Sanders

Jerry Sanders, AMD's charismatic founder, steered the company through both great achievements and significant challenges. His leadership during AMD's early years was marked by a blend of visionary strategies and sometimes precarious decisions that shaped the company's future.

Founded in 1969, AMD was formed under Jerry Sanders and a team of former Fairchild Semiconductor colleagues. Sanders, who served as AMD's first CEO, quickly distinguished the company through a focus on quality and reliability, targeting sectors that valued these traits, such as military equipment and high-end computing systems. This strategy allowed AMD to carve out a niche in a market dominated by larger competitors like Intel.

Despite often being viewed as a secondary choice to Intel, AMD emerged as a significant player in the microprocessor industry under Sanders' leadership. This relationship allowed AMD to gain technological prowess while also positioning itself as a constant underdog striving for innovation. Sanders' approach was marked by aggressive marketing, innovation and quality, which helped AMD differentiate itself from competitors and maintain a reputation for reliability in high-value markets.

He believed in the power of salesmanship and public relations to elevate the company's profile. His approach involved direct competition through improved product offerings and emphasized AMD's reliability and performance, challenging the industry's giants on their own turf.

Sanders' tenure at AMD was a mix of proactive initiatives and missed opportunities. While he was adept at seizing market opportunities, such as AMD's entry into the microprocessor market and its competitive positioning against Intel, his management style sometimes lacked the proactive measures necessary to streamline operations and address inefficiencies. This oversight became particularly evident as AMD struggled with operational challenges that hindered its ability to compete effectively, especially during the critical periods of intense competition with Intel.

Sanders was known for his commitment to proprietary technologies, which was both a strength and a weakness. On one hand, this focus led to innovative products that distinguished AMD in the competitive marketplace. On the other hand, it sometimes resulted in overcommitment to certain technologies without sufficient flexibility to adapt to rapidly changing market conditions. This approach occasionally isolated AMD from mainstream trends that were vital for its survival and growth, particularly as the semiconductor industry evolved towards more standardized technology platforms.

Sanders' charismatic and flamboyant leadership style was a double-edged sword. On the one hand, it infused AMD with a culture of creativity and risk-taking, leading to significant techno- logical innovations such as the K6 and Athlon processors, which were critical in AMD's history. On the other hand, his approach sometimes resulted in strategic missteps, particularly his failure to fully anticipate and adapt to market changes, such as the shift towards mobile computing and energy-efficient processors.

His approach was epitomized by extravagant events, such as the massive party at the San Jose Arena featuring Faith Hill and Tim McGraw. This event celebrated AMD's significant achievements under Sanders' leadership, particularly the success of the Athlon chips, which posed a serious challenge to Intel's dominance. These celebrations were not just about revelry; they symbolized Sanders' philosophy of making big bets and rallying his workforce behind AMD's vision. This approach did translate into periods of financial success, such as in 2000 when AMD saw nearly $1 billion in profits.

Sanders promoted a culture of innovation, pushing AMD into significant technological advancements. However, his focus on outshining competitors sometimes prioritized short-term tech- nological gains over long-term financial sustainability. This was evident in AMD's rapid expansion and ambitious projects, which, while innovative, often strained the company's financial resources. The acquisition of NexGen and the push into new processor tech- nologies under Sanders' guidance were pivotal but also came with high financial stakes.

Sanders' tenure, while visionary, was also marked by significant strategic challenges, often lacking the financial discipline required for long-term corporate stability. His leadership saw AMD through cycles of technological success and financial instability, a pattern that ultimately led to AMD struggling with consistency. The high costs of innovation without equally rigorous financial oversight led to significant losses over the years despite the occasional peaks in profitability.

This was evident in AMD's strategic decisions and missteps that did not always align with market realities in the 1980s and 1990s,when the company struggled with financial stability and market position amid rapid technological changes. While some of these decisions were rooted in a proactive vision for the company, they often lacked the necessary foresight regarding their long-term impact on AMD's financial health. This included significant investments in areas that did not yield expected returns and, at times, a cavalier approach to competition and market demands.

This pattern manifested in a cycle of technological successes followed by financial difficulties, exacerbated by intense competition and price wars with Intel. The cycle described by an industry analyst, where "AMD has one good year and three bad years" versus Intel's "three good years and one bad year," highlights the challenges AMD faced in maintaining market consistency and growth.

The microprocessor market has been highly competitive since its inception in the 1970s and 1980s, with AMD often finding itself in a reactive position to Intel's advancements. The tumultuous relationship between AMD and Intel, particularly under Sander's leadership, had its ups and downs. In the 1990s, AMD attempted to carve out its niche within the microprocessor market. However, the legal battles between the two companies culminated in a cross-licensing pact in 1995, allowing them to build each other's designs. This agreement was crucial for AMD to continue competing in the high-stakes processor market.

AMD's people-centric culture, initiated by Sanders, emphasized the importance of putting employees first, with the belief that prioritizing the workforce would lead to better products and profitability. This philosophy has endured, influencing AMD's corporate practices and contributing to a workplace environment that values employee contributions and fosters growth. However, this approach also faced criticism, particularly when short-term financial pressures were intense, highlighting a tension between long-term cultural commitments and short-term financial realities.

Jerry Sanders' leadership at AMD encapsulates the complexities of steering a pioneering technology company through the vicissitudes of a highly volatile industry. His legacy underscores the profound impact leadership can have on a company's direction, highlighting the delicate balance between bold innovation and disciplined execution that might have positioned AMD more favorably amid industry upheavals. While Sanders' visionary approach set the foundational pillars for AMD's resilience and adaptability, his story highlights the importance of strategic agility and the need to maintain a strong operational focus to ensure sustained competitive advantage in the high-stakes semiconductor industry. His story offers crucial lessons on the importance of aligning visionary leadership with robust management practices to ensure sustainable success.

As AMD transitioned leadership from Sanders to successors like Hector Ruiz and, later, Lisa Su, the company faced the need to balance its foundational strategies with new market realities. This transition highlighted the challenges of maintaining a visionary yet sustainable strategic direction. The transition in leadership to Lisa Su marked a strategic shift towards a greater focus on consistent execution and strategic diversification rather than high-risk maneuvers. Su's leadership is credited with fostering a more stable and focused approach, balancing innovation with strategic execution, and strengthening AMD's position in high-performance computing. The emphasis on a balanced approach to innovation and execution under her leadership suggests that AMD may continue to strengthen its market position in the top 3 in the semiconductor industry.

Sanders was known for his visionary approach, particularly in his early days at AMD when he foresaw the potential of the semiconductor industry. However, as AMD grew, its ability to anticipate market needs seemed to falter, particularly in adjusting AMD's strategies in the rapidly evolving tech landscape. His commitment to proprietary technologies might have been an initial attempt to differentiate AMD from competitors but failed to align with the broader industry's shift towards standardized technologies, which could have better-anticipated customer and market needs.

One of the critical aspects where Sanders' leadership might be critiqued is in the prevention of potential risks. AMD under Sanders faced significant financial difficulties, partly due to heavy investments in proprietary technologies that did not yield the expected market share. Additionally, the operational inefficiencies that plagued AMD were a danger that was not adequately addressed, leading to financial vulnerability. This approach suggests a gap in fostering a culture of continuous learning and adaptation.

Sanders' deep dedication to AMD and its people was evident. He was known for his loyalty to employees and his desire to make AMD a significant player in the semiconductor industry. However, his approach sometimes reflected a greater focus on personal or immediate business goals rather than a long-term, sustainable responsibility toward the organization's health.

Jerry Sanders and Lisa Su

Jerry Sanders and Lisa Su's leadership styles at AMD showcase a vivid contrast in strategic focus, execution, and company culture, illustrating different eras and challenges within the semiconductor industry. Two different people, two different styles.

Jerry Sanders, AMD's founder, was known for his charismatic and flamboyant leadership style. He played a crucial role in AMD's early days, emphasizing aggressive marketing and innovation. Sanders was known for his belief in the power of salesmanship and public relations, using these tools to elevate AMD's profile against stiff competition from Intel. His approach involved direct competition through improved product offerings and emphasized AMD's reliability and performance, which helped AMD carve out a niche in high-value markets.

In contrast, Lisa Su's tenure, beginning in 2014, marked a strategic shift towards stability, consistent execution, and strategic diversification. Su focused on high-performance computing, targeting growth areas like gaming, data centers, and AI technologies. Under her leadership, AMD has seen a resurgence by prioritizing product quality and technological leadership, emphasizing the development of products like the Ryzen and EPYC processors, which have been pivotal in regaining market share and competing more effectively against Intel.

In comparison to Sanders 'leadership, Lisa Su,has been lauded for her methodical and measured approach to leadership. Recognizing the shifts in the semiconductor market, Su strategically steered AMD away from less profitable ventures like mobile chips, which were outside AMD's core competencies, and instead doubled down on areas where AMD could truly excel and compete. Her leadership is credited with navigating AMD through a landscape dominated by Intel and new market entrants like ARM-based chip manufacturers.

Her approach has been more conservative and focused on financial health. Her strategic decisions, particularly around cost management and investment in R&D, have led to steady and sustained financial improvement, helping AMD build a solid financial base and invest in future growth areas.

Lisa Su's leadership has been marked by a focus on cultivating a disciplined, inclusive, and innovation-driven culture. Her emphasis on a people-centric approach similar to Sanders, while also focusing on execution and strategic investments, has helped stabilize AMD and foster a culture that drives consistent technological advancement and market responsiveness.

In summary, while Jerry Sanders helped establish AMD as a significant player through his charismatic and visionary style, his approach sometimes led to strategic missteps and financial volatility. Lisa Su's tenure, by contrast, has been characterized by strategic prudence, focused execution, and a steady hand, which has repositioned AMD as a competitive force in the semiconductor industry with a more stable financial outlook and a clear strategic direction. This comparison underscores the evolution of AMD's leadership philosophy from a founder to a CEO, which was in response to changing industry dynamics and internal corporate needs.

CHAPTER 10

Nurturing Behavior

"Ninety-five percent of my assets drive out the gate every evening. It's my job to maintain a work environment that keeps those people coming back every morning."

—James Goodnight

THE ROYAL MILITARY ACADEMY'S guiding principle, "Serve to Lead," epitomizes the essence of effective leadership and serves as an exemplary foundation for discussing nurturing behavior within the realm of leadership and organizational dynamics. This venerable motto underscores the belief that true leadership is derived from a selfless commitment to serving others, fostering an environment where growth, development, and well-being are at the forefront.

At the heart of this philosophy lies the conviction that the mark of a genuine leader is not wielded through authority or dominance but through their ability to uplift, guide, and enhance the lives of those they lead. It is this service-first approach that molds character and cultivates an enduring sense of loyalty and camaraderie amongst teams and organizations. Such an ethos aligns seamlessly with the principles of nurturing behavior, which posits that loyalty, both within and towards an organization, stems from a leader's unwavering dedication to the support and empowerment of their team members.

Nurturing behavior, as a behavioral determinant of loyalty, embodies a comprehensive approach that plays a significant role in fostering loyalty within an organization, team, or relationship. This approach is underpinned by its focus on providing support, encouragement, and facilitation of growth and development of others.

Central to nurturing behavior is the provision of support and encouragement, extending beyond mere verbal affirmations to the creation of an environment where individuals feel genuinely valued and understood. This approach is akin to Robert Greenleaf's servant leadership philosophy, where leaders prioritize the needs, growth, and well-being of their team members. By offering both emotional and practical support, nurturing behavior participates in establishing a foundation of trust and understanding. Such an environment is essential for loyalty to thrive, as it assures individuals that their contributions and welfare are recognized and appreciated.

Robert K. Greenleaf's concept of Servant Leadership was introduced through his first essay, "The Servant as Leader," published in 1970. This foundational work challenged traditional leadership models that emphasized command and control, proposing instead that the most effective leaders are those who prioritize the needs of others. Greenleaf's servant leadership is characterized by a deep sense of humility, altruism, and a commitment to the growth of people. According to him, a servant leader focuses on listening actively to and empathizing with their team members, understanding their needs, and helping them achieve their full potential, both personally and professionally. This approach requires leaders to shift their mindset from being the most important person in the room to being a facilitator of their team's success, which is similar to Collins' leadership model.

Such leaders have a great impact on their organizations, leading to more cohesive teams, increased trust, and stronger community spirit. They, in turn, enhance individual well-being and organizational performance.

Cognitive empathy and understanding constitute another key aspect of nurturing behavior. Exhibiting cognitive empathy involves a genuine effort to understand the perspectives, challenges, and aspirations of others. The environment that team leaders create should both internalize the company's cause and principles but also foster interpersonal relationships which enable the recognition of the professional and human side of the team members. This empathetic approach builds lasting, meaningful connections. It entails recognizing the individuality of each member of the team or the organization and responding to their unique needs and concerns in a thoughtful, practical manner. This resonates with the empathetic and attentive leadership style advocated by Greenleaf.

The concepts of emotional and social intelligence have rich historical roots. **Emotional Intelligence (EI)** prominently emerged through the work of psychologists Peter Salovey and John Mayer in 1990, who first formally defined it as the ability to recognize, understand, and manage one's own emotions and those of others. Daniel Goleman later popularized EI in the mid-1990s, extending its scope and impact by highlighting its relevance both to personal effectiveness and to organizational success. Goleman emphasized aspects such as self-awareness, self-regulation, motivation, empathy, and interpersonal skills as critical components for leaders and organizations aiming to foster meaningful, supportive environments. Goleman later further clarified these concepts, explicitly distinguishing between emotional and social intelligence in his subsequent book, *Social Intelligence: The New Science of Human Relationships*.

The concept of **Social Intelligence (SI)** has deep historical roots, initially shaped by educational reformer John Dewey. In his work, *Moral Principles in Education* (1909), Dewey argued that social intelligence underpins moral behavior, stating: *"Ultimate moral motives and forces are nothing more or less than social intelligence—the power of observing and comprehending social situation,—and social power—trained capacities of control—at work in the service of social interest and aims."* Dewey highlighted SI as fundamental to both effective social interaction and principled decision-making.

Building on these insights, psychologist Edward Thorndike introduced and formally defined **Social Intelligence** in the early 1920s as the distinct capability to understand, navigate, and manage interpersonal relationships successfully: *"the ability to understand and manage men and women and boys and girls, to act wisely in human relations."* Thorndike positioned SI clearly as an independent dimension of intelligence, emphasizing the importance of perceiving social dynamics, responding effectively to interpersonal cues, and adeptly managing social interactions.

Both emotional and social intelligence significantly contribute to nurturing behavior, which is essential in effective leadership, mentoring, and coaching. Organizational psychologist Richard Boyatzis has extensively studied these dynamics, highlighting how leaders who possess strong emotional and social intelligence naturally foster supportive and growth-oriented environments. Boyatzis emphasizes that when leaders practice empathy, genuine care, and interpersonal awareness, they create conditions that significantly enhance learning, growth, and sustained personal development among team members.

Leaders equipped with emotional and social intelligence authentically understand individual and group needs, cultivating environments of trust and psychological safety. Through constructive feedback and cognitive empathy, leaders can thoughtfully respond to emotional and social cues, further improving the well-being of their people and their results.

By investing in the personal and professional development of individuals, nurturing behavior exemplifies a dedication to their success and also fosters a sense of reciprocal loyalty. This is particularly evident in organizations that prioritize the growth and well-being of their members over profits—though profitability is, of course, necessary for survival.

Being responsive to the needs and concerns of others is also a hallmark of nurturing behavior. This responsiveness manifests in actions taken to address the issues and challenges faced by individuals within the organization, which is akin to the empowerment approach discussed by Liz Wiseman in "Multipliers." Wiseman's concept of the Multiplier effect posits that these leaders create environments where ideas flourish, people feel valued, and the collective intelligence of the team is leveraged. Her perspective aligns with the notion that nurturing leadership is not just about directing but also about empowering and enabling team members to reach their full potential. Such attentiveness reinforces the notion that the organization cares about its members, which, in turn, is a powerful driver of loyalty. It creates a reciprocal relationship where loyalty is not just expected but is fostered through genuine care and concern.

Additionally, nurturing behavior contributes to creating a positive, supportive environment. This involves promoting a culture of open communication, collaboration, and inclusiveness, where individuals feel they are an integral part of the organization. This sense of belonging and inclusiveness creates a sense of being part of something larger than oneself.

In leadership roles, nurturing behavior involves leading by example. Leaders who demonstrate behaviors that exemplify dedication and integrity, set a standard for the rest of the team or organization. By modeling desirable behaviors, such leaders inspire loyalty, as team members are more inclined to emulate and respect leaders who embody the values they advocate.

Their leadership model is inherently people-centric, growth-oriented, and enabling. This integrated approach to leadership promotes individual development and well-being and drives organizational success and innovation. By focusing on serving others, understanding and managing emotions, and amplifying the abilities of team members, leaders can cultivate environments where individuals feel valued and are encouraged to contribute their best.

Nurturing behavior as a determinant of loyalty is more than just occasional gestures of support or encouragement. It is an all-encompassing approach that involves actively contributing to the well-being and development of individuals, fostering strong relationships based on mutual respect and cognitive empathy, and creating an environment conducive to the growth of loyalty. This multifaceted approach nurtures the individual members and enhances the overall cohesion and loyalty within the organization, establishing itas a vital component in the dynamics of organizational and relational loyalty.

A few years ago, I met a German team leader working for a German engineering company operating in Europe. For the past two years, his main focus has been on French business clients, and his trips to Paris have become more frequent. He told me he realized that speaking in English wasn't the best way to build rapport with his clients, as informal conversations in English often felt awkward and brief. Conversations were usually cut short and their relationship remained strictly formal. He expressed his observations to his team leader and the company hired a French language tutor and he and his colleagues who had travelled to Paris started French classes twice a week for an hour and a half during their work hours. Him and I met in a French language school in France for which the company paid all expenses for him spending two weeks there. Both the company and he were invested in the process, because as he said if he improves, the company will improve its position in the French-speaking market.

One might say that nurturing behavior is too complex or too encompassing. Though it is its essence that contributes to its applicability because it is founded upon the principle that what we do to others, we do to ourselves. Most importantly, we should do to others what they want us to do to them which is strongly connected to the psychological contract agreed upon by both parties. An organization should strive to create a positive environment—free of negative associations—where people are encouraged and supported in their growth by leaders who value and respect them while having the integrity to do what they say in a nurturing, not a toxic, way.

The Antithesis of Nurturing Behavior

Toxic behavior within an organization encompasses a range of actions and attitudes that degrade both individual morale and collective performance. Understanding these toxic behaviors is critical for identifying and addressing the underlying issues that contribute to an unhealthy workplace which in the long-term would damage the organization's performance.

Authoritarian leadership extends beyond strict control, often manifesting in an environment where feedback is disregarded or punished, and creativity is stifled. Leaders who adopt this style typically see their authority as absolute, leaving little room for collaboration or innovation. This results in a culture where employees feel undervalued and reluctant to contribute ideas, fearing retribution or dismissal. According to the Situational Leadership Model, authoritarian leadership may be effective with novice employees lacking the necessary skills or in industries requiring manual labor.

Similarly, micromanagement signals a lack of trust in employees' abilities and judgment. This excessive oversight burdens leaders with unnecessary details and also demoralizes employees, who may feel they are not trusted or respected. The constant scrutiny can inhibit initiative, discourage innovation, and lead to a culture of dependency where employees are hesitant to make decisions or act without explicit direction.

Furthermore, demeaning communication is not merely rude or unprofessional; it systematically breaks down an individual's sense of worth and belonging within the team. Regular exposure to such negativity can lead to decreased self-esteem and mental well-being among employees, fostering an environment where disrespect becomes the norm rather than the exception. This degrading atmosphere erodes the foundational trust necessary for effective teamwork and collaboration.

Intimidation and fear-mongering are used to maintain control through psychological oppression, leading to an environment where employees are constantly on edge, fearing the consequences of even minor mistakes. This atmosphere stifles open communication and honest feedback, critical components of a thriving workplace. The prevalence of fear undermines employee confidence and can lead to a range of negative outcomes, from ethical breaches to mental health issues, which all ultimately lead to subpar organizational performance.

A lack of cognitive empathy in the workplace transcends indifference. It involves a blatant disregard for the personal and professional challenges faced by employees. In such environments, team members may struggle in silence, feeling unseen and unheard, which can exacerbate stress and reduce overall job satisfaction. The absence of cognitive empathy leads to a breakdown in team solidarity, as individuals feel increasingly disconnected from the organizational support system.

Additionally, toxic workplaces often stifle employee growth. This involves limiting professional opportunities and creating a culture where employees are discouraged from seeking new challenges or expanding their skill sets. This stagnation breeds frustration and hopelessness, as employees see no clear path for advancement or personal development, leading to increased turnover and a loss of valuable talent.

Manipulation and deception destroy an organization's ethical backbone. These toxic behaviors create an environment where truth is malleable, and honesty is undervalued, leading to widespread cynicism and a lack of faith in leadership. As these practices become ingrained, the organization risks legal and reputational damage, further undermining its stability and success.

Guidelines

Creating an organizational culture that genuinely values nurturing behavior is fundamental to developing a successful and resilient organization. This culture should permeate every aspect of the organization, from the highest levels of leadership to the newest team members. By ingraining nurturing and empowering behaviors into the core values of the company, these principles become more than just guidelines—they become a way of life within the organization.

For nurturing behavior to be truly effective, it must be consistently modeled by all levels of leadership and embraced by all employees. This requires a commitment to nurturing as a core cultural value, actively promoted and lived by everyone within the organization. Leaders should set the tone by demonstrating nurturing behaviors, recognizing and rewarding those who contribute to a supportive and empowering workplace, and making these values a central part of all training and development programs.

Balance Nurturing with Empowerment

While nurturing leadership is fundamental to fostering a positive organizational environment, it is crucial to recognize the risk of dependency that may arise when employees become too reliant on their leaders for direction and validation. This dependency can inadvertently hinder the development of employees' own decision-making skills and reduce their autonomy. To mitigate this, leaders should strive to balance their nurturing behaviors with empowerment strategies. Encourage employees to take initiative and make decisions within a supportive framework. This can be achieved by setting clear objectives, providing the necessary resources, and then stepping back to allow employees to navigate their own path to these goals. Regularly assess and adjust the level of support and guidance you provide to ensure that it promotes independence rather than dependence. Create opportunities for employees to lead projects, solve problems, and make decisions, and ensure that they feel supported to succeed in these endeavors.

Address Misunderstandings and Prevent Favoritism

Nurturing behavior must be applied consistently and fairly to prevent any misunderstandings or perceptions of favoritism, which can erode trust and loyalty within the team. It is imperative that all team members feel equally valued and supported by their leaders. Implement clear guidelines and provide training for leaders on how to apply nurturing behaviors effectively and equitably. This training should include practical tips on providing unbiased support, recognizing and celebrating diverse contributions, and ensuring that all team members have equal access to growth and development opportunities. Leaders should be trained to be mindful of their interactions and to check their biases, ensuring that their support is not disproportionately directed towards certain individuals or groups.

Ultimately, the goal is to cultivate an organizational culture where nurturing behaviors empower individuals to grow, contribute, and succeed, fostering a collective sense of loyalty and shared success.

The SAS Institute and Jim Goodnight

"While we say we have a 35-hour workweek ... I don't know anybody who really works 35 hours. The reality is if you trust people, and you ask them to do something–and you treat them like a human being as opposed to a commodity where you try to squeeze something out–they're going to work all sorts of hours. But they're going to enjoy those hours as opposed to 'slaving in the office.'"

Jim Goodnight, CEO and co-founder of SAS Institute, has been instrumental in cultivating one of the most innovative and employee-focused organizational cultures in the technology sector. His leadership philosophy is centred on the principle that employees are a company's most valuable assets and that their welfare directly impacts the organization's success and sustainability.

Goodnight has maintained a visionary approach towards business analytics long before the terms "artificial intelligence" and "machine learning" became industry buzzwords. For over 50 years, Goodnight's focus has been on developing software that utilizes statistical methods to enable better decision-making—essentially what today is often termed as AI. SAS Institute, founded in 1976, has grown under Goodnight's leadership to become a global leader in business analytics software and services. The company is renowned for its products and also its unique approach to employee welfare and organizational culture.

Jim Goodnight has been instrumental in defining what SAS cause is about - leveraging data to drive better decision-making. His leadership style is deeply nurturing, focusing on creating an engaging and supportive work environment. He famously stated, "95% of my assets drive out the gate every evening. It's my job to maintain a work environment that keeps those people coming back every morning." This philosophy can be observed in all aspects of the business, from strategic planning to daily operations.

SAS invests a quarter of its annual expenses in research and development, a strategy reflecting Goodnight's commitment to innovation. This approach is about keeping up with technological advances and foreseeing customer needs. When the need for faster data processing was recognized, SAS began adapting its software to perform high-performance analytics by running in parallel on many processors—significantly speeding up customer data operations.

Goodnight is renowned for his philosophy that "if you treat employees like they make a difference, they will." This belief has led to unique workplace practices at SAS, including extensive employee benefits like on-site childcare, healthcare services, and even amenities like dry cleaning, which contribute to a high level of job satisfaction, less time spent on driving to town, and low employee turnover.

SAS's success is also a product of Goodnight's prudent financial management. He humorously notes that "revenue growth should always be higher than expense growth," a basic yet often overlooked principle. This old-fashioned approach to business growth—coupled with a resistance to unnecessary rapid expansion—has allowed SAS to prepare for economic downturns more effectively than many of its peers. While the company's private status has enabled long-term planning free from the pressures of outside investors.

The company has seen consistent growth year after year, a rarity in the volatile tech industry. This is attributed to a methodical approach to innovation and expansion, eschewing the typical Silicon Valley mantra of rapid scaling in favor of steady, manageable growth. The focus remains on the core of SAS's business—data analytics—while ensuring the company adapts to new technological paradigms, such as cloud computing and real-time data processing.

The company has a nominal 35-hour workweek, which allows for flexibility, recognizing that creativity and productivity are not strictly tied to longer hours. The company culture discourages excessive overtime such as 70 hour weeks, based on the understanding that prolonged work hours often lead to diminishing returns and increased errors.

During the height of the recent economic downturn, Jim Goodnight, the CEO of SAS, took a bold step that set the company apart from its competitors. While other companies were resorting to layoffs to cut costs, Goodnight made a commitment to his employees that would secure their jobs and consequently boost company morale and productivity.

In January 2009, amidst growing concerns about potential job cuts due to the economic crisis, Goodnight addressed his employees through a companywide webcast. He made a reassuring promise: there would be no layoffs at SAS for the entire year. However, he emphasized the need for everyone to contribute to reducing expenses and to halt hiring processes wherever possible.

Fostering a sense of security among employees, Goodnight saw an increase in productivity across the company. Notably, 2009 proved to be one of SAS's top three most profitable years. This outcome highlighted how a nurturing work environment, coupled with job security, could lead to higher employee output and company profitability.

Goodnight was openly critical of the common practice among firms to handle economic pressures by reducing their workforce. He argued that companies that quickly resort to layoffs are admitting to poor management skills. Interestingly, while such companies often see a temporary rise in stock prices post-layoffs, Goodnight pointed out the paradox in rewarding companies for what he viewed as short-sighted management decisions.

The no-layoff policy was not a one-off decision but part of a broader strategy to maintain an employee-centered work environment. Goodnight's approach was shaped by his early career experiences working on the Apollo space project, where he observed the detrimental effects of treating skilled workers as if they were on an assembly line. This led him to ensure that SAS employees enjoyed benefits such as individual offices, well-stocked break rooms, on-site health facilities, and recreational amenities.

This nurturing approach has reaped significant financial benefits for SAS. With an employee turnover rate significantly lower than the industry average—only 3% to 4% compared to 17%-25%—SAS saves approximately $100 million annually on recruitment and training costs. These savings underscore the financial efficacy of investing in employee satisfaction and stability. This strategy was rooted in Goodnight's belief that maintaining a stable workforce was essential for nurturing creativity and productivity, particularly during tough economic times.

Goodnight's no-layoff pledge aligns with his broader philosophy that companies thrive by keeping their workers content. He believes that the respect and security provided to employees translate into higher loyalty and productivity, which in turn drive profitability and innovation. This approach challenges the short-term, cost-cutting tactics prevalent in many corporations, suggesting a sustainable model that values human capital as the key asset.

A few years back, SAS announced a new video game division, and managers let developers migrate there. When the department ended up failing, the developers were welcomed back where they came from. Even though the initiative didn't succeed, it taught management some valuable lessons and reminded employees that their company supported them, earning their loyalty.

Interestingly, SAS does not use stock options as incentives. Instead, the company believes in rewarding employees with more challenging and engaging projects. This method of acknowledgment aligns with the company's emphasis on intellectual satisfaction as a primary motivator for its employees. Further, the method has been talked about in the context of knowledge workers by researchers such as Mihaly Csikszentmihalyi, Teresa Amabile and Robert Sternberg, and Peter Drucker.

Under Goodnight's leadership, SAS has consistently been listed among the best places to work. The company boasts one of the industry's lowest turnover rates, a testament to employee satisfaction and loyalty. Furthermore, the nurturing environment has led to high levels of innovation, as employees feel secure and supported to explore new ideas.

CHAPTER 11

Shared Values

"Every enterprise requires commitment to common goals and shared values. Without such commitment there is no enterprise; there is only a mob."

—Peter F. Drucker

SHARED VALUES STRENGTHEN ORGANIZATIONS WHEN they are not simply adopted officially but are embraced by individuals at a personal level. As previously discussed through the different examples and behavioural determinants, shared values are recognized as a cornerstone in the building of an organization. From the process of socialization, identification, and internalization through reciprocity and Asabiyyah which cannot function unless the members of the organization are confident in the invisible bond that moves them toward their cause.

Values and integrity are part of the psychological contract, discussed with reciprocity, because how can the contract be fulfilled unless the parties have decided in their hearts that they will act on their words? Hence, shared values are more than pretty, simple words written on a wall or a banner. Their daily embodiment is what defines an organization, whether the outside world agrees or not with them. The members of the organization and especially its leadership should begin defining them and acting according to them. The only way they can be successfully spread not as a pamphlet that is remembered but as words that define actions in any moment, is for them to be beneficial to the organization's actions and goals. Thus, the members have to understand that acting in a certain way, for example in an honest one, can bring more benefits compared to the old practices.

The introduction of new values or the modification of existing ones often encounters resistance. This resistance can stem from a variety of sources, including fear of the unknown, perceived threats to job security or working conditions, or preservation of the status quo because it works or it is comfortable. Overcoming this resistance requires transparent communication and the involvement of employees in the change process to align everyone with the new values. Leadership must be proactive in demonstrating integrity to these values through actions, not just words, to overcome skepticism and build trust.

The effectiveness of shared values hinges on their consistent application across all levels of the organization. This requires continuous reinforcement through communication and example. *Lead by example* can sound too ideal or something that came from a fortune cookie. But if one leads by example in every single moment based on the values that one has declared and does not betray them, then the members of the organization will believe and act. A consistent value system supports a strong organizational culture and identity.

While leadership is crucial in defining and endorsing shared values, an over-reliance on a top-down approach can stifle the necessary commitment from lower-level employees. This method often overlooks the practical insights and day-to-day experiences of non-executive employees, potentially leading to a disconnect between stated and lived values. Encouraging a bottom-up flow of ideas and feedback can mitigate this by ensuring that the values resonate at all levels and are practical and applicable across the organization.

A robust organizational culture, cultivated through shared values, directly impacts the organization's external reputation. As employees embody these values, they act as brand ambassadors to the outside world, enhancing the organization's public image. A positive reputation attracts both potential employees, customers and investors who share or support these values, thereby driving the organization's success in a globally competitive market.

At the end, it is about choosing the values, embodying them through daily actions, and making sure that the values are practical for the members and this is recognized throughout the organization not just by a group of people.

Ford Motor Company

The turnaround of Ford Motor Company under the leadership of Alan Mulally is a compelling case study in the impact of principled leadership on corporate revival and success. When Mulally become CEO in 2006, Ford was facing a dire financial crisis. His approach to transforming the company was grounded in upstanding leadership practices, emphasizing transparency, accountability, and collaboration, which were instrumental in Ford's recovery.

One of Mulally's first actions was to cultivate a culture of openness and transparency within Ford. He implemented the Business Plan Review (BPR) meetings, where managers were encouraged to openly discuss challenges without fear of retribution. This was a significant shift from Ford's previous culture, which often penalized honesty about setbacks. By fostering an environment where problems could be openly discussed, Mulally enabled quicker identification and resolution of issues, thereby improving operational efficiency.

Mulally emphasized accountability at all levels of the organization. He streamlined Ford's operations, focusing on its core brand

and divesting from other brands like Jaguar, Land Rover, and Aston Martin. This strategic refocusing required making tough decisions that were not always popular but necessary for the company's long-term health. Mulally's commitment to making decisions that were in the best interest of the company, even when difficult, demonstrated a high level of ethical responsibility and accountability.

Mulally's leadership style was highly collaborative. He broke down silos within the company and encouraged a more integrated approach to problem-solving. He fostered a team-oriented culture, where the success of one division was seen as beneficial for the entire company. This approach improved internal collaboration and led to more innovative solutions to the company's challenges.

During the 2008 financial crisis, Mulally's principled leadership was particularly evident. While other major automakers sought government bailouts, Mulally decided to mortgage all of Ford's assets for $23.6 billion to fund a business transformation. This bold move, driven by a commitment to self-reliance and principled financial management, enabled Ford to avoid bankruptcy and government bailouts.

Mulally's leadership restored pride and morale among Ford's employees and stakeholders. By successfully navigating the company through a financial crisis, he preserved Ford's legacy and enhanced its reputation for integrity and principled business practices. Employees took pride in being part of an organization that could weather such a significant crisis through responsible leadership. The company's renewed focus on quality, innovation, and customer satisfaction bolstered this sense of pride, aligning with Mulally's vision of building cars that people wanted and valued. The transformation under his leadership led to a resurgence in employee morale, as they witnessed first-hand the positive outcomes of a culture rooted in transparency, accountability, and principled decision-making.

Mulally's leadership also had a ripple effect on Ford's external stakeholders. Investors and customers saw a company committed to ethical practices, financial stability, and long-term growth, which helped to rebuild trust and loyalty towards the Ford brand. Under his tenure, Ford saw improvements in vehicle quality and customer satisfaction ratings, further enhancing the brand's reputation.

The turnaround of Ford under Alan Mulally's leadership remains a benchmark in how upstanding leadership can positively influence a company's fortunes. His focus on management practices demonstrated that responsible leadership could be a catalyst for not just surviving a crisis but emerging stronger from it. The legacy of his leadership at Ford is a testament to the power of principled leadership in creating sustainable business success and a loyal, engaged workforce. It underscores the notion that upstanding leadership and business success are not mutually exclusive but can indeed be synergistically achieved.

KONE Corporation

KONE Corporation, established in 1910 in Finland, has emerged as a global frontrunner in the elevator and escalator industry. Renowned for its dedication to quality, safety, and customer service, KONE provides a comprehensive range of products including elevators, escalators, and automatic building doors, alongside solutions for maintenance and modernization. Operating across over 60 countries and catering to more than 400,000 customers worldwide, the company prides itself on its robust research and development initiatives. Their mission is to improve the flow of urban life.

In 2020, KONE embarked on a transformative journey to reassess and reshape its organizational values, aligning them more closely with the collective aspirations and experiences of its diverse global workforce. This extensive initiative involved the analysis of over 35,000 of their employees, reflecting a wide array of employee insights. This participative approach was instrumental in ensuring that the revamped values were not merely theoretical concepts but tangible reflections of the daily realities and beliefs of KONE employees.

By integrating real-life employee experiences and insights into its core values, KONE transitioned towards a more inclusive organizational culture. Employees were encouraged to move beyond the role of passive policy recipients, becoming active contributors to the company's strategic direction and cultural ethos. This shift bolstered organizational identification and also cultivated an environment where employees felt genuinely valued and heard.

Implementing large-scale initiatives in a global company with tens of thousands employees comes with its set of challenges, particularly in maintaining focus and consistency across diverse teams. Furthermore, instilling new values in a workforce spread across various regions, each with its distinct cultural nuances, can be daunting. The complexity of ensuring genuine buy-in from all employees, especially in an established organization with deep-rooted cultural practices, should not be underestimated. Moreover, the effectiveness of digital platforms in fostering true engagement, as opposed to mere compliance, remains a subject for ongoing scrutiny.

Despite these challenges, KONE's efforts have borne fruit, with the company making significant strides towards the desired positive direction. Proactively promoting core principles and values such as safety and mutual care, KONE has implemented numerous initiatives, including a global safety management system based on ISO 45001 standards. Programs like the 'KONE Way for Safety', global safety weeks, and the 'Safety in Mind' interactive learning application have collectively contributed to a remarkable 91% reduction in work-related incidents. Additionally, the 'Elevate

Your Health' program underlines KONE's commitment to holistic employee well-being, encapsulating both physical and mental health initiatives.

The experience of KONE highlights the complexity and necessity of embedding shared values within an organization, which, while challenging, particularly in a diverse and global team, yields significant benefits in terms of employee satisfaction, performance, and overall organizational cohesion. This case serves as a testament to the fact that in the heart of every successful organization lie shared values that resonate with its members, propelling them towards common goals while adhering to the envisioned standards and fostering an environment ripe for innovation and sustained excellence.

CHAPTER 12

Benevolence

"Leadership must be based on goodwill. Goodwill does not mean posturing and, least of all, pandering to the mob. It means an obvious and wholehearted commitment to helping followers."

—Vice Admiral James Stockdale

BENEVOLENT BEHAVIOR IS ONE OF the recognized consequences of loyalty strongly connected to the shared values in the organization on a daily basis and psychological safety. Benevolence could sound like a complex term but its essence is the simple goodwill towards the fellow members of the organization. Benevolence is connected with a long-term perspective, as discussed, because goodwill towards others and the subsequent support of their-well-being creates a more productive work environment.

In the Confucian Analects, benevolence is viewed as faithful behavior in interacting with other people. In this context, benevolence encompasses actions and attitudes aimed at the well-being and support of others. It's an expression of goodwill and kindness that is beyond professional obligation. Such behavior nurtures a positive and supportive environment, essential for loyalty to thrive. While nurturing behavior as a determinant of loyalty is about nurturing growth and development, benevolence is a consequence of loyalty which defines a supportive culture.

It's not merely about being kind; it's about integrating cognitive empathy and support into the fabric of organizational practices in a way that advances the collective objectives. This involves understanding the unique dynamics and requirements of different sectors and tailoring benevolent practices that reinforce professional effectiveness without compromising the competitive edge of the business. Such practices include active listening and using social intelligence to discern whether a colleague needs to share, seeks advice, or is indirectly signaling a need for time off. Being generous with one's own time, especially as leader or an experienced colleague, is another practice which both supports other members and increases their confidence in the organization's long-term perspective towards them. It's not about spending long periods listening or helping—it's about managing your time effectively to remain approachable and available when needed.

Moreover, benevolence in leadership or group dynamics encourages resilience and a shared sense of purpose, aligning with the core principles of Josiah Royce's philosophy of loyalty and Ibn Khaldun's concept of Asabiyyah. In this context, benevolence extends beyond altruism—it reflects a strategic alignment between leadership and organizational culture, which, when effectively implemented, can significantly enhance loyalty among stakeholders. This reinforces the idea that loyalty is not a one-way street; it's nurtured through mutual respect, understanding, and acts of kindness and support.

In a business setting, this can be translated into building strong team dynamics where benevolence is a shared value. Encouraging teamwork, collaboration, and mutual support among employees strengthens group cohesion, which in turn reinforces loyalty to the organization. The application of benevolent practices should be strategically aligned with business objectives to avoid challenges such as complacency or misalignment with market demands. Leaders should foster a positive work environment regardless of organizational pace, as this has been shown to boost both creativity and productivity—while also enhancing leadership effectiveness. A culture characterized by benevolent actions where employees feel safe and supported, pays off during times of organizational stress or change.

Helping others is a practice for sustainable growth and the realisation of organizational goals because people feel valued and cared for. The implementation of benevolence varies across industries and cultures; what works in a non-profit organization may not be directly applicable in a financial firm. In the past few years, a company might offer flexible work policies to support employee well-being, but doing so, it must also ensure that these policies do not hinder productivity or operational efficiency. This balance is essential to maintain market competitiveness.

Risk of Misinterpretation and Exploitation

The risk that benevolent actions might be misinterpreted or exploited is a real concern in any organizational setting. Transparency in intentions and clarity in communication are essential to mitigate these risks. Leaders and peers alike must ensure that their benevolent actions are consistent with the organization's stated values and goals. Establishing clear guidelines and boundaries around benevolent practices can help prevent misunderstandings and ensure that such measures are seen as integral to the organization's ethos, rather than as arbitrary or manipulative.

To mitigate this, companies should communicate their intentions clearly, first spoken and then in writing, and ensure their actions align with their stated values. The organizations set the culture and the tone, but if unattended, external culture and personal habits will take over. Regularly set feedback mechanisms and open dialogues can help in continuously refining these practices.

Thus, while Royce's and Ibn Khaldun's philosophies provide a solid theoretical foundation, the application of benevolence in business requires a nuanced understanding of organizational dynamics and market realities.

George Washington serves as a prominent example of a military leader who demonstrated benevolence towards his men. As the commander-in-chief of the Continental Army during the American Revolutionary War, Washington's leadership was not just about strategic brilliance but also about his ability to inspire and connect with his troops. He was known for his capacity to adapt and improvise, which was crucial in rallying his soldiers during challenging times. For instance, Washington's daring maneuvers during the crossing of the Delaware River and the subsequent attack on the Hessian garrison at Trenton were strategic masterstrokes that showcased his inner resolve and commitment to his men's welfare. His leadership style was characterized by principled decision-making and a deep concern for the well-being of his soldiers, which in turn inspired their loyalty and dedication.

George Washington

George Washington's crossing of the Delaware River on the night of December 25-26, 1776, stands as a remarkable event that underscores his resolve and commitment to his men's welfare. This daring maneuver was a testament to Washington's leadership in extremely challenging conditions.

Washington's army, encamped near McConkey's Ferry, was a diminished force, with many soldiers unfit for duty and needing hospital care. Despite the setbacks, including lost battles, the loss of New York, and low morale, Washington persisted. He was able to procure supplies and recruit new members for the militia, partly due to the behavior of British and Hessian soldiers in New

Jersey and Pennsylvania, which turned public sentiment in favor of the Patriots.

The morale of the Patriot forces was significantly boosted by the publication of Thomas Paine's "The American Crisis" on December 19, which Washington ordered to be read to all of his troops. It encouraged the soldiers and improved their tolerance of difficult conditions. This was followed by the arrival of reinforcements and provisions, including much-needed blankets, on December 24, further bolstering the army's spirits.

The plan for the attack involved three crossings. Washington led the main attack on Trenton, with other columns creating diversions or guarding escape routes. Preparations for the attack began on December 23, and on Christmas Day, the plans were finalized. A wide variety of watercraft were assembled for the crossing, managed by experienced watermen, including the men of Captain Daniel Bray and others, who supervised the transport of infantry, cavalry, and artillery.

The crossing itself was a monumental task, hindered by a severe winter storm of wind, rain, snow, hail, and sleet. Despite the delays caused by the weather and the necessity to use larger ferries for artillery, Washington decided against retreating and continued with the operation, which was more than three hours behind schedule.

Once on the Jersey shore, the exhausted and freezing Continental Army reassembled and marched to Trenton, securing the first major military victory of the war. Without Washington's determination, resilience, and leadership, this critical victory, which had a substantial impact on the course of the American Revolutionary War, would not have been possible.

CHAPTER 13

Pride and Advocacy

*"To win in the marketplace you must first win
in the workplace."*

—Doug Conant

IN THE REALM OF ORGANIZATIONAL behavior, the concepts of pride and advocacy emerge as behavioral consequences of loyalty. When employees exhibit pride in their organization and engage in advocacy, this behavior reflects an identification and possibly internalization with the organization, contrasting starkly with toxic behaviors. Advocacy for an organization alone could be a defence of one's own choice to join and work there. It can be an act of self-defence or rationalization. Some people might not have anything else to defend, thus they have chosen to defend their organization, hence their choice. Subtle or explicit pride in the organization can be a powerful tool for countering toxic language and its dangerous consequences for the people in the organization. Through it, the organization's cause can be advocated. Pride is a behavioral consequence which, if not associated with the organization's cause, can be easily influenced by team dynamics, direct management, and/or external recognition.

Social Identity Theory, developed by Henri Tajfel and John Turner, offers a perspective on this phenomenon. The self-concept of employees, deeply influenced by their membership in the organization, fosters a unique group identification. They categorize themselves as part of the 'us' – the organization – as opposed to 'them' – other organizations. This isn't just belonging; it's integral to their self-concept. By defending the organization, employees reinforce their own sense of self and belonging. The organization's status and prestige contribute to employees' self-esteem, enhancing this pride.

The process of socialization plays a crucial role in shaping this identification and internalization. Socialization, as discussed, is the structured and unstructured way in which new employees learn the norms, values, and required behaviors of their organization. This process starts from the moment an employee decides to join the organization and continues as they assimilate the corporate culture. Effective socialization ensures that employees understand and internalize the organization's values and mission, making these an integral part of their own identity.

As employees progress through the stages of socialization, they begin to identify more strongly with the organization. This identification signifies a deeper alignment where the organization's successes and challenges become personal as it builds on the identification prior to the job interview process. Employees start to see the organization's goals as their own, leading to a natural inclination to advocate for it. This strong identification promotes pride and a protective stance towards the organization.

Internalization, the deepest level of this process, occurs when employees fully embrace the organization's values and mission as their own. At this stage, the organization's cause is passionately championed. Employees internalize the purpose of their work, seeing it as contributing to something greater than themselves. This is reflected in their advocacy and pride, driving them to promote and defend the organization with genuine conviction.

Pride in an organization is not just about defending its image; it's about defending one's identity. When the organization's actions and culture align with employees' personal values and ethics, defending and advocating for it becomes a personal mission. This alignment leads to an authentic advocacy and a sense of fulfilment, as employees feel they are contributing to a cause they believe in and the organizational achievements become their own.

Leadership plays a critical role in shaping these behaviors. Leaders who demonstrate pride in the organization inspire similar feelings in employees. They help employees see their role in achieving organizational goals, making their pride and advocacy powerful tools against internal toxicity on all levels. External recognition also plays a part. When organizations are recognized for their achievements and innovation, employee pride swells, motivating them to advocate and defend it publicly. This satisfaction stems from being part of a well-regarded organization, as posited by social comparison and organizational prestige theories.

Professional identity evolves through work experiences and career transitions. This evolution links professional growth with organizational pride, further explored in career development and employee engagement literature. Their perception of long-term career development opportunities influences employees' pride and willingness to advocate for their organization.

Growth, learning, and advancement enhance these feelings. However, such professional development can be horizontal or vertical. There are people who do not want to climb the corporate ladder or assume positions of further responsibility. Such employees could want to grow their competencies and develop their expertise horizontally and still exhibit loyal behaviour as found through our research and practice. This is completely fine and a personal career choice.

In analyzing pride and advocacy, the distinction between extroversion and introversion is evident. Extroverts might display their advocacy more visibly, engaging in networking and social activities that promote the organization. They might lead in boosting team morale. Introverts, conversely, might advocate quietly but impactfully, through dedicated work and deep, thoughtful contributions. It should be noted that rarely people are 100 percent introverted or extroverted, though they lean towards one or the other. Both extroverts and introverts find common ground in taking pride in personal and team achievements and adapting to organizational values.

The distinction between analytical and intuitive thinkers should be considered. Analytical thinkers base their advocacy on data and logic, focusing on the organization's achievements and market position. Intuitive thinkers, conversely, advocate based on the organization's vision and emotional aspects of work. Additionally, the contrast between task-oriented and relationship-oriented individuals highlights different advocacy styles. The former demonstrates loyalty through work ethic, while the latter focuses on interpersonal connections and a positive work environment.

Finally, the emotionally focused versus logically focused dichotomy, influenced by bounded rationality and social intelligence, reveals how decision-making can oscillate between emotional appeal and rational arguments. Adapters and innovators, as per Kirton's Adaption-Innovation theory, show loyalty differently: Adapters improve existing systems, while innovators challenge the status quo, advocating for change and new ideas. Both of these behaviours can stem from loyalty, but they have to be understood in the context of the behavioral determinants underlying loyalty's definition. As discussed, it is a reciprocal relationship and clear communication through psychological safety will facilitate the understanding of the different expressions of acts of pride and advocacy.

In conclusion, pride and advocacy are not only outcomes of loyalty; they are deeply intertwined with the processes of socialization and its effectiveness together with the processes of identification and internalization. By fostering a strong sense of belonging and aligning organizational values with personal values, leaders can cultivate genuine pride and advocacy among employees, transforming the organization into a thriving, resilient entity.

CHAPTER 14

Long-Term Perspective

"People have to see how in the process of becoming a we,
they could also be their best me."

—Phil Jackson

EMPLOYEES EXHIBITING LOYALTY TO THEIR organization's cause often adopt a long-term perspective towards their defined and agreed role and position. This orientation towards the future rather than immediate rewards underscores a strategic alignment with the organization's long-term objectives. As discussed earlier, the reasons for the alignment of individual and organizational goals can be due to the processes of identification and/or internalization of values, or refined egoism. The long-term perspective is a behavioural consequence of loyalty, however, it is dependable on the presence of loyalty's determinants and their individual level of development. Employees with a long-term perspective are predisposed to undertake activities that, while not immediately beneficial, are vital for sustained organizational success. Examples include mentoring junior colleagues and engaging in professional development activities that align with evolving organizational goals.

Furthermore, a long-term perspective promotes resilience among loyal employees against short-term adversities. This resilience is anchored in the understanding that setbacks are temporary and integral to the broader trajectory towards achieving organizational goals, similar to the SAS Institute example in 2008-2009. The reciprocity principle underscores the importance of maintaining clear communication during periods of change to preserve loyalty. Such communication acts as a safeguard for loyalty by ensuring employees and their teams are not left in ambiguity regarding shifts in leadership's priorities or organizational direction, thus mitigating potential impacts on their dedication and morale. Social Intelligence, objectivity, WE thinking, and Accountability are the identified underlying elements of long-term perspective.

Social Intelligence

The role of social intelligence involves an understanding of the other side's position, facilitating the discovery of common ground and mutual understanding. It allows for the identification of shared interests and goals, essential in formulating solutions that resonate with all parties. Social intelligence involves the ability to understand and manage interpersonal relations judiciously and empathetically. At its core is empathy, the ability to understand and share the feelings of another through an appreciation of differing viewpoints for the realization of shared objectives.

Connected to social intelligence is objectivity which is about focusing on interests rather than positions and is rooted in looking beyond the immediate demands that are often subjective and tied to emotional stakes. It helps to depersonalize conflicts and focus on the underlying needs that are driving demands, hence its closeness to social intelligence. Objectivity allows for more creative and effective solutions that can potentially meet the needs of all parties or defend one's own viewpoints without moving away from a constructive debate into an open conflict.

It encourages individuals to consider facts, data, patterns etc. in their decision-making, rather than being swayed by personal feelings or unfounded opinions. It fosters an environment where all parties feel heard and understood. This impartial stance encourages open dialogue, where ideas and solutions are evaluated on their merits rather than who proposed them, previously highlighted by the concept of psychological safety. This approach increases the likelihood of achieving outcomes that are both fair and aligned with the strategic goals of the organization.

I vs. We Thinking

Building on social intelligence, there is a recognition of the value of integrating the WE mind-set for the sustainability of the organization. Such a mind-set encapsulates the indispensability of the success and well-being of each member to the collective success of the team and/or the organization. Such a perspective cultivates a sense of belonging and value among members, as they perceive themselves as essential contributors to shared objectives.

This requires a shift from individualistic to systemic thinking underlying the WE mind-set, in which decisions are made with consideration for the wider impact on all stakeholders, especially internal ones. Leaders and peers can instill a sense of investment and ownership among team members by promoting an atmosphere where successes are shared, echoing the principle of reciprocity. This can be achieved through exemplary behavior, on-time feedback, and open recognition.

Ongoing regular dialogue and constructive feedback help in adjusting strategies and behaviors to better meet the needs of all stakeholders. Through these, people can feel more secure in their job roles, have predictability of the future and where the organization/team is handing. Understating the context of the company, their social intelligence can better adjust their behavior and a long-term perspective will be born.

Accountability

By being accountable for their actions, employees build trust with their peers and supervisors as stakeholders can rely on one another to fulfill their obligations. This is a cornerstone of fostering a trustworthy and predictable environment within an organization. When employees are held accountable for their actions, it establishes a culture of responsibility and reliability. Job security and the knowledge that colleagues are equally dedicated to upholding standards of performance and ethics, preserves their long-term dedication.

Accountability aligns with the cultural expectations of integrity within an organization. It's a reflection of an organization's commitment to upholding its values, which resonates deeply with employees who share similar principles through the processes of identification and/or internalization. When employees see that their leaders and peers are held accountable, it reinforces their sense of fairness and justice within the workplace, which is crucial for maintaining morale and loyalty. This strengthens their work relationships and reinforces their alignment with values and the cause of the organization.

Challenges and Pitfalls

Power Dynamics and Imbalances

The challenge of power dynamics and imbalances in achieving Win/Win outcomes is particularly nuanced. In any collaborative setting, disparities in power—whether arising from organizational hierarchies, control over resources, or differing levels of expertise—can skew negotiations and interactions. When one party holds more power than another, it can create an environment where the less powerful feel they have no choice but to accept less favorable terms.

In organizational contexts, for example, employees may feel pressured to agree to terms set by higher management, even if these are not in their best interest. In such cases, the apparent agreement may mask underlying dissatisfaction, leading to issues like reduced morale, decreased loyalty, and even increased turnover. Addressing these imbalances requires conscious efforts by those in positions of power to level the playing field. This can involve measures like ensuring equal participation in decision-making processes, actively seeking and valuing input from all levels of the organization, and creating safe spaces for open and honest communication.

Short-Term vs. Long-Term Focus

The conflict between short-term gains and long-term benefits represents another significant challenge in implementing a long-term mentality. Often, the pressure to achieve immediate results can overshadow the importance of building sustainable, mutually beneficial relationships. This short-term focus can lead to decisions that, while beneficial in the immediate term, might undermine long-term collaboration and trust.

For instance, in a business setting, a focus on quarterly profits might drive decisions that are at odds with longer-term strategic partnerships, employee development, or customer satisfaction. While such decisions might deliver short-term wins, they can erode trust and loyalty, which are crucial for long-term success. Shifting focus to long-term relationship building requires a reevaluation of success metrics, incentivizing and rewarding not just immediate results but also efforts that contribute to sustained mutual benefit and loyalty.

Competing and Comparing

Focusing on competition and comparison can often go against the long-term perspective. While a certain level of competition can drive innovation and improvement, it may also foster an environment where individual achievements overshadow collective progress. Conversely, the long-term approach fosters collaboration and alignment of individual goals with collective objectives. In competitive scenarios, adopting a long-term approach could involve shifting the emphasis from "defeating" other teams within the organization to creating value that benefits all stakeholders. Similarly, moving away from constant internal or external comparison and instead recognizing and valuing each individual's unique strengths and contributions fosters an environment of complementary assets rather than one of rivalry.

Over-Compromise and Loss of Individual Goals

The risk of over-compromise in pursuit of a long-term approach outcome is a delicate balance. While compromise is essential for collaboration, there is a fine line between healthy compromise and over-compromise, where parties feel they are conceding too much. This over-concession can lead to solutions that might be equitable on the surface but leave all parties feeling unfulfilled or even resentful.

It is imperative to ensure that compromises do not lead to the loss of essential individual or organizational goals. It requires a careful assessment of what each party values most and finding ways to accommodate these core needs while still finding common ground. For example, in a team project, this might involve balancing the diverse working styles and priorities of team members to ensure that the project's goals are met without compromising individual members' key needs or preferences.

The long-term approach, due to loyalty, encapsulates a focus on social intelligence, WE thinking, objectivity, accountability.

CHAPTER 15

Building Culture

*"What is honored in a country
is cultivated there."*

—Plato

A business that makes nothing, but money is a poor business."
—Henry Ford

HENRY FORD'S STATEMENT UNDERSCORES HIS conviction that businesses need to have a purpose beyond profit. He believed that the social roles of business were crucial, advocating for a broader mission that prioritizes creating value for society, providing quality products or services, and caring for employees and customers. According to Ford, focusing solely on financial gain risks long-term failure, as such businesses may lose touch with the needs of people and society.

This philosophy of responsible entrepreneurship is evident in Ford's revolutionary approach to employee welfare. By significantly increasing workers' wages to $5 per day—an amount that allowed them to not only live better but also afford the products they produced—Ford demonstrated a belief that businesses thrive when they invest in their employees. This move not only boosted worker morale and productivity but also stimulated economic demand, as workers could now participate as consumers in the marketplace, thus benefiting the business in return.

Though his relationship with unions was marked by conflict and differing perspectives, Ford's approach aligns with modern concepts of corporate social responsibility (CSR). His belief that businesses should function in the interest of their employees, customers, and society as a whole points to a longer-term view of success and sustainability. He recognized that when businesses prioritize people and social well-being, they promote resilience and cultivate a loyal customer base.

In today's business landscape, where consumers and employees increasingly value purpose-driven organizations, Ford's philosophy resonates more than ever. Companies that balance profit with social responsibility, just as Ford envisioned, often secure greater long-term success by nurturing the communities they serve. Businesses that focus on people—not just profits—create lasting impact, sustainable growth, and a stronger social fabric, ensuring they remain relevant in a rapidly changing world.

For over 25 years, my father has developed his expertise in various fields of psychology. He began his career in military and social psychology as an officer and head of the National Army Psychology Centre in Bulgaria. During this period, he served as the psychologist for the first Bulgarian Army battalion in Iraq during Operation Iraqi Freedom. His early specialization in crisis situations proved invaluable, particularly when working closely with special forces and during a terrorist attack around Christmas Day 2003.

During this attack, the Bulgarian base was targeted, resulting in a bomb truck explosion that claimed soldiers' lives. In the aftermath, a mutiny loomed due to the servicemen's anger towards their commanders' decisions prior to the attack. My father's words and actions calmed the armed and angry soldiers who were ready to hijack a military aircraft, ensuring the battalion safe return to Bulgaria on the designated date.

Following these events, my father led a team of IT professionals in developing a machine learning software aimed at revolutionizing the recruitment and hiring process for future officers in Bulgaria. This software addressed psychological biases and potential manipulation by interested parties. Soon after, he shifted his focus to private business and founded the Aleksiev Group. Over the years, nearly 100 clients from 46 different industries have benefited from the firm's consultancy.

Drawing from his background as an electrical engineer and associate professor in psychology, my father's research has bridged various client experiences, leading to the creation of proprietary diagnostic tools. These tools have improved Leadership Self-Awareness®, Team Intelligence Model®, and most recently, the Loyalty Quotient to Loyalty® in organizations.

The development of the Loyalty Quotient to Loyalty® tool began in 2018, prompted by a challenge from one of Bulgaria's largest furniture manufacturers. The company wanted to replace its policy of using lie detectors on high management due to the issues it posed. The resulting tool, now in version 2.0, is a web-based application, ArtaPava that measures the loyalty of key employees, such as decision-makers and those with access to sensitive information, once or twice a year. The goal is to assess and either maintain or further develop their loyalty. Unlike a binary yes-or-no structure, loyalty is categorized into seven different levels, one output value, and two reports.

Unique Features and Benefits of the Loyalty Quotient to Loyalty® (LQL) Instrument

1. Based on a Comprehensive Concept

The LQL instrument is based on a thoroughly researched and well-documented concept that encapsulates the multifaceted nature of loyalty within organizations. This comprehensive foundation ensures that the tool is theoretically robust and aligns with the latest insights in psychology, sociology, and organizational behavior. The written concept provides a clear framework that guides the development and application of the instrument, ensuring consistency and reliability in measuring loyalty to loyalty.

2. Grounded in Past Practical Experience

The development of the LQL instrument draws heavily on extensive practical experience accumulated over decades. This includes my father's pioneering work in military and social psychology, his leadership in crisis situations, and his vast experience in the private sector. This rich practical background ensures that the LQL instrument is theoretically sound and deeply rooted in real-world applications. The lessons learned from these diverse experiences have been integrated into the tool, making it highly relevant and effective in various organizational contexts.

3. Research Conducted with Real Professionals

Unlike many instruments that rely on studies involving paid groups or college students, the LQL instrument is based on research conducted with real professionals. Our field research involved working directly with our clients, who represent a wide range of 46 different industries and organizational levels. This approach ensures that the data and insights gained are highly applicable and reflective of real-world scenarios. The use of actual professionals in our research adds significant credibility and validity to the instrument's findings and recommendations.

4. Output Simplicity

One of the standout features of the LQL instrument is its output simplicity. Despite the complexity of the factors it measures, the results are presented in a clear and straightforward manner. This simplicity ensures that leaders and managers can easily interpret the findings and make informed decisions without needing extensive training or expertise. The user-friendly reports and visualizations facilitate quick understanding and actionable insights, making it easier to integrate the tool's output into everyday organizational practices.

5. Practicality

The LQL instrument is designed with practicality in mind. ArtaPava is a web-based application that can be seamlessly integrated into an organization's existing systems. The tool is structured to be used once or twice a year, making it easy to implement without causing disruption. The practical nature of the instrument means that it provides actionable insights that can be directly applied to understanding the organization's members, enhance or effectively maintain their loyalty and improve organizational performance. Areas of concern, areas needing more attention, and those that need to simply be maintained or have the opportunity to be developed are identified. Further, the instrument has been used to drive specific initiatives, such as improving team cohesion and addressing turnover rates. Its practical design ensures that it meets the needs of busy professionals and fits smoothly into the workflow of organizations.

6. Uniqueness

What sets the LQL instrument apart is its uniqueness. No other instrument on the market offers the same comprehensive and nuanced approach to measuring loyalty to loyalty. The LQL instrument categorizes loyalty to loyalty into seven different levels, with one output value, and two reports, providing a detailed and multi-dimensional view of employee loyalty. This unique approach allows organizations to understand the nuances of loyalty to loyalty and address specific areas for improvement. The tool's distinctive methodology and innovative features make it an unparalleled resource for organizations seeking to measure and foster loyalty effectively. This uniqueness is highlighted by the lack of comparable tools on the market and the positive feedback from clients who have experienced its benefits first-hand.

Building a Culture: How Can a Leader Create an Environment, Develop, and Maintain It?

Organizational culture serves as the backbone of a company's identity, shaping behaviors, attitudes, and the overall environment within which employees operate. A strong organizational culture fosters loyalty by promoting integrity, mutual respect, psychological safety, proactivity, nurturing behavior, and shared values. These behavioral determinants of loyalty are foundational for both the organization and its members, guiding their interactions and commitments.

Loyalty, as defined in this book, is "the willing, practical, and thoroughgoing dedication of a person to a cause in the presence of reciprocity and Asabiyyah." This definition highlights the reciprocal nature of loyalty and the sense of oneness (Asabiyyah) that binds individuals to the organization. A well-defined culture promotes these principles through routine daily practices, ensuring that loyalty is both fostered and maintained.

Key Characteristics of a Loyalty-Fostering Culture

The key characteristics of a loyalty-fostering culture are derived from the behavioral determinants of loyalty which are further explored in the book. These characteristics are essential in creating an environment where loyalty can thrive, aligning with the overall definition of loyalty. Each of the following is visualized through examples of best practices and not so best ones. Each example is tied to specific loyalty determinants or parts of the definition of loyalty, providing practical insights and detailed analysis.

Integrity involves consistent adherence to moral principles. When an organization and its members act with integrity, trust is built, fostering a loyal environment.

Mutual Respect ensures that all members feel valued and heard. This respect underpins positive relationships and a supportive work environment.

Psychological Safety allows employees to take risks and express their ideas without fear of retribution. A culture of psychological safety encourages innovation and loyalty due to open expression of opinions and the courage to act within the job's parameters.

Proactivity involves anticipating and addressing potential issues before they become problems. A proactive culture supports continuous improvement and a forward-thinking mindset.

Nurturing Behavior focuses on supporting the growth and development of employees. Organizations that invest in their people promote a sense of loyalty and commitment.

Shared Values align the organization's mission with its members' personal values. This alignment strengthens the connection between the individual and the organization.

Internal Foundation and Specific Steps to Create a Loyalty-Fostering Culture

Building and maintaining a loyal culture starts from within, both at the individual and organizational levels. This internal foundation is exemplified through the routine daily practices that reinforce the organization's values and foster a culture of loyalty. Leadership and key decision-makers must embody the desired cultural traits, setting an example through their actions and decisions.

Internal Foundation

The internal foundation of a loyalty-fostering culture is built on the principle that everything first comes from within. Whether we are talking about an individual or an organization, the core values and behaviors must be internalized and consistently demonstrated. For leaders and key decision-makers, this means exemplifying the culture through their daily practices and interactions.

Loyalty, as defined in this book, is "the willing, practical, and thoroughgoing dedication of a person to a cause in the presence of reciprocity and Asabiyyah." The definition highlights that loyalty exists in practical and reciprocal terms, where both the organization and its members exhibit behaviors that reinforce mutual dedication.

A culture of loyalty is not created overnight. It requires a consistent and deliberate effort to embed the desired behaviors into the fabric of the organization. This involves a dedication to the principles of integrity, mutual respect, psychological safety, proactivity, nurturing behavior, and shared values. Leaders must consistently model these behaviors and ensure that they are reinforced through the organization's structures, processes, and routines, because in the end loyalty exists in practical and reciprocal terms.

Specific Steps to Create a Loyalty-Fostering Culture

Once loyalty is measured, specific steps are taken to enhance it based on individual reports and the broader organizational culture. These steps are grounded in our research and best practices from organizational management.

Cause (Purpose), Mission, and Vision

Cause (Purpose)

A cause is often the core reason for an organization's existence beyond profit. It embodies a higher calling, something the organization stands for and aims to contribute to the world. While mission and vision often have more operational or strategic components, a cause is rooted in values and beliefs. It's about why the organization exists on a deeper, emotional level. A cause remains constant over time, providing a compass for all decisions and strategies. It doesn't change easily, as it reflects the organization's long-term values and reason for being.

Mission

The mission, on the other hand, describes what the organization does, who it serves, and how it operates. It's more immediate and actionable compared to a cause, focusing on the organization's day-to-day activities and practical goals. While the cause speaks to the bigger "why," the mission defines the operational aspects of how the organization fulfills that reason. The mission can evolve as market conditions or internal capabilities change, but it remains anchored to the cause.

Vision

The vision represents where the organization wants to go in the future. It is aspirational, outlining the desired future state the organization strives to reach. A good vision is forward-looking and ambitious, motivating stakeholders toward a common future goal. The vision gives people an image of the change the organization aims to make, guiding long-term planning and setting a benchmark for success.

Examples

Mondelez International

Purpose: We empower people to snack right.

Mission: To create delicious moments of joy by providing the world's favorite snacks.

Vision: To be the leading global snacking company, offering the right snack at the right moment, made the right way, with a commitment to sustainability and inclusivity.

ING Group

Purpose: Empowering people to stay a step ahead in life and in business.

Mission: To be the preferred bank of our customers through operational excellence and international service quality; and of our employees with the highest level of ethical and moral values.

Vision: To provide our customers with the most effective solutions to help them best manage their financial futures, while creating long lasting value for all stakeholders.

Establish a Cause

When a company without prior experience in articulating a cause starts the process, the challenge is identifying the underlying values and motivations that may not yet be clear. Many companies focus on financial objectives, products, or market positioning without digging deeper into their purpose. Here's how to establish a cause in these organizations:

Internal Exploration

The first step is deep introspection and engagement with the leadership team to discuss core values. In companies without a tradition of causes, it's vital to look at the history of the organization, trends in its development, and the societal context in which it operates. Often, a company's cause is not immediately apparent, so discussions should revolve around what the organization stands for, what it believes in, and the lasting impact it wants to create in the world.

Employee and Customer Input

Employees and customers are often a rich source of insight into the potential cause. They can reflect on the unique qualities and motivations of the organization, helping to uncover a cause that resonates emotionally and practically. This engagement builds collective ownership of the cause and integrates diverse perspectives into the formation process.

Linking Cause to Strategy

Once the cause is identified, it is a foundation to which the organization's strategic goals and business model can be linked. The cause should influence the development of the mission and vision, ensuring alignment across all aspects of the business. Even in its early stages, the cause must be genuine and lived by the organization through its practices and culture.

Establishing a Cause in Start-Ups or Newly Founded Companies

For start-ups or newly founded companies, establishing a cause is a unique challenge. Unlike more mature organizations, start-ups typically operate in highly dynamic environments with evolving products, strategies, and business models. However, this lack of established norms or processes presents an opportunity to embed a cause from the very beginning, ensuring it becomes an integral part of the company's DNA rather than an afterthought.

Defining the Cause Early

In start-ups, the cause needs to be established early—ideally, during the company's formation. At this stage, founders have the opportunity to align their business model, product/service development, and culture with the cause from the ground up. Since start-ups are often driven by passionate founders with a vision to solve specific problems, the cause tends to naturally align with the founder's personal values and the business's reason for being. A cause in a start-up context should speak directly to the problem the company is trying to solve in the marketplace.

Maintaining Flexibility

Unlike more established companies, start-ups often pivot their business models, products, or target markets based on market conditions or emerging opportunities. This flexibility is essential for survival, but it can also pose challenges for maintaining alignment with the cause. Start-ups need to ensure their cause is broad and adaptable enough to withstand these pivots while still remaining a guiding principle for decision-making. This flexibility allows the cause to remain relevant even as the business evolves.

Cause-Driven Culture and Growth

Start-ups are typically small, lean, and agile, which means they have the opportunity to build a cause-driven culture from the outset. The founder(s)'s role in shaping this culture is crucial, as their passion and dedication to the cause can inspire employees and partners. As the company grows, it's important that new hires and investors understand and embrace the cause, ensuring that it spreads to all new organization's members.

Start-ups that successfully embed their cause into the fabric of the organization are better positioned to attract like-minded employees, customers, and investors who share their values.

Balancing Financial Pressures with Purpose

Start-ups often face intense financial pressures, especially in their early stages. The need to secure funding, generate revenue, and reach profitability can sometimes overshadow the company's cause. However, staying true to the cause can actually be a strategic advantage. Many modern investors and consumers are drawn to purpose-driven businesses that align with their values.

Start-ups need to balance short-term financial goals with long-term dedication to their cause. For example, a start-up may be tempted to take on a high-revenue contract that doesn't align with its cause, but this could lead to long-term brand dilution or internal cultural conflicts. By staying focused on their cause, start-ups can build a loyal customer base and attract investors who are in it for the long haul, ensuring financial sustainability and purpose alignment. This pressure can sometimes lead founders to make decisions that conflict with their cause to survive in the short term.

Strategies for Balancing Financial Survival with Purpose

- **Prioritize Core Values:** While start-ups need to be adaptable and flexible, it's critical that they remain anchored to their core values. Founders should identify non-negotiable aspects of their cause early on.

- **Long-Term Investor Relations:** Early-stage funding often comes from investors who prioritize rapid growth and quick returns. Start-ups need to carefully choose investors whose values align with the cause. It's tempting to take capital from any willing source, but accepting funding from investors who push for growth at the expense of the company's core values can lead to a conflict of interest, brand dilution, and even employee dissatisfaction.

- **Develop Cause-Centric Revenue Streams:** One way to bridge the gap between short-term financial pressures and long-term dedication to the cause is by developing early revenue streams that align with the cause.

- **Stay Transparent with Stakeholders:** Being upfront with investors, employees, and customers about the company's financial and cause-related challenges is essential. Transparency builds trust and allows stakeholders to better understand short-term decisions without assuming that the cause is being compromised.

Evolving the Cause Over Time

While start-ups should establish a cause early, it's important to recognize that this cause may evolve as the company matures. As the start-up gains traction, scales its operations, and expands its product/service offerings, the expression of the cause together with the mission and vision might need to be refined to reflect the current leadership and the organization's impact. However, the core values and beliefs that underpin the cause should remain consistent, providing a stable foundation even as the business grows and evolves, because in times of doubt going back to the root can serve as a reminder of the reason for being and why all was started.

Pitfalls

- Over-Pivoting Away from the Cause: It's normal for start-ups to pivot in response to market demands or feedback but pivoting too far away from the original cause can lead to brand confusion and loss of focus.

- Misaligned Hiring Practices: A critical pitfall is hiring employees who don't align with the company's cause or values, especially in the early stages. If early hires are primarily chosen based on technical skills or immediate needs, without considering their cultural fit, it can create friction as the company grows.

- Ignoring Cause in Marketing or Branding: Start-ups can also fall into the trap of developing marketing strategies or branding that downplay or misrepresent their cause in an effort to attract a wider audience.

Some Advice

- Frame the Cause as a Competitive Advantage: Start-ups can demonstrate to investors that the cause isn't just an ethical stance but also a competitive differentiator. By framing the cause as a market opportunity, start-ups can attract investors looking for long-term growth.

- Provide Metrics that Connect Cause to Financial Performance: To bridge the gap between investor expectations and the company's mission, founders should develop measurable metrics that show how the cause contributes to profitability. For example, demonstrating that customer loyalty and retention increase due to cause alignment, or that sustainable practices reduce costs in the long run, provides a compelling case for investors.

Establishing a Cause in Companies with Market History

When it comes to establishing a cause within an organization, the journey can vary depending on the company's background, yet many of the core principles remain the same. Whether a company is completely new to the concept of articulating a cause or has a long history with traditions, successes, and failures, the process of defining and integrating a cause requires careful consideration. In both cases, the establishment of a cause needs to reflect the organization's core values, serve its stakeholders, and align with its overall strategy for the future.

Internal Exploration and Introspection

The starting point for any company, experienced or not, is deep introspection. Companies without prior experience articulating a cause may find this process to be one of discovery, as they often focus primarily on operational or financial objectives without having defined a deeper purpose. These companies need to begin by asking fundamental questions: What do we believe in? What lasting impact do we want to have beyond profit? What value do we create?

For companies with a rich history, the challenge lies in revisiting their past to uncover the implicit values and beliefs that have driven their successes and failures. These organizations need to look back at key moments that define their journey, identifying patterns where they have aligned with or deviated from what might be their true purpose. Successes that resonate emotionally with customers or stakeholders often point toward a cause that has been there all along but not formally articulated. Similarly, failures provide valuable insights into moments when the organization lost touch with its core values. Whether the company is new to the idea of a cause or has long-standing traditions, the process of introspection helps uncover the deeper motivations that guide the organization and its people.

Engaging Employees and Stakeholders

A cause must be a shared, collective understanding within an organization. In both types of companies, whether experienced with causes or not, engaging employees, customers, and stakeholders is critical. These groups provide diverse perspectives on what the organization stands for and how it impacts the world around it. In companies without prior experience in defining a cause, this engagement helps leaders see beyond the immediate financial or operational goals and recognize the unique aspects of the company's culture, identity, and market presence. Engaging key stakeholders in the process fosters a sense of collective ownership of the cause, ensuring it is not just a leadership-driven initiative but something that resonates across the organization.

Leveraging Tradition While Navigating Change

Companies with deep-rooted traditions face a specific challenge when defining a cause: how to honor the past while evolving to meet the demands of the present and future. A cause needs to reflect the organization's heritage, but it needs to also be adaptable enough to remain relevant in modern contexts. The task for these organizations is to distill the essence of their traditions and values and embed them into a cause that serves as a guiding principle moving forward.

For companies without this history, the challenge is different. They need to ensure that they aren't reactive or overly influenced by short-term market trends or competitive pressures. Instead, these companies have the freedom to define a cause that is forward-thinking and aligned with the opportunities and challenges of today's business landscape, building something new and authentic that can guide their long-term direction. Both types of organizations need to strike a balance: leveraging their history and current market position to shape a cause that is both enduring and adaptable.

Aligning Cause with Strategy

No matter the background, a cause cannot exist in isolation; it needs to be integrated into the company's broader strategic framework. In companies without prior experience in this area, the articulation of a cause often requires a realignment of their mission, vision, and strategic objectives. The cause should influence the organization's strategic decisions and priorities, ensuring that every action supports the larger purpose (cause).

For companies with a long history, this alignment may require reevaluating certain legacy products, services, or processes that no longer reflect the evolving cause. These companies may have successful business units (e.g., cash cows) that generate significant revenue but do not align with the newly defined cause. Managing this misalignment is a key challenge. The company needs to decide whether to phase out or adapt these legacy units to better align with the cause, while also ensuring they don't undermine financial stability.

In both cases, the cause should act as a filter through which strategic decisions are made, helping the company focus on long-term impact rather than short-term gain. This ensures coherence across the organization's activities, enabling it to operate with purpose and direction.

Learning from the Past, Planning for the Future

Whether a company is new to defining a cause or has a rich history to draw from, the process is iterative and evolves over time. Companies with no experience in defining a cause should remain mindful of their growth trajectory and external trends that will shape their future. The cause needs to be based on lasting values and concept of how business should be done yet specific enough to provide clarity and direction which can be further used in the crafting of the mission statement.

For companies with a market history, questions that apply are related to lessons learned. What worked well before, and why? What failed, and what lessons can we extract from those failures? How has the market changed, and what role can our company play in addressing emerging societal needs?

The BCG Matrix and the Cash Cow in the Context of Cause Establishment

The Boston Consulting Group (BCG) Matrix is a strategic tool that helps companies analyze their product portfolios and business units based on market growth and market share. It divides products into four categories: Stars, Cash Cows, Question Marks, and Dogs. Each of these categories plays a role in the company's overall strategy and resource allocation.

Understanding the Cash Cow's Role in Business

The cash cow is a product or business unit that consistently generates significant revenue with little need for further investment. It typically exists in a mature market where the company has a strong market share. Cash cows are critical for providing financial stability and enabling the company to fund other ventures, such as innovations or high-growth projects that align with its long-term strategic objectives.

In the context of establishing a cause, the cash cow can be both a strength and a challenge. The stable revenue it provides can fund initiatives that support the cause, making it easier for the organization to invest in purpose-driven projects. However, if the cash cow operates in a way that conflicts with the company's new or emerging cause, it creates a tension between financial sustainability and purpose alignment.

Conflict Between Cause and Cash Cow

A significant challenge arises when a company's cash cow operates in a way that contradicts the values or objectives of its cause. For example, if a company's cause is centered around sustainability and reducing environmental impact, but its cash cow relies on practices that are environmentally harmful, this creates a clear conflict. Such a scenario demands careful navigation. The company needs to determine whether it can modify the operations of the cash cow to align with the cause or whether it should gradually phase out that business unit and replace it with new ventures that are more aligned.

This is where the importance of structure and planning comes. Companies need to avoid adopting a cause that directly fights against their key business units—especially the cash cow—without a clear structure, plan, and timeline for resolution. Sudden decisions that drastically alter or cut off a cash cow could harm the organization's financial health and create instability, which is why strategic planning is crucial.

Evaluating Alignment Between Cash Cow and Cause

When a company establishes or redefines its cause, it needs to evaluate how well the cash cow aligns with this cause. This process involves:

- **Assessing** whether the current cash cow aligns with the cause or whether it contradicts the values the organization aims to promote.

- **Determining** whether operational changes can be made to bring the cash cow more in line with the cause.

- **Creating** a plan for transitioning away from the cash cow if it cannot be aligned, with a focus on developing new sources of revenue that are compatible with the cause.

This evaluation should also consider the broader business strategy and the role the cash cow plays in funding other aspects of the organization's growth. A company cannot afford to hastily dismantle its primary source of income without a clear strategy for replacing it or managing the financial impact.

BCG Matrix as a Tool for Strategic Planning

The BCG Matrix itself serves as a useful framework for companies to evaluate how each product or business unit supports or detracts from the overall cause. When aligning the company's portfolio with its cause, the BCG Matrix helps determine where to focus investment and which units should be phased out or repositioned. For example:

- **Stars:** High-growth products with significant market share are often natural candidates for alignment with the company's cause. They can be future cash cows and fund continued cause-driven growth.

- **Question Marks:** These products are in high-growth markets but have low market share. The company needs to decide whether they have the potential to grow into stars (and eventually cash cows) and whether they support the cause. For example, a "question mark" product may align with the cause but require investment, while a cash cow might not support the cause but provides critical funding.

- **Dogs:** Low-growth, low-market-share products often consume more resources than they generate. If they do not align with the cause, these should be prime candidates for divestment.

By using the BCG Matrix to evaluate alignment with the cause, companies can strategically allocate resources to the units that best serve both financial goals and long-term purpose.

The BCG Matrix and the Cash Cow: Employee Well-being vs. High-Stress Cash Cow in a Manufacturing Company. A Fictional Example

A manufacturing company produces high-end industrial equipment, sold predominantly through its in-house sales department. The company's flagship product—reliable, high-demand machinery—is the company's cash cow, driving substantial and consistent revenue. However, the sales team responsible for moving this product operates under immense pressure to meet demanding sales quotas, leading to long hours, stress, and high turnover rates.

Recently, the company adopted a cause centered on employee well-being and sustainable productivity, aiming to balance high performance with a healthier, more supportive work environment. This creates a tension between the new cause and the company's existing sales-driven cash cow, where productivity and revenue have been historically tied to high-pressure, high-stress conditions.

Strategic Planning Options and From a Cause – Mission – Vision – Strategic Objectives to a New Business Model.

1. **Modify Operations to Align the Cash Cow with the Cause.**

In light of the new cause, the company needs to rethink its traditional sales model without reducing the effectiveness of its cash cow. Instead of relying on aggressive sales tactics and stress-inducing quotas, the company can shift toward a culture of sustainable, relationship-driven sales, focusing on:

- Long-term client relationships over short-term wins, emphasizing trust and retention rather than high-pressure, quick sales.

- Empowering the sales team to focus on strategic account management rather than just transactional selling, allowing them more control over their workflows.

By revamping the sales process, the company leverages its cash cow's strong market position while focusing on longer-term customer loyalty and reducing stress on the sales team. The cash cow continues to generate revenue, but following a pre-approved plan to change to a more sustainable model for employees, aligning with the cause of well-being.

Moving toward a relationship-based sales culture might initially slow down sales cycles. However, the lifetime value of customers increases, as satisfied clients stay longer and purchase more over time, compensating for any short-term dip. Further, less turnover in the sales department reduces recruitment and training costs, improving profitability in the long run.

Convincing the sales team to embrace this new approach could be difficult, as it moves away from a quota-based model they may be accustomed to. It also requires leadership to manage expectations during the initial adjustment period, where results may not be as immediately apparent. This change in thinking pushes the company to redefine success metrics—not just based on immediate revenue but also on client satisfaction and employee retention, which create more sustainable long-term growth.

2. Gradually Phase Out the High-Stress Sales Model

The company could implement a more holistic approach to managing both the production and sales cycles by creating cross-functional teams. These teams would include sales, production, and customer support representatives working together to achieve shared goals, rather than focusing on isolated, department-specific targets. This would involve:

- Collaborative problem-solving: Salespeople would have direct input from the production team, allowing them to set realistic expectations for clients and better manage the sales process.

- Cross-team accountability: Each team member contributes to meeting customer needs, meaning the burden isn't solely on the sales department to generate revenue quickly.

The creation of cross-functional teams distributes the stress of maintaining high sales volumes and production schedules across departments. This collaborative structure ensures that the cash cow operates more smoothly, reducing inefficiencies and relieving pressure on individual teams, all while maintaining profitability.

Cross-functional teams can improve operational efficiency, as real-time collaboration between sales and production eliminates bottlenecks and reduces miscommunication. This approach also helps with resource allocation, leading to smoother workflows and fewer production delays. However, the initial restructuring could slow the sales cycle as teams learn to collaborate effectively.

This method requires breaking down long-standing departmental silos, which may face resistance from employees accustomed to traditional roles and the status quo. Training and managing these new teams could be resource-intensive initially, but the long-term gains in efficiency and employee satisfaction outweigh the costs. It is difficult to implement and requires significant preparation, training and change management. This shift in organizational structure creates a work environment where employees are more involved in decision-making, reducing individual pressure and promoting a sense of shared responsibility.

Be-Do-Have

In both personal development and organizational growth, success often stems not from what we do or what we achieve, but from who we are at our core. The Be-Do-Have model captures this philosophy, emphasizing that identity drives actions, which ultimately lead to outcomes. This concept has been embraced by leaders and organizations as a way to ensure that their actions (the "do") and outcomes (the "have") are consistently aligned with their deeper purpose (the "be").

At its essence, the Be-Do-Have model suggests that to achieve the desired results, an organization must first focus on being the kind of organization that naturally produces those results. It starts with clearly defining who you are and your core values (being), then taking aligned actions based on that identity (doing), and ultimately achieving the desired outcomes (having). This process ensures that success is built on a foundation of authenticity and integrity.

The German social psychologist and philosopher, Erich Fromm, extensively explored the tension between being and having in his work, including in his book *To Have or To Be?* (1976). Fromm critiques modern society for its obsession with material possessions and consumerism and suggests that people are increasingly focused on having—acquiring and owning material goods—as a means to define themselves and measure success. According to Fromm, this focus on having created an alienated, anxious society where true fulfillment and self-actualization remain elusive.

Fromm contrasts this with the idea of being, which he defines as a state of authentic living, where individuals are connected to their deeper values, emotions, and relationships. In the being mode, people live through active participation, personal growth, and meaningful engagement with others and the world. This mode of living prioritizes personal development, self-expression, and ethical behavior over accumulating wealth or status.

Fromm's concept of being as central to a fulfilling life is foundational to the Be-Do-Have model. In this sense, Fromm's philosophy can be seen as an articulation of the model whose creator is unknown. He suggests that individuals need to first be—that is, connect deeply with their authentic selves and values—before they can meaningfully do so in the world, which will ultimately lead to a more fulfilling having (a state of contentment or success). Resonating with the model are Albert Schweitzer's words: *Success is not the key to happiness. Happiness is the key to success.*

As my father says, the **Be** can either open your wings or put you in shackles. The **Be** can originate externally and become something we adopt or internalize without awareness. Alternatively, we can consciously cultivate our **Be** through deliberate self-programming and a clear mindset. While this conscious development is often personal, it can equally become part of a broader organizational culture. The essential question is: How do we help others discover their own **Be**, enabling them to spread their wings?

Yet, the **Be** we create is never permanent—just as our levels of self-awareness and reflection, which guide our growth, fluctuate over time. This impermanence allows us continual choices and ongoing opportunities for self-programming. Herein lies the true magic of the **Be**. It empowers us to become better people, both to ourselves and others. Through this process, we come to understand the saying, "If you want to go fast, go alone; if you want to go far, go together."

When we focus on developing ourselves authentically, we realize that each of us is a unique creation of nature. We also recognize that there are other genuinely good people in the world with whom we can align our cause. Only when we cease to compete and compare can we genuinely create something greater and connect deeply with others. Ultimately, we cultivate an independent will—acknowledging that what truly matters is not who we once were, but who we are now.

The Be-Do-Have concept is a timeless principle found in ancient philosophies in the East and the West. Thinkers like Aristotle, Cicero, and Laozi all explored the cultivation of one's inner character as the foundation for meaningful action and fulfillment. Aristotle emphasized that cultivating virtues such as courage and wisdom (being) naturally leads to virtuous actions (doing), which ultimately cause happiness and flourishing (having). Similarly, Cicero argued that integrity and responsibility guide leaders and citizens alike, which allows their actions to contribute to their common good and harmony. In the East, Laozi, in his teachings of Taoism, stressed the importance of aligning with the Tao (being), which leads to effortless, harmonious action (doing) and the attainment of fulfillment (having). This ancient wisdom, reflected in the inscription "Know thyself" at the temple of Delphi, reminds us that understanding and cultivating who we are at our core is the true path to meaningful action and success, a timeless human truth.

It is imperative to keep in mind the context of these philosophers and the goals they set for themselves and their concepts. Every organization including yours operates in a specific market with its objectives and plans for future development. Therefore, the application of such concepts depends both on the current organizational culture and the organizational members whose desire for a change together with the influence the decision-makers can exert, can be the triggers or the breaks of the process.

The Marketing Industry's Use of the Be-Do-Have Model

Interestingly, the marketing industry has often flipped this model into a more consumer-driven approach, using the Do-Have-Be or Have-Do-Be variations. These versions encourage customers to do something (buy a product), have the desired outcome (status, results), and then be something (successful, happy, or fulfilled). This reversal emphasizes immediate consumption and achievement over long-term identity-building.

Companies, however, need to be cautious when using this approach internally. The goal should be for the organization to be purpose-driven primarily, rather than starting from a "do" or "have" mindset that seeks short-term gains at the expense of long-term values.

In a business context, the Be-Do-Have model becomes a powerful tool for aligning an organization's identity, actions, and outcomes. Companies, particularly those focused on a cause, should ensure that their core values and purpose (being) drive the actions they take (doing), ultimately leading to the outcomes they seek (having). This alignment is critical for creating a coherent strategy that promotes long-term success and resilience.

1. Be: Define the Organization's Identity (Cause)

In the Be phase, a company needs to clearly define its identity—its cause, values, and long-term purpose. This is the foundation on which the organization operates. Rather than focusing solely on short-term profits or market trends, the company needs to root its mission in something larger than its products or services.

2. Do: Act in Line with the Identity (Mission)

Once the company has established its identity, it needs to translate this being into doing—taking actions that are in harmony with its cause. These actions should reflect the company's values and support its mission. In this stage, the company's mission becomes a guide for decision-making, ensuring that the business consistently operates in ways that align with its purpose.

3. Have: Achieve the Desired Outcomes (Vision)

When a company focuses on being the right kind of organization and doing the right things (efficiency), it naturally has the outcomes it seeks (effectiveness). The company's vision becomes a reality, driven by a combination of its values and its actions. In the Have phase, the company experiences the results of aligning its operations with its cause—whether that's customer loyalty, market leadership, or financial success.

In the fast-paced world of business, it's easy to get caught up in short-term goals and market pressures, which can lead companies to drift away from their cause. The Be-Do-Have model acts as a framework for keeping the company focused on its long-term purpose.

Key Benefits of Applying the Model

1. **Alignment Between Vision and Strategy:** By starting with the company's being (identity), the actions taken (doing) naturally support the company's vision. This ensures that the company remains aligned with its cause, integrity, avoiding the disconnect that often occurs when short-term decisions are prioritized over long-term goals.

2. **Sustainable Growth:** Companies that build their actions around their core values are better positioned for

long-term success. Their consistent actions create a strong brand reputation and promote customer loyalty and drive sustainable growth.

3. **Employee Engagement and Loyalty:** When employees understand and believe in the company's identity and cause, they are more likely to feel engaged with their set goals and loyal to the cause of the company. They know their actions contribute to a larger purpose, leading to higher proactivity and retention.

4. **Resilience:** In times of market volatility or crisis, companies with a strong sense of identity are more resilient. They can weather short-term challenges without losing sight of their long-term vision, as their actions are guided by deeper values rather than reactive, profit-driven decisions.

Drucker, OKRs and more

One effective way to implement the Do phase of the Be-Do-Have model in the long-term is through the use of Objectives and Key Results (OKRs) and Peter Drucker's concept of Management through Objectives together with fostering reciprocity and oneness.

In applying the Be-Do-Have model, companies can maintain a clear sense of direction, ensuring that every action taken supports their larger cause and long-term vision. It serves as a strategic compass, keeping the organization aligned with its values while still pursuing measurable, ambitious goals. This approach builds authenticity, fosters sustainable growth, and ensures that the company's outcomes reflect its identity and purpose.

OKRs: Aligning Cause, Mission, and Vision

Objectives and Key Results (OKRs) are a great tool for aligning a company's strategic objectives with its cause, mission, and vision. By breaking down ambitious goals (Objectives) into measurable outcomes (Key Results), OKRs provide a structured way to track progress and ensure that the organization's actions remain focused on its long-term purpose. This makes OKRs particularly useful for companies working within the Be-Do-Have framework, as they link identity (being) to action (doing) and outcomes (having).

OKRs: The Basics

Objective (O): An ambitious, clearly defined goal that aligns with the company's mission and vision. It represents what the company wants to achieve. The objective should be inspirational, time-bound, and action-oriented.

Key Results (KRs): Specific, measurable outcomes that indicate progress toward achieving the objective. These represent how the company will achieve the objective. Each key result should be quantifiable, time-bound, and verifiable, allowing the company to assess whether it's on track to meet its goals.

Alignment with the Cause

In cause-driven companies, OKRs ensure that the company's actions are consistent with its core values. Objectives rooted in the company's identity keep the organization aligned with its mission, while Key Results ensure accountability and track the company's progress toward its vision.

Clarity and Focus

OKRs provide a clear roadmap for employees at all levels of the organization, helping them understand how their actions contribute to the company's mission and vision. By focusing on a small number of high-impact objectives, OKRs prevent organizations from getting overwhelmed by too many initiatives. This helps keep everyone focused on what matters most.

Agility and Adaptation

OKRs allow agility in the face of changing circumstances. Because OKRs are typically set on a quarterly or yearly basis, they provide a framework for regular reassessment. This flexibility allows companies to adjust their Key Results or set new Objectives as market conditions, technologies, or societal needs evolve—while still keeping their actions aligned with their cause.

Measuring Success

Cause-driven companies often face challenges when trying to measure the impact of their cause on their overall business success. OKRs provide a clear, measurable way to assess progress and outcomes. By breaking down the cause through the strategic objectives that support it and from there into smaller objectives, the respective results can be tracked over time.

How Can Decision-Makers Apply Some of the Behavioral Loyalty Determinants to the Cause?

Integrity: Embedding Accountability

When setting OKRs, ensure that integrity is embedded by establishing clear accountability measures. This can be done by assigning ownership of key results to specific individuals or teams and ensuring that these individuals understand how their actions tie directly to the company's cause. OKRs should reflect values-driven objectives, a result of system-based decision-making procedures. For example, quarterly reviews should include a "values check", where teams assess not only whether they are meeting goals but the way they do it. These checks will focus on ensuring that the decisions made together with their work process align with the company's cause.

During milestone reviews, leaders could ask, "Have the actions taken thus far aligned with our values and mission?" This creates a culture of accountability without constant oversight, allowing employees to make independent decisions while keeping them accountable at critical moments. "How was the process aligned with the company's values?" This creates a culture where meeting targets is important, but how they are met is equally critical.

Psychological Safety

To promote psychological safety, ensure that during the OKR setting and review processes, there are clear avenues for open feedback without repercussions. Leaders should regularly seek and ask for feedback on whether employees feel safe in expressing concerns.

During monthly or quarterly OKR check-ins, dedicate time for an open discussion where team members can raise concerns about progress, process, or the direction of the objectives. Leaders need to ensure that these discussions are focused on solving problems rather than assigning blame.

Proactivity: Encouraging Initiative

In the OKR process, proactivity can be encouraged by asking team members to propose their own OKRs within the larger strategic framework. This increases ownership and ensures that employees are actively seeking out opportunities to further the company's cause. Employees can also be encouraged to lead initiatives that help the organization meet key results, fostering a sense of leadership at all levels.

Proactivity needs to be encouraged but made optional, meaning employees can propose their own OKRs or lead initiatives if they are ready to do so, but without pressure. The focus will remain on giving those who are naturally proactive the space to contribute, while others are not obligated to take on extra responsibility if it does not align with their current capacity.

Shared Values: Alignment through Communication

Rather than regularly reaffirming shared values through repetitive monologues, the focus will be on ensuring that OKRs themselves remain aligned with the shared values. The values should be implicitly integrated into the goals, ensuring that they are relevant to the task at hand and not treated as separate from the company's mission.

During OKR-setting sessions, check whether each objective and key result supports the company's shared values and does not contradict it. Instead of re-stating the values, emphasize how the current goals reflect those values. This ensures that teams do not stray from values while pursuing operational goals.

Strategic Objectives As OKR in the Cause-Mission-Vision Framework

Strategic objectives are the actionable steps organizations take to fulfill their cause, mission, and vision. When aligned properly, strategic objectives support the mission and vision and serve as direct extensions of the cause, ensuring that every operational goal contributes to the larger purpose of the organization.

The alignment between cause, mission, and vision ensures that strategic objectives don't become isolated or purely profit-driven. This coherence guarantees that all organizational efforts move towards a unified purpose, sustaining long-term success and impact.

Understand Culture

Leaders must thoroughly understand the existing culture within their organization to foster a loyalty-fostering environment effectively. This involves a deep dive into the current practices, behaviors, and values that define the organization. Understanding the culture is not just about recognizing what is visible on the surface; it requires an examination of the underlying norms, unwritten rules, and shared beliefs that drive employee behavior.

The first step is to assess the current state of the culture. This can be achieved by observing daily practices, including feedback from third parties who are not part of the process or communication.

These observations help gather insights from employees at all levels, providing a practical and holistic view of the cultural dynamics. Leaders should pay attention to how employees perceive the culture, what they value, and any existing gaps between the current culture and the desired one.

It is also crucial to understand the cultural historical context. Organizations often carry forward practices and behaviors influenced by past leaders, significant events, or long-standing traditions. These historical elements can have a lasting impact on how employees interact and perform. Recognizing these influences helps leaders understand why certain behaviors persist and how they can be aligned with the desired cultural changes. Additionally, it's important to acknowledge the past behavior of the management and leadership, including your own. Even if you have changed or are working to change, your past behavior is likely still remembered by employees and continues to influence the current culture.

Analyzing the impact of current cultural practices on employee behavior and loyalty is another essential aspect. Leaders must identify which practices are fostering loyalty and which are detracting from it. The determinants and consequences of loyalty explored in this book provide a framework for this analysis. For instance, if a culture of micromanagement is prevalent, it may lead to disengagement and high turnover rates. Conversely, a culture that promotes autonomy and empowerment may cause higher levels of loyalty and commitment.

Communicating the findings of the cultural assessment to the organization is a crucial step. Transparency in this process builds trust and demonstrates a commitment to improvement. Leaders should share the insights gathered, highlighting both the strengths and areas for improvement. This communication should also outline the steps that will be taken to address any gaps and enhance the culture. Additionally, it should address how current practices are hindering growth, sustainability, and work harmony.

If changes are needed, selecting new practices that align with the desired culture is vital. These new practices should be clearly articulated and their benefits communicated to all members of the organization. Employees need to understand how these changes will positively impact their work environment and contribute to their overall well-being and success. Employees not involved in the decision-making process should have the decision explained to them, particularly the reasons behind it and the expected benefits. Involving employees in this process can promote a sense of ownership and facilitate smoother implementation of new cultural practices.

Moreover, leaders must be aware of the external influences that shape the organizational culture. These can include industry trends, competitive pressures, and societal expectations. Understanding these external factors helps leaders anticipate changes and adapt the culture proactively, ensuring it remains relevant and supportive of organizational goals.

Understanding the culture also involves recognizing and addressing any resistance to change. Cultural shifts can be challenging, and some employees may be reluctant to embrace new practices. Leaders need to listen to their concerns, provide reassurances, and involve their direct leaders in articulating the decisions. Asking for feedback both for the leader and other key decision-makers helps to mitigate resistance and promotes a smoother transition.

Finally, leaders should continuously monitor and evaluate the culture. This ongoing assessment helps ensure that the culture evolves in alignment with organizational goals and employee needs. Regular check-ins, feedback sessions, and cultural audits can provide valuable insights into the effectiveness of the cultural initiatives and identify areas for further refinement.

For instance, a company might find through observation that its current culture emphasizes strict hierarchy and rigid procedures, which stifles innovation and employee engagement. Recognizing this, the leadership team decides to shift towards a more inclusive and flexible culture. This step could not be the most efficient way because first the underlying cause has to be found and understood. The process might be fine and such a big change can lead to a culture which is not manageable and even worse, employees feel so much free choice or responsibility that they find it counterproductive. Thus, the specific reason has to be found and analysed.

Understanding the culture of an organization is a multifaceted process that requires thorough assessment, transparent communication, and continuous monitoring. By deeply understanding the current cultural dynamics, historical influences, and external factors, leaders can identify the necessary changes to foster a more loyal and engaged workforce. Involving employees in the process, addressing resistance constructively, and ensuring that all members understand the reasons and benefits behind changes are critical to successfully embedding new cultural practices. This comprehensive understanding and proactive management of culture lay the groundwork for sustained loyalty in organizations and their success.

Define Desired Behaviors

Clearly articulating the behaviors that support the desired culture is essential. These behaviors should reflect the organization's values and goals, providing a clear standard for employees to follow. Defining desired behaviors is a critical step in shaping a culture that promotes loyalty, and it requires a thoughtful and strategic approach.

The key to defining desired behaviors lies in aligning them with the organization's core values and purpose. These behaviors should not be abstract ideals but practical actions that employees can incorporate into their daily routines. The desired behaviors should be specific, observable, and actionable, making it easy for employees to understand what is expected of them.

It is important to recognize that desired behaviors are reinforced through everyday practices, behaviors, and words of the decision-makers and leaders. Employees closely observe these actions, and if there is a dissonance between what leaders say and what they do, the entire effort to define and instill desired behaviors will be perceived as inauthentic and resisted by the workforce. Therefore, leaders must consistently model the behaviors they want to see in their teams. This "lead by example" approach is critical for setting the standard and showing dedication to the defined values, culture, and cause. When leaders exemplify integrity, mutual respect, psychological safety, proactivity, nurturing behavior, and shared values, they signal to employees that these traits are valued and expected.

To ensure that desired behaviors are effectively integrated into the organizational culture, it is crucial to align structures and processes with these behaviors. This includes performance management systems, reward and recognition programs, and feedback mechanisms. When organizational systems support and reinforce the desired behaviors, employees are more likely to adopt and sustain them. Loyalty is a reciprocal process which requires the members and organization alike to treat each other in a loyal manner as defined in the book. It should not be a one-sided effort.

Involving employees in defining desired behaviors can also enhance their acceptance and integration. When employees participate in identifying and shaping the behaviors that will drive the culture, they are more likely to feel a sense of ownership and dedication to these behaviors. This participatory approach can be facilitated through workshops, focus groups, and collaborative sessions where employees can voice their perspectives in a psychologically safe manner and contribute to the development of the desired behaviors.

Hence, effective communication plays a pivotal role in defining and reinforcing desired behaviors. Leaders should use various communication channels to consistently convey the importance of these behaviors, provide examples of what they look like in practice, and highlight how they contribute to the organization's success, the benefits. Regularly sharing success stories and recognizing employees who exemplify the desired behaviors can reinforce their importance and encourage others to follow suit.

The hiring process is equally crucial in ensuring that new employees have the skills required for their jobs, share the values of the organization and fit into the work culture. Hiring candidates who align with the organization's values helps prevent potential conflicts and ensures a smoother integration into the team. If there is a distinct misalignment between the values of new hires and the current culture, it can lead to direct confrontations and either immediate problems or unresolved issues down the road. Therefore, the hiring process should thoroughly assess both the technical competencies and the cultural fit of candidates.

The socialization process is vital for new hires to assimilate into the organizational culture. Effective socialization, managed by both HR and current employees who have direct contact with new hires, helps newcomers understand and adopt the desired behaviors and values. HR should ensure that socialization practices are comprehensive and supportive, while team members and direct leaders should take responsibility for mentoring and integrating new employees to the culture and the desired behaviors. This dual approach ensures that new hires quickly become productive members of the organization, aligned with its cultural values.

In conclusion, defining desired behaviors is a foundational step in building a loyalty-fostering culture. By aligning these behaviors with the organization's values and purpose, ensuring consistency between words and actions, and integrating them into organizational structures and processes, leaders can create an environment where desired behaviors are naturally adopted and sustained. Engaging employees in the process, providing effective communication and training, and establishing feedback mechanisms further support the successful integration of these behaviors into the organizational culture. Additionally, a rigorous hiring process and effective socialization practices are essential to maintaining cultural alignment and fostering long-term loyalty.

Align Structures and Processes

Organizational structures and processes must support the desired culture and behaviors. This alignment ensures that the systems in place reinforce the values and practices the organization wants to promote, thereby embedding the desired culture into the daily operations. The key is to integrate cultural values into all aspects of the organization's structure, from performance management and rewards to communication and decision-making processes.

- **Step 1: Conduct a Comprehensive Review**

Begin by conducting a thorough review of existing systems, policies, and procedures to identify areas that support or hinder the desired behaviors. This involves mapping out current workflows, performance management systems, reward and recognition programs, communication methods, and decision-making processes. Documenting these processes helps decision-makers visualize where alignment with the desired culture is lacking.

- **Step 2: Redesign Performance Management Systems**

Performance management systems should be redesigned to recognize and reward behaviors that align with the organization's values. This includes setting cultural goals that incorporate cultural priorities into performance objectives. Managers should provide regular feedback that addresses both performance and adherence to cultural values, ensuring that employees understand how their actions contribute to the organization's cultural goals and organizational cause. Employees, on the other hand, have the opportunity to provide their views and also feedback on their perceptions of the management's actions or inactions. Cultural metrics should be integrated into performance reviews to evaluate how well employees embody the desired behaviors.

- **Step 3: Align Reward and Recognition Programs**

Develop reward and recognition programs that incentivize behaviors supporting the desired culture. This involves creating recognition criteria that align with cultural values, ensuring that both formal and informal rewards are in place. The former such as bonuses and promotions can be formalized in written formats, while the latter such as public recognition and appreciation can be ritualized in the company culture, creating a unique atmosphere and feeling. The way one feels is what one remembers, not the words or the money, but the feeling is always remembered. Recognizing employees who exemplify the desired behaviors reinforces their importance and encourages others to follow suit. For example, recognizing exceptional teamwork or innovative contributions can promote a culture of collaboration and innovation.

- **Step 4: Enhance Communication Processes**

Ensure all communication processes reflect and reinforce the desired culture. Develop consistent messaging that highlights the importance of cultural values through visualized examples centred on benefits and use various platforms such as team meetings, newsletters, and digital tools to disseminate these messages. Encourage open dialogue by creating forums, formal and/or informal, for employees to share their ideas and feedback.

Transparent communication is crucial, so clearly explain the reasons behind decisions and how they align with cultural values. It involves ensuring that the language, tone, and channels used for internal communication reflect the organization's values. This builds trust and ensures everyone is on the same page.

- **Step 5: Adjust Organizational Structures**

Adjust the organizational communication structure to support the desired culture. This might involve making the communication structure more hierarchical or less so, depending on what aligns best with the organization's values and goals. Integrate new decision-making practices that emphasize inclusivity of all interested members and transparency. For instance, involve employees in decisions that affect their work, seek input and feedback, and ensure decisions are made based on the organization's values. After decisions are made, communicate the results and rationale to the rest of the organization, ensuring that the process and outcomes align with the declared culture and values. This approach shows commitment to the organization's values.

Training and development programs should be aligned with the desired culture to equip employees with the skills and knowledge needed to embody the organization's values. These programs should focus not only on technical skills but also on cultural competencies, such as communication, teamwork, and leadership. Continuous learning opportunities help employees grow in ways that support the desired culture.

Ritualize Behaviors

Creating routines and rituals to consistently reinforce desired behaviors is crucial in embedding the desired culture into the daily life of the organization. Rituals and routines make the culture more tangible and provide a unique identity that distinguishes the organization from others. Here's a detailed, practical approach to achieving this:

- **Step 1: Identify Key Behaviors**

Begin by identifying the key behaviors that align with the organization's values and desired culture. These behaviors should be specific, observable, and actionable. For example, if teamwork is a core value, key behaviors might include regular team check-ins, collaborative problem-solving sessions, and shared decision-making.

- **Step 2: Design Meaningful Rituals**

Design rituals that reinforce these key behaviors and make them a regular part of the organizational routine. Rituals should be meaningful and engaging, helping to instill a sense of pride and belonging among employees. For instance, if innovation is a desired behavior, establish a weekly "Innovation Hour" where employees can brainstorm and present new ideas. If customer focus is a core value, start each team meeting with a customer success story.

- **Step 3: Integrate Rituals into Daily Operations**

Integrate these rituals into the daily operations and schedules of the organization. Ensure they are easy to follow and become a natural part of the workday. For example, implement a daily stand-up meeting where team members briefly discuss their goals and any obstacles they face, promoting transparency and teamwork.

- **Step 4: Celebrate Milestones and Achievements**

Use rituals to celebrate milestones and achievements that exemplify the desired behaviors. Recognize and reward employees who consistently demonstrate these behaviors, reinforcing their importance. For example, hold a monthly recognition ceremony to honor employees and/or teams who have embodied the organization's values.

- **Step 5: Create Symbolic Gestures**

Incorporate symbolic gestures that reinforce the desired culture and values. These gestures can be small but significant acts that remind employees of the organization's dedication to its cause. For instance, if environmental sustainability is a core value and part of the cause, you might start meetings with a brief update on the company's sustainability efforts or encourage employees to participate in green initiatives.

- **Step 6: Practice Daily**

Ensure that these rituals and behaviors are practiced daily to reinforce their importance and make them an integral part of the organizational culture. Daily practice solidifies these behaviors, making them second nature to employees and ensuring that the culture is consistently reinforced. However, this is as much an organizational process as a natural one. Nothing forced works greatly, meaning that the ritualization process should be conducted step by step with patience and an approved plan. If not, there will be a resistance to it and it will be trivialized and eventually forgotten. Once one of our clients prior to working with The Aleksiev Group, was advised by other consultants to incorporate Lego into its creative process. The constructors that were bought cost almost six figures but after one week they were all put back in their boxes and left aside because none of the organizational members wanted to use it. For example, daily team check-ins or stand-up meetings can promote regular communication and collaboration, while daily recognition of small achievements can continuously boost morale and reinforce desired behaviors.

- **Step 7: Encourage Storytelling**

Encourage employees to share stories that highlight how the desired behaviors have positively impacted their work and the organization. Create platforms for storytelling, such as internal newsletters, intranet sites, or dedicated time during specific meetings. Sharing these stories helps reinforce the desired behaviors and demonstrates their real-world application.

- **Step 8: Embed Rituals in Training and Development**

Incorporate rituals into training programs and the socialization process to ensure that new employees understand and adopt the desired behaviors from the outset. Include cultural orientation sessions that explain the importance of these rituals and how they contribute to the organization's overall success. This helps new hires internalize the culture quickly and effectively.

Step 9: Regularly Review and Adapt Rituals

Regularly review and adapt rituals to ensure they remain relevant and effective. Solicit feedback from employees to understand what works well, what could be improved, and what is unnecessary and troublesome. This continuous improvement process ensures that rituals stay fresh and meaningful, maintaining their impact over time.

Overcome Resistance

Addressing resistance to cultural change is crucial for successful implementation. Resistance can arise from various sources, including fear of the unknown, discomfort with new practices, and skepticism about the benefits of the change.

- **Step 1: Understand the Sources of Resistance**

Start by identifying sources of resistance within the organization. This can be achieved through surveys, interviews, and focus groups. For real success, any of those methods should be conducted in a psychologically safe environment without the slightest possibility of punishment. Understanding the underlying concerns and reasons for resistance helps tailor strategies to address them effectively. It is important to keep in mind that not all members would be sincere and some might exaggerate the situation, while others would prefer the status quo for different reasons. Common sources of resistance include fear of job loss, increased workload, loss of control, and distrust of management's intentions.

- **Step 2: Communicate the Vision and Benefits**

Clearly communicate the vision and benefits of the cultural change to all employees. Use transparent and open communication to explain why the change is necessary, how it aligns with the organization's goals, and what benefits it will bring to both the organization and its members. There is no need to highlight the stories of other organizations, but instead focus on the people within yours and how their work life and consequently their private one can be improved.

- **Step 3: Involve Employees in the Change Process**

Involve organizational members in the change process, either in the planning or (and) the implementation. Utilize their strengths and how each of them could be part of the process. This participatory approach helps reduce resistance by giving them a sense of ownership and control over the changes rather than being passive observers. Form cross-functional teams to gather input and develop a strategy. Encouraging participation demonstrates that members' opinions and contributions are valued especially when they are applied in some form.

- **Step 4: Address Concerns Directly**

Listen to all concerns and address them directly, without diminishment or avoidance. Create forums for open dialogue where employees can express their fears and frustrations without fear of retribution. Such can be a weekly or a monthly meeting or direct communication with them. Acknowledge their concerns and provide clear, honest answers. When people feel heard and understood, they are more likely to trust the process and support the initiative.

- **Step 5: Highlight the Long-Term Benefits**

Always emphasize the long-term benefits of the cultural change, both for the organization and its members. Discuss how the changes will lead to a better work environment and specify exactly how. Providing a clear picture of the future and the various small milestones along the way helps people see beyond the immediate discomfort and focus on the potential gains.

- **Step 6: Engage Middle Management**

Middle managers play a crucial role in influencing their teams and driving the change process. Engage middle management by involving them in planning and decision-making through their practical experience. Provide them with the necessary support to lead their teams through the transition. Middle managers can act as change champions, helping to communicate the vision and immediately address resistance within their teams. They can act on the spot and handle most daily challenges.

- **Step 7: Monitor Progress and Adapt**

Regularly monitor the progress of the cultural change and be prepared to adapt strategies as needed. This can be done through the middle management, feedback channels, and informal panels such as weekly/monthly short meetings. Use feedback from all members to identify areas where resistance persists and adjust tactical and operational approaches accordingly. Continuous monitoring and flexibility ensure that the change process remains effective and responsive to employees' needs.

- ### Step 8: Provide Ongoing Communication

Maintain ongoing communication throughout the change process. Keep employees informed about progress, upcoming steps, and any adjustments to the plan. In essence, keep people informed because imagine how would you feel if you are in their place? Regular updates help maintain transparency and trust, ensuring that employees feel involved and informed, which leads to predictability at the workplace.

Select Cultural Fit

Hiring and promoting individuals who align with the company's cultural values ensures that the culture is perpetuated and strengthened over time. This process is closely tied to socialization and identification, where new members are integrated into the organizational culture. Ensuring cultural fit during recruitment and promotion processes supports long-term cultural integrity and helps embed desired behaviors from the start.

The importance of selecting for cultural fit cannot be overstated. When new hires and promoted individuals embody the organization's values, they reinforce the cultural framework, making it stronger and more resilient. This alignment ensures that employees are not just skilled, but also committed to the same principles that drive the organization forward. It creates a cohesive work environment where everyone is working towards their shared goals with a shared sense of purpose.

Cultural fit also plays a critical role in loyalty and retention. When employees feel that their personal values align with those of the organization, they are more likely to be satisfied with their job and loyal to the cause. This alignment fosters a sense of belonging and pride in the organization, which can lead to higher productivity and lower turnover rates.

Moreover, selecting for cultural fit enhances team dynamics. Teams composed of individuals who share the same values tend to collaborate more effectively, communicate more openly, and resolve conflicts more efficiently. This harmonious work environment boosts morale and drives innovation and performance.

The recruitment process should be designed to identify candidates who not only possess the necessary skills and experience but also resonate with the company's cultural values. This involves incorporating cultural fit assessments into interviews, using behavioral questions to gauge alignment with values, and involving team members in the hiring decision to ensure a well-rounded evaluation. Similarly, promotion decisions should consider cultural fit as a key criterion. Employees who have demonstrated a dedication to the organization's values and behaviors should be recognized and rewarded with opportunities for advancement. This reinforces the importance of cultural fit and sets a standard for others to follow.

Ultimately, focusing on cultural fit from the outset and throughout an employee's career with the organization helps build a strong, unified culture. This culture becomes a competitive advantage, attracting like-minded talent and driving sustained organizational success. By prioritizing cultural fit in hiring and promotions, companies can ensure that their core values are lived out in every aspect of their operations, leading to a more loyal and high-performing workforce.

Measure and Improve

Regularly assessing the culture and making adjustments as needed ensures that it remains relevant and effective. This involves using tools like the Loyalty Quotient to Loyalty® (LQL) instrument to measure loyalty levels and identify areas for either maintenance or improvement. Continuous evaluation and refinement of cultural practices help maintain a dynamic and responsive organizational culture. Measuring loyalty provides a clear picture of where the organization stands and informs the approach needed for ongoing development.

The importance of measuring and improving organizational culture cannot be overstated. It is through consistent assessment that an organization can truly understand the effectiveness of its cultural initiatives. Tools like the LQL instrument offer invaluable insights into the levels of loyalty within the organization, highlighting both strengths and potential areas for growth. By regularly collecting and analyzing this data, organizations can make informed decisions that drive cultural evolution and improvement.

Continuous evaluation ensures that cultural practices do not become stagnant or outdated. In the fast-paced and ever-changing business environment, what works today might not be as effective tomorrow. Regular assessments allow organizations to stay ahead of the curve, adapting their cultural practices to meet new challenges and opportunities, and being proactive instead of reactive. This proactive approach helps maintain a culture that is not only current but also anticipates future trends, needs, and challenges.

Moreover, measuring loyalty specifically provides a clear benchmark for organizational health. Loyalty levels can directly impact various performance metrics such as productivity and retention. By understanding these dynamics, organizations can tailor their strategies to enhance loyalty, thereby improving overall performance. It also helps in identifying specific behaviors and practices that either contribute to or detract from loyalty, allowing for targeted interventions.

Refinement of cultural practices based on regular assessments fosters a culture of continuous improvement. Employees see that the organization is dedicated to its values and is willing to evolve and improve, which can enhance their own dedication. This cycle of assessment and improvement keeps the culture dynamic and responsive, ensuring that it meets the needs of both the organization and its members.

Finally, measuring and improving culture supports long-term organizational success. It ensures that the culture remains aligned with the organization's strategic goals and objectives. This alignment is crucial for achieving sustained performance and competitive advantage.

Concluding Remarks

Creating and maintaining a loyalty-fostering culture is a multifaceted process that starts from within the organization. By establishing a strong internal foundation and following specific steps to embed the desired culture, leaders can create an environment where loyalty thrives. This involves setting a clear purpose, understanding and aligning the existing culture, defining and modeling desired behaviors, and continuously reinforcing these practices through daily routines and effective communication. By overcoming resistance, selecting for cultural fit, and regularly measuring and improving the culture, organizations can foster long-term loyalty among their employees. Of course there will be people just for the money, but what a company could consider is striving for a long-term development together with its people.

CHAPTER 16

Conclusion

"In this world I value only loyalty.
Without it, you are nobody and you have no one.
In life, it is the only currency that will never be devalued."

—Vladimir Vysotsky

IN *THE SECOND PART OF King Henry* the *Sixth*, Shakespeare poignantly captures the fragility and significance of loyalty through Gloucester's lamentation: "O, where is loyalty? If it be banished from the frosty head, where shall it find a harbor in the earth?"

This line, uttered by Gloucester, speaks volumes about the disillusionment and despair that arise when loyalty is absent, especially among those who are expected to embody wisdom and stability. The "frosty head" symbolizes the statesmen and leaders, whose experience and age should ideally be the bedrock of loyalty and integrity. When these figures, who hold the moral compass with its values and principles, forsake loyalty, the very foundation of trust and honor within any organization begins to crumble.

Gloucester's rhetorical question underscores the pervasive impact of such a loss. Loyalty is a cornerstone of social and organizational oneness like Ibn Khaldun's Asabiyyah and not a personal only a personal virtue. If loyalty is missing from those at the helm, its absence ripples through the entire structure, leaving no place untouched by distrust and fragmentation. This absence creates a vacuum, challenging the very existence of loyalty elsewhere in a society or organization.

In the context of leadership and organizational dynamics, Gloucester's lament serves as a reminder of the critical role that leaders play in fostering and upholding loyalty. Leaders are the harbingers of culture and values within an organization. When they exemplify loyalty through their actions and decisions, it instills a sense of trust and commitment throughout the organization. Conversely, when leaders falter in their loyalty, it sets a precedent that can lead to widespread disillusionment and disengagement.

Furthermore, the imagery of finding "a harbor in the earth" suggests the necessity of a safe haven for loyalty to flourish. A harbor represents safety, security, and a place of refuge. In an organizational context, this translates to creating an environment where loyalty is nurtured and protected. Such an environment is characterized by mutual respect, integrity, and psychological safety, where employees feel valued and their dedication is reciprocated.

Gloucester's words also prompt reflection on the broader societal implications of loyalty. In any community, be it a family, a business organisation, or a nation, the erosion of loyalty among its leaders can lead to a breakdown in social cohesion and trust. The fabric of any collective endeavour is woven through the threads of loyalty and mutual support. When these threads are weakened or severed, the entire fabric risks unravelling.

In today's rapidly changing world, where the dynamics of the workforce and organizational structures are continually evolving, the essence of Gloucester's lament remains relevant. The challenge for modern leaders is to ensure that loyalty is not seen as an outdated or expendable virtue but as a fundamental pillar that supports long-term success and stability.

Although Shakespeare's *The Second Part of King Henry the Sixth* was written in 1591, its themes are more than relevant nowadays. The alignment between values, words, and actions by organization's members is crucial in creating, maintaining, and preserving a culture for long-term sustainable success. Loyalty can indeed be a harbor, providing a stable foundation upon which trust, commitment, and collective success can be built.

In McKinsey's 2022 Great Attrition research, employees identified three equally important factors—lack of caring leaders (35%), unsustainable work expectations (35%), and insufficient career development opportunities (35%)—as the most critical reasons for leaving their jobs. Leaders should focus on four primary strategies to create the human-centered experience that employees crave.

First, they should personalize relationships and avoid transactional interactions. Second, prioritizing social interactions is crucial. Third, providing room for growth is essential in today's dynamic labor market. Thus, employers must treat their employees as long-term assets, investing in their development and showing a clear career path within the organization. Lastly, creating sustainable working models is vital to address disengagement and burnout.

In 2021, Australian workplaces lost $17 billion due to absenteeism and mental health issues. In contrast, Italy is very different. In addition to dozens of national and municipal holidays, paid days-off for life events such as marriage, and a 13th-month salary for Christmas—standard benefits in Italy—the Lardini family, owners of the Lardini fashion house with hundreds of employees, believe that what they provide for themselves should also be provided for their employees. They see vacation not as a luxury, but as a necessity for everyone to relieve stress and maintain well-being. Importantly, these days off are fully paid by the company.

Employees at Lardini report they rarely get sick, attributing this to the low levels of stress supported by the company's approach to balance. One striking example is the daily two-hour lunch break, during which employees often return home to have lunch with their families—a practice deeply embedded in the company culture. Other Italian companies, such as Ducati Motor Holding echo this sentiment, insisting there is no contradiction between employee well-being and business profitability. Despite these generous policies, Italy consistently ranks among the top 20 most productive countries in terms of GDP per hour worked.

Of course, these practices exist within the context of Italy's unique culture and labor laws, which support a more human-centered approach to productivity. Still, the example of Lardini challenges the assumption that long hours and constant pressure are prerequisites for high performance.

While it is relatively easy for organizations to raise salaries and offer flexible schedules, the World Economic Forum has recognized that creating a purposeful and meaningful environment is the hardest challenge. Competitors willing to pay more for top talent compound the issue and some have equated it to transforming one company as the training ground of theirs. Although employees need a decent paycheck and value a flexible working model, many hunger for something more. One in five cited a lack of fulfillment as their reason for leaving their jobs. The antidote is the creation of an organizational cause and fostering a company culture where employees feel their work is meaningful, their contributions valued, and they experience a sense of belonging.

To create a cause is to answer the question *Why are we here?* and in answering it the key characteristic is simplicity because causes which resonate with organizational members are first communicated to them. When a cause is simple and tied to the core line of business of the company, one can more easily identify with it and the process of fostering loyalty begins.

Building this sense of meaning requires time and commitment, and opportunities for employees to feel valued. Remote work has made it harder to build a shared cause, but the rewards are immense—a rekindling of the bonds of loyalty. Wharton management professor Matthew Bidwell highlights the high costs associated with turnover, including recruitment, training, and lost productivity, which makes it essential for employers to invest in retaining their employees rather than paying attrition's high cost. Organizations need people who are committed to looking out for the organization's interests and doing the right thing, because if everybody is out for themselves, what will get done?

Brief Summary of Loyalty Definition

"All truths are easy to understand once they are discovered; the point is to discover them."

—Galileo Galilei

Our definition of loyalty is the willing, practical, and thoroughgoing dedication of a person to a cause in the presence of reciprocity and Asabiyyah. True loyalty involves a conscious, voluntary decision to dedicate oneself to a cause. This dedication is a recognition of one's alignment with its values and objectives and not merely an attraction to the cause. The process of loyalty begins with socialization, a planned process of introducing a person to the organizational culture, job position, and all of its details. Identification may begin even before socialization, when a person identifies similarities between their current values and some of the organization's values. The final process is internalization, where the person recognizes the practicality and value of organizational values, which were initially new to them, and these values become deeply ingrained, guiding all actions and decisions. If you want to foster loyalty, it is key to reciprocate loyalty, thus Loyalty to

Loyalty. To desire or demand loyalty from others without reciprocating it, is not practical and not sustainable.

Role of Reciprocity and Asabiyyah

Reciprocity, partly inspired by Confucius's Analects, is a foundational element of loyalty, characterized by mutual trust and support. It ensures that loyalty is not one-sided but a balanced and equitable relationship, where each party fulfills their role and supports the other. Asabiyyah, derived from Ibn Khaldun's work, refers to social cohesion and oneness within a group. It emphasizes the importance of acting as one, understanding and respecting each other, and fostering a sense of unity. This collective identity and mutual commitment are crucial for the long-term success and stability of any group, creating an environment where everyone feels valued and understood.

Importance of Behavioral Determinants

Behavioral determinants such as integrity, mutual respect, psychological safety, proactivity, and nurturing behavior play a crucial role in fostering and sustaining loyalty. Integrity ensures that loyalty is grounded in agreed-upon principles—doing what one has dedicated to and not deviating from it in a predictable business relationship. Mutual respect and psychological safety create an environment where loyalty can thrive, as individuals feel safe to express their opinion and feel valued. Direct communication and feeling part of the process are vital; they enhance transparency and ensure everyone is aligned with the cause. Proactivity and nurturing behavior actively support and sustain dedication to the cause, ensuring that loyalty is not passive but dynamic and ongoing.

The Cause

In essence, these behavioral determinants transform the organizational culture into one where loyalty to the cause is a natural outcome of everyday interactions and practices.

At the heart of any successful organization lies a compelling cause—a purpose that transcends day-to-day operations and inspires collective dedication. This cause is the guiding star that aligns the efforts, aspirations, and values of all members of the organization, creating a unified direction.

The cause acts as a cohesive force, bringing together diverse talents and perspectives into a harmonious effort towards common goals. It serves as a rallying point during times of change or challenge, offering a clear reminder of why the organization exists and what it strives to achieve. Ultimately, the cause is the lifeblood of the organization, infusing every aspect of its operations with purpose and passion.

Loyalty and Business

For even the most skeptical organizations, fostering loyalty is possible. It starts within you, the leader, by committing to the principles and practices outlined in this book. By creating a culture of integrity, mutual respect, psychological safety, proactivity, nurturing behavior, and shared values, leaders can inspire their teams and cultivate a loyal, dedicated workforce. This commitment to loyalty will drive performance, innovation, and long-term sustainability, ensuring that your organization remains competitive and successful in the future.

A key takeaway from this book is the critical role of organizational culture in fostering loyalty. Building a culture that promotes loyalty involves understanding the existing culture, defining desired behaviors, aligning structures and processes, and over-coming resistance. It requires a commitment from leadership to model the desired behaviors, communicate transparently, and support employees' growth and development. By doing so, orga-nizations can create a positive, predictable and productive work environment that attracts and retains top talent.

Success Stories from the Book

Phil Jackson

Phil Jackson's coaching philosophy with the Chicago Bulls and Los Angeles Lakers was deeply rooted in Zen principles and oneness which closely resembles the concept of Asabiyyah. By promoting mindfulness and collective responsibility, Jackson transformed teams of highly successful individuals into cohesive units. Under his leadership, players like Michael Jordan, Scottie Pippen, and Dennis Rodman for the Bulls, and Kobe Bryant and Shaquille O'Neal for the Lakers, transcended their individual talents to achieve collective greatness. Jackson's ability to manage the dynamics between such strong personalities, under the intense pressure of media scrutiny and public expectations together with social circles reminding the players that they are "the man", exem-plifies how fostering a sense of oneness and shared purpose can lead to sustained success. His cause was about creating a team ethos that emphasized harmony, mutual respect, and a singular focus on the collective goal and winning championships.

Tata Group

Tata Group, with a history spanning over 150 years, has consis-tently preserved its mission and vision, embodying the cause of improving the quality of life for the communities it serves. This foundational principle has guided the company's evolution and strategic objectives, ensuring that Tata remains committed to innovation, sustainability, and long-term business practices. The Tata Group's ability to maintain its core values while adapting to changing market conditions demonstrates how a long-standing mission can inspire loyalty and drive organizational success across generations. Tata's cause of community welfare and ethical excellence remains as relevant today as it was at its early years, reflecting a deep-rooted commitment to making a positive impact on society.

Ralph Lauren

Ralph Lauren's journey in fashion is driven by a cause that precedes commercial success—creating a lifestyle that embodies the American dream. His dedication to authenticity, quality, and attention to detail has made the Ralph Lauren brand a symbol of aspiration and inclusivity. By staying true to his vision and consistently delivering a recognizable style, his cause is recognizable and easily identifiable by those with similar values. The work environment and the organizational members have internalized the cause evident by their actions and words fuelled by passion and determination. This authenticity creates a meaning, a clear purpose for all stakeholders. Lauren's cause is reflected in every aspect of his brand, making it a powerful example of how a clear, consistent vision can drive long-term success.

Hubert Joly

Hubert Joly's leadership at Best Buy focused on placing people at the center of the corporate strategy. By prioritizing a culture of transparency and mutual respect, Joly transformed Best Buy into a thriving organization. His initiatives, such as the "Discover Your Purpose" program, helped employees align their personal aspirations with the company's mission, creating a sense of shared purpose. This reciprocal loyalty, where the company supports its employees and they, in turn, are motivated and proactive, underscores the importance of a people-centric approach. Joly's leadership practically demonstrates how clear communication of the cause and consistent support for employees can drive organizational success in a corporate business environment.

Cynthia Cooper

Cynthia Cooper's role in uncovering the WorldCom accounting fraud is a powerful example of integrity and dedication to core principles. Faced with significant pressure to ignore the discrepancies, Cooper initiated an internal investigation, driven by her unwavering commitment to corporate governance and dedication to her beloved company. Her actions prevented further damage to the company and restored trust in the organization. Cooper's integrity and courage in addressing the issues internally highlight the importance of principled leadership in maintaining loyalty in organizations and ensuring long-term sustainability. Her story emphasizes that even when some leaders stray from core principles, individuals committed to integrity can restore trust and secure the organization's future.

Lou Gerstner

Lou Gerstner's leadership at IBM demonstrates the transformative power of inclusive communication and cultural change. When Gerstner took over, IBM was struggling with internal silos and bureaucratic inertia. By engaging directly with employees and fostering a sense of collective purpose, he dismantled these barriers and created a unified vision for the company's future. Gerstner's hands-on approach, which included regular town halls and direct feedback sessions, ensured that employees felt included in the change process. Internal communication was improved and a culture of oneness and mutual support was fostered. Gerstner's ability to instill the underlying elements of Asabiyyah in a large international corporation proves that creating a unified and cohesive team is possible.

Anne Mulcahy

Anne Mulcahy's leadership during Xerox's financial crisis showcased the power of proactive leadership and transparent communication. Upon assuming the role of CEO, Mulcahy focused on understanding the challenges faced by employees, traveling extensively to gather insights and foster direct communication of the company's direction. Her straightforward approach, which emphasized honesty and clear expectations, reassured and united employees. By addressing the company's issues openly and involving employees in the turnaround strategy, Mulcahy built a cohesive and dedicated team. Her leadership highlights that proactive measures, combined with transparency and genuine engagement, can restore confidence and drive organizational success

Jim Goodnight

Jim Goodnight's leadership at SAS Institute is a testament to the impact of a nurturing work environment on fostering loyalty. Goodnight's belief that employees are a company's most valuable asset led to the creation of an environment where employees feel secure, valued, and supported. SAS offers extensive benefits, but it is the management's attitude and behavior towards the organizational members that contributes more to the low turnover rates and the organization's productivity. The benefits are a consequence of the said attitude. Goodnight's no-layoff policy during economic downturns reinforced trust and loyalty among employees. His

---

leadership style, which emphasizes standing by stated principles, essentially your word, and creating a supportive culture, fosters reciprocal loyalty, where employees are motivated to contribute their best to the organization. This approach demonstrates that a culture of mutual respect and shared values can drive innovation and long-term success.

Today's Quest and Actions

In today's competitive and rapidly evolving market, businesses face unprecedented challenges in attracting and retaining top talent. The COVID-19 pandemic has reshaped employees' priorities as they have experienced what it is like to commute less and spend more time with their loved ones, emphasizing the importance of family time and work-life balance. Generational differences have increased as priorities both in personal and professional lives have changed for a significant majority of the people in highly industrialized economies. Simultaneously, the competition for skilled personnel has intensified, with more companies vying for the same talent pool. In this context, building a company culture that promotes loyalty is both a strategic advantage and a necessity for long-term success.

The quest for meaningful work has intensified. Due to the said shifts in views, the perceived sense of security and the greater choice of workplaces, employees today seek more than just a paycheck. They want to be part of an organization with a clear purpose and values that resonate with their own. This calls for a renewed focus on corporate purpose, vision, and values visualised in practise not just on the wall. Companies need to articulate their mission and vision in a way that connects with employees on a personal level, fostering a sense of pride and ownership in their work. By aligning organizational goals with the personal values of their workforce, businesses can deepen the emotional engagement of their employees, thereby enhancing internalization and loyalty.

In this new landscape, leadership is paramount. Leaders have to model the desired behaviors and values, embodying the principles of integrity, mutual respect, and psychological safety. Transparent communication from leaders about the organization's direction, challenges, and successes helps build trust and fosters a sense of inclusion (being informed and as a consequence predictability in the workplace). When leaders are accessible and empathetic, they can better understand and address the concerns and aspirations of their teams, reinforcing a culture of loyalty.

Creating a culture that prioritizes loyalty involves fostering a sense of community and connection among employees, particularly in a remote or hybrid work environment. Regular team-building activities, virtual coffee chats, and collaborative projects can help maintain strong interpersonal relationships and a sense of belonging, even when employees are physically dispersed. Technology plays a crucial role in facilitating these connections, enabling seamless communication and collaboration across different locations and time zones.

As organizations navigate this new era, it is essential to continuously measure and evaluate the impact of their cultural initiatives. Tools like the Loyalty Quotient to Loyalty® can provide valuable insights into the levels of loyalty within the organization and highlight areas for improvement. By regularly assessing the effectiveness of cultural practices and making necessary adjustments, companies can ensure that they remain responsive to the needs of their employees and aligned with their strategic objectives.

The Aleksiev Group through its web application, Artapava, offers a tool set of diagnostics about Leadership Self-Awareness®, Team Intelligence Model®, and the Loyalty Quotient to Loyalty®. The name Artapava is inspired by the Vedic traditions with Rta referring to the cosmic order (rhythm), Pava to Pavamana – purification or cleansing, and A for Aleksiev. The goal is to improve clarity and business practises as pavamana mantra says:

> From falsehood lead me to truth,

> From darkness lead me to light,

> From death lead me to immortality.

After years of research, we have developed the Loyalty Quotient to Loyalty® 2.0 which builds on the previous version with improved wordage and reports to simultaneously facilitate a better understanding of the questionnaire and the meaning of the results in the reports. More actionable insights are added which can be implemented into the decision-making process and the targeted strategies. With the number of clients from different industries increasing and the ability to have anonymized longitudinal research based on the raw data, we have improved the metrics and the models behind the questionnaire.

What to Expect Next?

The Team Intelligence Model® (TIM) is a thoroughly new concept developed over the past 30 years and now it is fully available for all teams around the world. The model and its quotient measure the team's ability and potential to function synergistically and achieve sustained success in a changing environment. It values the team's collective ability to combine individual skills, knowledge and experience in a creative process that leads to excellence and solutions that exceed the capabilities of individual members.

TIM is based on eight key elements of development: Choice, North Star, Trust, Purpose, Commitment, Accomplishment, Selfless Union and Evolution. Each of these elements is linked to specific indicators that assess different aspects of team dynamics and interaction.

In our quest to develop the concept of Team Intelligence Model® for how teams can grow and achieve sustainable success, we found that the model we developed (based on our knowledge of psychology, engineering, organizational development and behavior, military science, history, political science, behavioral economics, people management and leadership together with our on ground experience - as business consultants, in building, diagnosing and developing teams and organizations) connections can be found with the Pythagorean teaching, the Musical Octave, the Hermetic principles and the model Be-Do-Have.

Although Pythagorean ideas and hermetic principles are ancient, they continue to find application in modern scientific and technological research, such as quantum physics and the study of vibration and resonance. This shows that the deep connections between mathematics, music and cosmic laws continue to be relevant and provide valuable insights into the structure of reality. The connections between numbers, hermetic principles, and the musical octave have a metaphorical and symbolic value that transcends rigorous scientific evidence. They can be used as tools to better understand the world and stimulate creative thinking.

The Team Intelligence Model® is a validated model and tool developed by Ivaylo Aleksiev. The research is based on nearly 30 years and field experience (teams, both in the military and on combat missions and in business organizations) that support team effectiveness and efficiency. The generated report explains every element, each's four characteristics and respective measurements thoroughly, and offers practical tools for improvement, which can be utilized by you. The report you receive is 45 pages of explanatory insights, your results, and actionable tools. Quantitative representation enables a qualitative perspective, which is a platform for discussion among team members, how to use their strengths and provoke development decisions.

Just as the dancers' competence in moving in unison determines the grace of their performance, so your team's ability to collaborate determines its team intelligence and performance. Our diagnostics illuminate different aspects of your team – degree of unison, collaboration, points of vulnerability, ways to foster an environment of trust and understanding – creating a dance of efficiency and creativity. In this dance, loyalty is the rhythm that synchronizes the movements, ensuring that each step is taken with trust and mutual respect, leading to a harmonious and high-performing team.

As you conclude this book, reflect on the principles and practices discussed and consider how they can be applied within your organization. Engage your team in conversations about loyalty, listen to their feedback, and take actionable steps to create a supportive and loyal work environment. Remember, fostering loyalty starts with you and can transform your organization into a thriving, resilient entity ready to face the challenges of tomorrow and become your legacy for the future.

The loyalty you cultivate today will become the cornerstone of your organization's success, fostering a culture of trust, innovation, and sustained performance. May your efforts to foster loyalty transform your organization into one, where every member feels valued, respected, and dedicated to a common cause.

In closing, my wish for you is to see your organization flourish, built on the bedrock of loyalty and dedication. May the principles and practices discussed in this book guide you towards creating an environment where every team member feels a sense of belonging and purpose. Thank you for embarking on this journey!

References

PART ONE

- Mayer, J. D., Salovey, P., & Caruso, D. R. (2004). Emotional intelligence: Theory, findings, and implications. *Psychological Inquiry, 15*(3), 197-215. https://doi.org/10.1207/s15327965pli1 503_02

SECOND PART

Aristotle:

- Aristotle. "Nicomachean Ethics." Translated by W.D. Ross. The Internet Classics Archive. Web Atomics.

- Aristotle. "Politics." Translated by Benjamin Jowett. The Internet Classics Archive. Web Atomics.

- Kraut, Richard. "Aristotle's Ethics." The Stanford Encyclopedia of Philosophy, Fall 2018 Edition, edited by Edward N. Zalta.

- Miller, Fred D. "Aristotle's Political Theory." The Stanford Encyclopedia of Philosophy, Winter 2017 Edition, edited by Edward N. Zalta.

Ibn Khaldun:

- Khaldun, I. (2005). The Muqaddimah: An introduction to history (F. Rosenthal, Trans.; N. J. Dawood, Ed.). Princeton University Press.

- Rosenthal, E. I. J. (1968). State and government in medieval Islam. In Political thought in medieval Islam: An introductory outline (pp. [specific pages]). Cambridge University Press.

- Lambton, A. K. S. (1981). The jurists. In State and government in medieval Islam: An introduction to the study of Islamic political theory (pp. [specific pages]). Oxford University Press.

- CBC Radio. (2021, June 28). Beware of bitter oranges: Modern lessons from a medieval thinker. Retrieved from https://www.cbc.ca/radio/ideas/beware-of-bitter-oranges-modern-lessons-from-a-medieval-thinker-1.6078888

- Demir, S. (2014). Ibn Khaldun's Asabiyya for social cohesion. Elektronik Sosyal Bilimler Dergisi, 13(51), 45-57. Retrieved from https://www.researchgate.net/publication/269992084_Elektronik_Sosyal_Bilimler_Dergisi_IBN_KHALDUN%27S_ASABIYYA_FOR_SOCIAL_COHESION

- Bartlett, B. (2012). The Laffer Curve, Part 2. *Tax Notes*, 136(10).

Confucius:

- IvyPanda. (2020, May 17). Confucianism and government: Chinese political system. Retrieved from https://ivypanda.com/essays/confucianism-and-government-chinese-political-system/

- Smithsonian Institution. (n.d.). Han dynasty. Retrieved from https://asia.si.edu/learn/for-educators/teaching-china-with-the-smithsonian/explore-by-dynasty/han-dynasty/

- Stanford Encyclopedia of Philosophy. (2017, March 15). Confucius. Retrieved from https://plato.stanford.edu/entries/confucius/

- Confucius. (1979). The Analects (Lunyu). (D. C. Lau, Trans.). Penguin Classics.

- Eno, R. (2015). The Analects of Confucius. Retrieved from https://scholarworks.iu.edu/dspace/bitstream/handle/2022/23420/Analects_of_Confucius_%28Eno-2015%29-updated.pdf?sequence=2

Japan's Shinise Companies and Their Longevity:

- I Done This Support. (2014). 3 lessons on business longevity from the oldest company in the world. I Done This. Retrieved from http://blog.idonethis.com/oldest-company-in-the-world/

- Lufkin, B. (2020). Why so many of the world's oldest companies are in Japan. BBC. Retrieved from https://www.bbc.com/worklife/article/20200211-why-are-so-many-old-companies-in-japan/%20target=

- Gren, C. (2020). Keeping it in the family: Japan's oldest companies have survived for 1000 years. Industry Leaders Magazine. Retrieved from https://www.industryleadersmagazine.com/keeping-it-in-the-family-japans-oldest-companies-have-survived-for-1000-years/

- Gren, C. (2022). World's oldest: How culture shaped Japanese companies. Industry Leaders Magazine. Retrieved from https://www.industryleadersmagazine.com/the-worlds-oldest-how-culture-shaped-japanese-companies/

- The Life Motivation. (n.d.). Want your business to last over 300 years? Learn from Japanese shinise companies. The Life Motivation. Retrieved from https://thelifemotivation.com/want-your-business-to-last-for-more-than-300-years-learn-from-japanese-shinise-companies/

- Encyclopædia Britannica. (n.d.). Second law of thermodynamics. Encyclopædia Britannica. Retrieved from https://www.britannica.com/science/second-law-of-thermodynamics

- Premier Family Business Consulting. (2021). Family firm longevity with Professor Toshio Goto. Premier Family Business Consulting. Retrieved from https://premierfamilybusiness.com/family-firm-longevity-with-professor-toshio-goto/

- Bandura, U. (1976) Empire of Three Brilliants. Partizdant.

- Mitsubishi. (n.d.). History outline. Mitsubishi. Retrieved from https://www.mitsubishi.com/en/profile/history/outline/

- Mitsubishi Corporation. (n.d.). Company guide. Mitsubishi Corporation. Retrieved from https://www.mitsubishicorp.com/jp/en/about/cguide/pdf/01.pdf

- Yamamotoyama. (n.d.). Company profile. Yamamotoyama. Retrieved from https://www.yamamotoyama.co.jp/about_en.html#link04

- Garelli, S. (2016, December). Why you will probably live longer than most big companies. IMD. Retrieved from https://www.imd.org/research-knowledge/articles/why-you-will-probably-live-longer-than-most-big-companies/

- Stanford Graduate School of Business. (2020). Secrets to corporate longevity. Retrieved from https://www.gsb.stanford.edu/insights/secrets-corporate-longevity

- Demir, S. (2020). Family business - Sustainability model. ResearchGate. Retrieved from https://www.researchgate.net/publication/341806627_Family_Business_-_Sustainability_Model [Accessed April 26, 2023].

- The Business Standard. (2020, August 16). Japanese mantra: Firms survive crises, last centuries. Retrieved from https://www.tbsnews.net/feature/panorama/japanese-mantra-firms-survive-crises-last-centuries-120862

Loyalty and Management:

- Schaufeli, W. B., & Salanova, M. (2011). Work engagement: On how to better catch a slippery concept. European Journal of Work and Organizational Psychology, 20(1), 39-46. DOI: 10.1080/1359432X.2010.515981.

- Schaufeli, W. B., & Bakker, A. B. (2010). Work engagement: A handbook of essential theory and research. Psychology Press.

- Mael, F., & Ashforth, B. E. (1989). Social Identity Theory and the Organization. Academy of Management Review, 14(1), 20-39.

- Schrag, C. O. (2001). The Self After Postmodernity. Yale University Press.

- Organ, D. W. (1988). Organizational citizenship behavior: The good soldier syndrome. Lexington Books.

- Gulati, R. (2012, November). The management century. Harvard Business Review. Retrieved from https://hbr.org/2012/11/the-management-century

- Great Managers. (n.d.). Where it all began: The origin of management theory. Retrieved from https://www.greatmanagers.com.au/management-theory-origin/

- Verywell Mind. (2021, June 22). Theories of intelligence. Retrieved from https://www.verywellmind.com/theories-of-intelligence-2795035

- HRZone. (n.d.). History of employee engagement: From satisfaction to sustainability. Retrieved from https://www.hrzone.com/engage/employees/history-of-employee-engagement-from-satisfaction-to-sustainability

- Gardner, H. (1983). Frames of mind: The theory of multiple intelligences. Basic Books.

- Gardner, H. (1993). Multiple intelligences: The theory in practice. Basic Books.

- APA PsycNet. (2020). Social knowledge and interpersonal interaction. Retrieved from https://psycnet.apa.org/record/2020-10981-031

- Drucker, P. F. (2008). Management by objectives and self-control. In Management: Tasks, responsibilities, practices (pp. 125-132). Routledge. Retrieved from https://www.taylor-francis.com/chapters/mono/10.4324/9780080939322-8/management-objectives-self-control-peter-drucker

Royce:

- Royce, J. (1908). The philosophy of loyalty. The Macmillan Company.

Collins:

- Collins, J. (2001). *Good to great: Why some companies make the leap... and others don't.* HarperBusiness.

Fraud:

- Association of Certified Fraud Examiners (2018) Fraud Examiners Manual: 2018 International Edition. ACFE.

THIRD PART

Socialization:

- Van Maanen, J., & Schein, E. H. (1979). Toward a theory of organizational socialization. Research in Organizational Behavior, 1, 209-264.

- Katz, D. (1980). Socializing academic and industrial scientists. Administrative Science Quarterly, 23(3), 404-423.

- Ashforth, B.E., & Mael, F. (1989). Social identity theory and the organization. Academy of Management Review, 14(1), 20-39.

- Bauer, T.N., Bodner, T., Erdogan, B., Truxillo, D.M., & Tucker, J.S. (2007). Newcomer adjustment during organizational socialization: A meta-analytic review of antecedents, outcomes, and methods. Journal of Applied Psychology, 92(3), 707-721.

- Kelman, H. C. (1958). Compliance, identification, and internalization: Three processes of attitude change. Journal of Conflict Resolution, 2(1), 51-60.

- McDavid, J. W., & Harari, H. (1974). Psychology and social behavior. Harper & Row.

- Thibaut, J. W., & Kelley, H. H. (1959). The social psychology of groups. John Wiley & Sons.

- Saks, M. J., & Krupat, E. (1988). Social psychology and its applications. Harper & Row.

- Leontiev, A. N. (1973). Activity, consciousness, and personality. Prentice-Hall.

- Piaget, J. (1970). Structuralism (C. Maschler, Trans.). Basic Books.

- Csikszentmihalyi, M. (1990). Flow: The psychology of optimal experience. Harper & Row.

- Andreeva, L. (1999). Social knowledge and interpersonal interaction (2nd ed.). Lik Publishing.

- Zhonev, S. (1996). Social psychology II. Sofi-R Publishing

- Zhonev, S. (1996). Social psychology III. Sofi-R Publishing.

- Clauss, G., et al. (1985). Wörterbuch der Psychologie. VEB Bibliographisches Institut Leipzig.

IBM:

- Gerstner, L. (2002). Who says elephants can't dance? Leading a great enterprise through dramatic change. HarperBusiness.

- Lagace, M. (2002, December 9). Gerstner: Changing culture at IBM - Lou Gerstner discusses changing the culture at IBM.

Harvard Business School Working Knowledge### Grouping of Citations Based on Table of Contents

Identification:

- Ashforth, B. E., & Mael, F. (1989). Social identity theory and the organization. Academy of Management Review, 14(1), 20-39.

- Deci, E. L., & Ryan, R. M. (1985). Intrinsic motivation and self-determination in human behavior. Plenum.

- Deci, E. L., & Ryan, R. M. (2000). The "what" and "why" of goal pursuits: Human needs and the self-determination of behavior. Psychological Inquiry, 11(4), 227-268.

- Meyer, J. P., & Allen, N. J. (1991). A three-component conceptualization of organizational commitment. Human Resource Management Review, 1(1), 61-89.

- Ryan, R. M., & Deci, E. L. (2000). Self-determination theory and the facilitation of intrinsic motivation, social development, and well-being. American Psychologist, 55(1), 68-78.

- Shamir, B., House, R. J., & Arthur, M. B. (1993). The motivational effects of charismatic leadership: A self-concept based theory. Organization Science, 4(4), 577-594.

- Tajfel, H., & Turner, J. C. (1979). An integrative theory of intergroup conflict. In W. G. Austin & S. Worchel (Eds.), The social psychology of intergroup relations (pp. 33-47). Brooks/Cole.

Internalization:

- Schafer, R. (1968). Aspects of internalization. International Universities Press.

- Kelman, H. C. (1958). Compliance, identification, and internalization: Three processes of attitude change. Journal of Conflict Resolution, 2(1), 51-60.

Definition of Loyalty:

- Schrag, B. (2001). The moral significance of employee loyalty. Business Ethics Quarterly, 11(1), 41-66.

- Merriam-Webster. (n.d.). Dedication. Retrieved from https://www.merriam-webster.com/dictionary/dedication

- Online Etymology Dictionary. (n.d.). Dedication. Retrieved from https://www.etymonline.com/word/dedication

- Oxford Learner's Dictionaries. (n.d.). Dedication. Retrieved from https://www.oxfordlearnersdictionaries.com/definition/american_english/dedication

- Royce, J. (1908). The philosophy of loyalty. The Macmillan Company.

- Khaldun, I. (2005). The Muqaddimah: An introduction to history (F. Rosenthal, Trans.; N. J. Dawood, Ed.). Princeton University Press.

A Cause:

- Frankl, V. E. (2006). Man's search for meaning. Beacon Press. (Original work published 1946)

Tata Group:

- Tata Group. (n.d.). *Our Heritage.* Retrieved from https://www.tata.com/about-us/tata-group-heritage

- Tata Group. (n.d.). *Our Mission and Vision.* Retrieved from https://www.tata.com/about-us/mission-vision

- Tata Group. (n.d.). *Leadership with Trust.* Retrieved from https://www.tata.com/about-us/leadership-with-trust

- Tata Group. (n.d.). *Sustainability.* Retrieved from https://www.tata.com/business/sustainability

- Britannica. (2024). Tata Group. Retrieved from https://www.britannica.com/money/Tata-Group

- StartupCityIndia. (2024). An In-Depth Exploration of Tata Group's History, Companies, and Values. Retrieved from https://www.startupcityindia.com/blogs/an-in-depth-exploration-of-tata-groups-history-companies-and-values

Ralph Lauren's:

- Lauren, R. (2019). *Ralph Lauren: In His Own Fashion.* Abrams.

- HBO. (2019). Very Ralph [Film]. Home Box Office. Retrieved from https://www.hbo.com/movies/very-ralph

Hubert Joly:

- Joly, H. (2021). The heart of business: Leadership principles for the next era of capitalism. Harvard Business Review Press.

Reciprocity:

- Biron, M. (n.d.). Negative reciprocity and the association between. Retrieved from https://www.semanticscholar.org/paper/Negative-reciprocity-and-the-association-between-Biron/e93a39fe0ce1e2fd4b403d1362e05408e063f819/figure/0

- Wang, S., Song, M., & Zhong, L. (2022). Unethical reciprocity. Journal of Management. Retrieved from https://scholars.cityu.edu.hk/files/124668851/Wang_Song_Zhong_JOM_2022_Unethical_reciprocity.pdf

- Negative reciprocity and the association between. (n.d.). Semantic Scholar. Retrieved from https://www.semanticscholar.org/paper/Negative-reciprocity-and-the-association-between-Biron/e93a39fe0ce1e2fd4b403d1362e05408e063f819/figure/0

Flavius Belisarius:

- Mark, J. J. (2019, September 20). Belisarius. World History Encyclopedia. Retrieved from https://www.worldhistory.org/Belisarius/

- Wikipedia. (n.d.). Belisarius. Retrieved from https://en.wikipedia.org/wiki/Belisarius

- Natsinas, K. (2024, January 31). Belisarius: The great commander of the Byzantine Empire. Greek Reporter. Retrieved from https://greekreporter.com/2024/01/31/belisarius-commander-byzantine-empire/

- Barber, M. (2016, September 26). Belisarius: The powerful general of the Byzantine Empire. Ancient Origins. Retrieved from https://www.ancient-origins.net/history-famous-people/belisarius-powerful-general-byzantine-empire-003870

The Cheesecake Factory:

- Halkias, T. (2023, January 26). The Cheesecake Factory focuses on employees. FSR Magazine. Retrieved from https://www.

fsrmagazine.com/feature/cheesecake-factory-puts-focus-employees/

- Weinberger, M. (2017, June 30). Cheesecake Factory's CEO: To have happier employees, do these 3 things. CNBC. Retrieved from https://www.cnbc.com/2017/06/30/cheesecake-factorys-ceo-to-have-happier-employees-do-these-3-things.html

- Mason, L. (2021, November 4). Cheesecake Factory cooks up a rigorous employee training program. Workforce. Retrieved from https://workforce.com/news/cheesecake-factory-cooks-up-a-rigorous-employee-training-program

- Yahoo Finance. (2021, August 30). Cheesecake Factory named to PEOPLE Companies that Care list. Retrieved from https://finance.yahoo.com/news/cheesecake-factory-named-people-companies-205800572.html

- BrightTALK. (2021, June 15). Creating a culture of learning at The Cheesecake Factory. Retrieved from https://www.brighttalk.com/webcast/18728/487614

- Franek, R. (2022, March 25). The surprising way Cheesecake Factory waiters learn the menu. Mashed. Retrieved from https://www.mashed.com/796822/the-surprising-way-cheesecake-factory-waiters-learn-the-menu/

Asabiyyah:

- Demir, S. (2014). Ibn Khaldun's Asabiyya for social cohesion. Elektronik Sosyal Bilimler Dergisi, 13(51), 45-57. Retrieved from https://www.researchgate.net/publication/269992084_Elektronik_Sosyal_Bilimler_Dergisi_IBN_KHALDUN%27S_ASABIYYA_FOR_SOCIAL_COHESION

- Khaldun, I. (2005). The Muqaddimah: An introduction to history (F. Rosenthal, Trans.; N. J. Dawood, Ed.). Princeton University Press.

- Rosenthal, E. I. J. (1968). State and government in medieval Islam. In Political thought in medieval Islam: An introductory outline (pp. [specific pages]). Cambridge University Press.

- Lambton, A. K. S. (1981). The jurists. In State and government in medieval Islam: An introduction to the study of Islamic political theory (pp. [specific pages]). Oxford University Press.

- CBC Radio. (2021, June 28). Beware of bitter oranges: Modern lessons from a medieval thinker. Retrieved from https://www.cbc.ca/radio/ideas/beware-of-bitter-oranges-modern-lessons-from-a-medieval-thinker-1.6078888

- Demir, S. (2014). Ibn Khaldun's Asabiyya for social cohesion. Elektronik Sosyal Bilimler Dergisi, 13(51), 45-57. Retrieved from https://www.researchgate.net/publication/269992084_Elektronik_Sosyal_Bilimler_Dergisi_IBN_KHALDUN%27S_ASABIYYA_FOR_SOCIAL_COHESION

HP and Carly Fiorina:

- Hall, A. (2023, August 24). Carly Fiorina's impact at HP: Bold leadership and controversial decisions. Retrieved from https://aaronhall.com/insights/carly-fiorinas-impact-at-hp-bold-leadership-and-controversial-decisions/

- Harvard Business Review. (2015, September). Carly Fiorina's legacy as CEO of Hewlett-Packard. Retrieved from https://hbr.org/2015/09/carly-fiorinas-legacy-as-ceo-of-hewlett-packard

- Fiorina, C. (2007). Tough choices: A memoir. Penguin Books.

- Stein, J. (2015, May 4). Carly Fiorina's tenure: What really happened at HP. Time. Retrieved from https://time.com/3845767/carly-fiorina-hp/

- Johnson, C. E. (2008). The rise and fall of Carly Fiorina: An ethical case study.

IBM and Lou Gerstner:

- Gerstner, L. (2002). Who says elephants can't dance? Leading a great enterprise through dramatic change. HarperBusiness.

- Lagace, M. (2002, December 9). Gerstner: Changing culture at IBM - Lou Gerstner discusses changing the culture at IBM. Harvard Business School Working Knowledge. Retrieved from https://hbswk.hbs.edu/archive/gerstner-changing-culture-at-ibm-lou-gerstner-discusses-changing-the-culture-at-ibm

PART FOUR

Integrity:

- Stevenson, H. H., Cruikshank, J. L., & Mihnea, C. (1998). Do lunch or be lunch: The power of predictability in creating your future. Harvard Business Press.

The Space Shuttle Challenger:

- Rossow, M. (2012) Engineering ethics case study: The Challenger disaster. Continuing *education and development, Inc.*

- Kahneman, D. (2003). A perspective on judgment and choice: Mapping bounded rationality. American Psychologist, 58(9), 697-720

WorldCom and Cynthia Cooper:

- Cooper, C. (2008). Extraordinary circumstances: The journey of a corporate whistleblower. John Wiley & Sons.

- CFO.com. (2023, February 13). WorldCom whistle-blower Cynthia Cooper. Retrieved from https://www.cfo.com/news/worldcom-whistle-blower-cynthia-cooper/673026/

- Carozza, D. (2008, March/April). Extraordinary circumstances: An interview with Cynthia Cooper. Fraud Magazine. Retrieved from https://www.fraud-magazine.com/article.aspx?id=210

Mutual Respect:

- Porath, C. (2018, July 25). Do your employees feel respected? Harvard Business Review. Retrieved from https://hbr.org/2018/07/do-your-employees-feel-respected

- Porath, C., & Pearson, C. (2013, January). The price of incivility. Harvard Business Review. Retrieved from https://hbr.org/2013/01/the-price-of-incivility

- Ascopubs. (n.d.). [Title of the article]. Retrieved from https://ascopubs.org/doi/10.1200/EDBK_249529

- Indeed. (n.d.). Mutual respect with employees. Retrieved from https://www.indeed.com/hire/c/info/mutual-respect-with-employees

Geert Hofstede:

- Hofstede, G. (1991). Cultures and organizations: Software of the mind. McGraw-Hill.

Alcibiades:

- Cartwright, M. (2013, February 8). Alcibiades. World History Encyclopedia. Retrieved from https://www.worldhistory.org/Alcibiades/

- Josho. (2021, February 19). Alcibiades: A controversial Athenian general. Ancient Origins. Retrieved from https://

Zappos:

- Rossi, J. (2020, December 3). How Tony Hsieh built Zappos—in his own words. Forbes. Retrieved from https://www.forbes.com/sites/jimrossi/2020/12/03/how-tony-hsieh-built-zapposin-his-own-words/

- CLS Blue Sky Blog. (2016, August 8). Culture and conduct: Beyond regulation and compliance. Retrieved from https://clsbluesky.law.columbia.edu/2016/08/08/culture-and-conduct-beyond-regulation-and-compliance/?noamp=mobile#comments

Psychological Safety:

- Newport Institute. (2024). What Is Psychological Safety? Retrieved from https://www.newportinstitute.com/resources/psychological-safety

- PagerDuty. (2024). The Role of Psychological Safety in Incident Response. Retrieved from https://www.pagerduty.com

- Rogers, C. R. (1951). Client-Centered Therapy: Its Current Practice, Implications, and Theory. Houghton Mifflin.

- Rogers, C. R. (1961). On Becoming a Person: A Therapist's View of Psychotherapy. Houghton Mifflin.

- LeaderFactor. (2024). Google and Psychological Safety. Retrieved from LeaderFactor.

- TechTarget. (2024). Google Project Aristotle - 5 Keys to Team Success. Retrieved from TechTarget.

- Positive Psychology. (2024). Psychological Safety & Positive Psychology: A Leadership Guide. Retrieved from Positive Psychology.

- Allspaw, J. (2013). *Learning from Failure at Etsy*. Retrieved from https://www.kitchensoap.com/2013/09/30/learning-from-failure-at-etsy/

Proactivity:

- Reference for Business. (n.d.). Mulcahy, Anne M. 1952—. Retrieved from https://www.referenceforbusiness.com/biography/M-R/Mulcahy-Anne-M-1952.html

- Vollmer, L. (2004, December 1). Anne Mulcahy: The keys to Xerox turnaround. Stanford Graduate School of Business. Retrieved from https://www.gsb.stanford.edu/insights/anne-mulcahy-keys-turnaround-xerox

- Knowledge@Wharton. (2018, May 29). The cow in the ditch: How Anne Mulcahy rescued Xerox. Retrieved from https://knowledge.wharton.upenn.edu/article/the-cow-in-the-ditch-how-anne-mulcahy-rescued-xerox/

- Moorhead, P. (2019, May 2). AMD's 50th anniversary reminds us why the company matters. Moor Insights & Strategy. Retrieved from https://moorinsightsstrategy.com/amds-50th-anniversary-reminds-us-why-the-company-matters/

- TechSpot. (2022, June 21). AMD: The rise, fall, and revival of a tech giant. Retrieved from https://www.techspot.com/article/2043-amd-rise-fall-revival-history/

- Company Histories. (n.d.). Advanced Micro Devices, Inc. - Company history. Retrieved from https://www.company-histories.com/Advanced-Micro-Devices-Inc-Company-History.html

- Kanellos, M. (2011, November 7). Where AMD failed. Forbes. Retrieved from https://www.forbes.com/sites/michaelkanellos/2011/11/07/where-amd-failed/

- Organizational Physics. (2013, April 25). A scathing portrait of the innovator leadership style at AMD. Retrieved from https://organizationalphysics.com/2013/04/25/a-scathing-portrait-of-the-innovator-leadership-style-at-amd/

- Forbes. (2001, February 14). How AMD beat Intel to 64 bits and Intel rebounded. Retrieved from https://www.forbes.com/2001/02/14/0214amd.html

- Newcomer, E. (2022, November 22). How AMD became a chip giant and leapfrogged Intel after playing catch-up. CNBC. Retrieved from https://www.cnbc.com/2022/11/22/how-amd-became-a-chip-giant-leapfrogged-intel-after-playing-catch-up.html

- Lee, T. B. (2020, March 27). Lisa Su's bold bet on AMD's future. CNN. Retrieved from https://edition.cnn.com/2020/03/27/tech/lisa-su-amd-risk-takers/index.html

- Hachman, M. (2020, March 27). End of an era as AMD's Sanders steps aside. CNET. Retrieved from https://www.cnet.com/tech/tech-industry/end-of-era-as-amds-sanders-steps-aside/

- TechSpot. (2015, January 24). AMD: The rise and fall (page 3). Retrieved from https://www.techspot.com/article/599-amd-rise-and-fall/page3.html

- La Pedrosa, M. (1988, December 5). End of an era as AMD's Sanders steps aside. Los Angeles Times. Retrieved from https://www.latimes.com/archives/la-xpm-1988-12-05-fi-622-story.html

- Caulfield, B. (2012, February 22). How AMD beat Intel to 64 bits and Intel rebounded. Forbes. Retrieved from https://www.forbes.com/sites/briancaulfield/2012/02/22/how-amd-beat-intel-to-64-bits-and-intel-bounced-back/

Schaufeli:

- Schaufeli, W. B. (n.d.). Tests. Retrieved from https://www.wilmarschaufeli.nl/my-publications/tests/

- Schaufeli, W. B. (n.d.). [PDF document]. Retrieved from https://www.wilmarschaufeli.nl/publications/Schaufeli/390.pdf

- Dewe, P. J., & Guest, D. E. (1990). Methods of coping with stress at work: A conceptual analysis and empirical study. Journal of Management Studies, 27(4), 367-385. Retrieved from https://www.jstor.org/stable/256287

- Schaufeli, W. B., & Bakker, A. B. (2010). Work engagement: A handbook of essential theory and research. Psychology Press.

Xerox and Anne Mulcahy:

- Reference for Business. (n.d.). Mulcahy, Anne M. 1952—. Retrieved from https://www.referenceforbusiness.com/biography/M-R/Mulcahy-Anne-M-1952.html

- Vollmer, L. (2004, December 1). Anne Mulcahy: The keys to Xerox turnaround. Stanford Graduate School of Business. Retrieved from https://www.gsb.stanford.edu/insights/anne-mulcahy-keys-turnaround-xerox

- Knowledge@Wharton. (2018, May 29). The cow in the ditch: How Anne Mulcahy rescued Xerox. Retrieved from https://knowledge.wharton.upenn.edu/article/the-cow-in-the-ditch-how-anne-mulcahy-rescued-xerox/

AMD and Jerry Sanders:

- Moorhead, P. (2019, May 2). AMD's 50th anniversary reminds us why the company matters. Moor Insights & Strategy. Retrieved from https://moorinsightsstrategy.com/amds-50th-anniversary-reminds-us-why-the-company-matters/

- TechSpot. (2022, June 21). AMD: The rise, fall, and revival of a tech giant. Retrieved from https://www.techspot.com/article/2043-amd-rise-fall-revival-history/

- Company Histories. (n.d.). Advanced Micro Devices, Inc. - Company history. Retrieved from https://www.company-histories.com/Advanced-Micro-Devices-Inc-Company-History.html

- Kanellos, M. (2011, November 7). Where AMD failed. Forbes. Retrieved from https://www.forbes.com/sites/michaelkanellos/2011/11/07/where-amd-failed/

- Organizational Physics. (2013, April 25). A scathing portrait of the innovator leadership style at AMD. Retrieved from https://organizationalphysics.com/2013/04/25/a-scathing-portrait-of-the-innovator-leadership-style-at-amd/

- Forbes. (2001, February 14). How AMD beat Intel to 64 bits and Intel rebounded. Retrieved from https://www.forbes.com/2001/02/14/0214amd.html

- Newcomer, E. (2022, November 22). How AMD became a chip giant and leapfrogged Intel after playing catch-up. CNBC. Retrieved from https://www.cnbc.com/2022/11/22/how-amd-became-a-chip-giant-leapfrogged-intel-after-playing-catch-up.html

- Lee, T. B. (2020, March 27). Lisa Su's bold bet on AMD's future. CNN. Retrieved from https://edition.cnn.com/2020/03/27/tech/lisa-su-amd-risk-takers/index.html

- Hachman, M. (2020, March 27). End of an era as AMD's Sanders steps aside. CNET. Retrieved from https://www.cnet.com/tech/tech-industry/end-of-era-as-amds-sanders-steps-aside/

- TechSpot. (2015, January 24). AMD: The rise and fall (page 3). Retrieved from https://www.techspot.com/article/599-amd-rise-and-fall/page3.html

- La Pedrosa, M. (1988, December 5). End of an era as AMD's Sanders steps aside. Los Angeles Times. Retrieved from https://www.latimes.com/archives/la-xpm-1988-12-05-fi-622-story.html

- Caulfield, B. (2012, February 22). How AMD beat Intel to 64 bits and Intel rebounded. Forbes. Retrieved from https://www.forbes.com/sites/briancaulfield/2012/02/22/how-amd-beat-intel-to-64-bits-and-intel-bounced-back/

Nurturing Behavior:

- Press, G. (2017, September 27). Ultimate entrepreneur: Jim Goodnight, SAS. Forbes. Retrieved from https://www.forbes.com/sites/g

- Press, G. (2017, September 27). Ultimate entrepreneur: Jim Goodnight, SAS. Forbes. Retrieved from https://www.forbes.com/sites/gilpress/2017/09/27/the-ultimate-entrepreneur-jim-goodnight-sas/

- High, P. (2014, May 12). An interview with the godfather of data analytics, SAS's Jim Goodnight. Forbes. Retrieved from https://www.forbes.com/sites/peterhigh/2014/05/12/an-interview-with-the-godfather-of-data-analytics-sass-jim-goodnight/

- Rogers, B. (2016, October 31). Tech titan Jim Goodnight positions SAS for the future. Forbes. Retrieved from https://www.forbes.com/sites/brucerogers/2016/10/31/tech-titan-jim-goodnight-positions-sas-for-the-future/

- Knowledge@Wharton. (2020). SAS Institute CEO Jim Goodnight on building strong companies and a more competitive U.S. workforce [Podcast]. Wharton School of the University of Pennsylvania. Retrieved from https://knowledge.wharton.upenn.edu/podcast/knowledge-at-wharton-podcast/sas-institute-ceo-jim-goodnight-on-building-strong-companies-and-a-more-competitive-u-s-workforce/

- SAS Blogs. (2014, July 21). At SAS, healthy employees, healthy business. Retrieved from https://blogs.sas.com/content/sascom/2014/07/21/at-sas-healthy-employees-healthy-business/

- Brandon, J. (2013, January 15). How SAS became the world's best place to work. Fast Company. Retrieved from https://www.fastcompany.com/3004953/how-sas-became-worlds-best-place-work

- Amabile, T. M. (2005, July). Managing for creativity. Harvard Business Review. Retrieved from https://hbr.org/2005/07/managing-for-creativity

- Mayer, J. D., Salovey, P., & Caruso, D. R. (2004). Emotional intelligence: Theory, findings, and implications. *Psychological Inquiry, 15*(3), 197-215. https://doi.org/10.1207/s15327965pli1503_02

- Dewey, J. (1909). *Moral principles in education.* Project Gutenberg. https://www.gutenberg.org/files/25172/25172-h/25172-h.htm

- Thorndike, E. L. (1920). Intelligence and Its Use. Harper's Magazine, 140, 227-235.

The Antithesis of Nurturing Behavior:

- Chiang, F. F. T., Liao, S., & Liang, T. (2020). Authoritarian leadership styles and performance: A systematic literature review and research agenda. Management Review Quarterly. Retrieved from Springer

Program on Negotiation at Harvard Law School. (2024). How an Authoritarian Leadership Style Blocks Effective Negotiation. Retrieved from Harvard Law School

Farh, J.-L., & Cheng, B.-S. (2000). A Cultural Analysis of Paternalistic Leadership in Chinese Organizations. Management and Organizations in the Chinese Context. Retrieved from SpringerOpen

Sipe, S. R., & Frick, D. E. (2009). The Seven Pillars of Servant Leadership. *Paulist Press.*

Edmondson, A. C. (1999). Psychological Safety and Learning Behavior in Work Teams. *Administrative Science Quarterly, 44*(2), 350-383.

Guidelines:

The SAS Institute and Jim Goodnight:

Included in Nurturing Behavior above.

Shared Values:

- Agile For All. (n.d.). Viktor Frankl's meaning triangle for organizations. Retrieved from https://agileforall.com/viktor-frankls-meaning-triangle-for-organizations/

- Culture Works HR. (n.d.). How aligning personal and company values leads to success. Retrieved from https://www.cultureworkshr.com/how-aligning-personal-and-company-values-leads-to-success/

- Culture Works HR. (n.d.). Why your company's core values are essential to success. Retrieved from https://www.cultureworkshr.com/why-your-companys-core-values-are-essential-to-success/

- Oxford Academic. (n.d.). [Chapter abstract]. Retrieved from https://academic.oup.com/edited-volume/36330/chapter-abstract/318713094?redirectedFrom=fulltext&login=false

Example Ford:

- Edmondson, A. C., & Jung, O. (2021). *The Turnaround at Ford Motor Company.* Harvard Business School Case 621-101.

- McKinsey & Company. (2024). Leading in the 21st century: An interview with Ford's Alan Mulally. Retrieved from McKinsey.

- Korn Ferry. (2024). Alan Mulally: The Man Who Saved Ford. Retrieved from Korn Ferry.

KONE Corporation:

- KONE Corporation. (n.d.). KONE culture playbook [PDF document]. Retrieved from https://www.kone.com/en/Images/KONE-Culture-Playbook_tcm17-113452.pdf

- KONE Corporation. (n.d.). Culture. Retrieved from https://www.kone.com/en/company/culture/

- Center for Creative Leadership. (n.d.). Strategic success: Real results by transforming the leadership culture. Retrieved from https://www.ccl.org/client-successes/case-studies/strategic-success-real-results-by-transforming-the-leadership-culture/

- Center for Creative Leadership. (n.d.). Toward interdependent leadership culture: A transformation case study of KONE Americas. Retrieved from https://cclinnovation.org/toward-interdependent-leadership-culture-a-transformation-case-study-of-kone-americas/

- Center for Creative Leadership. (2020). KONE Americas transformation story [PDF document]. Retrieved from https://cclinnovation.org/wp-content/uploads/2020/03/kone-americas-transformation-story.pdf

- KONE Corporation. (n.d.). History. Retrieved from https://www.kone.com/en/company/history/

Benevolence – Consequence:

- Likert, R. (1967). The Human Organization: Its Management and Value. McGraw-Hill.

- Greenleaf, R. K. (1977). Servant Leadership: A Journey into the Nature of Legitimate Power and Greatness. Paulist Press.

George Washington:

- Fischer, D. H. (2004). *Washington's crossing.* Oxford University Press.

- Alden, J. R. (1984). Washington's great gamble: The campaign to save the Revolution. *Military Affairs*, 48(4), 168-174. https://doi.org/10.2307/1987500

FIFTH PART

- Schein, E. H. (2010). Organizational culture and leadership (4th ed.). Jossey-Bass.

- Cameron, K. S., & Quinn, R. E. (2011). *Diagnosing and changing organizational culture: Based on the competing values framework* (3rd ed.). Jossey-Bass.

- Heskett, J. L. (2012). *The culture cycle: How to shape the unseen force that transforms performance*. FT Press.

- Lencioni, P. (2012). *Benefit: Why organizational health trumps everything else in business*. Jossey-Bass.

- Duhigg, C. (2012). *The power of habit: Why we do what we do in life and business*. Random House.

- Oxford Economics. (n.d.). Return on culture: Proving the connection between culture and profit. Retrieved from https://www.oxfordeconomics.com/resource/return-on-culture-proving-the-connection-between-culture-and-profit/

- Bluesky, C. L. S. (2016). Culture and conduct: Beyond regulation and compliance. Columbia Law School's Blog on Corporations and the Capital Markets. Retrieved from https://clsbluesky.law.columbia.edu/2016/08/08/culture-and-conduct-beyond-regulation-and-compliance/?noamp=mobile#comments

Conclusion

- Chodyniecka, E., De Smet, A., Dowling, B., & Mugayar-Baldocchi, M. (2022, March 28). Money can't buy your employees' loyalty. McKinsey & Company. Retrieved from https://www.mckinsey.com/capabilities/people-and-organizational-performance/our-insights/the-organization-blog/money-cant-buy-your-employees-loyalty

- Barton, Anne. "The King Disguised: Shakespeare's Henry VI." *Shakespeare Survey*, vol. 30, 1977, pp. 41-50.

- Shakespeare, William. *The Second Part of King Henry the Sixth.* Edited by Andrew S. Cairncross, Methuen, 1962.

- Muir, Kenneth. *Shakespeare's History Plays.* Hutchinson University Library, 1970.

About the Authors

YAVOR ALEKSIEV IS A BUSINESS Development Manager and leads Research and Development initiatives at The Aleksiev Group. A distinguished graduate of the Virginia Military Institute, he earned his Bachelor's degree in International Studies and Political Science with a Quadruple minor in Economics, Leadership Studies, National Security, and History. Yavor was instrumental in securing the first-ever military debate team victory against the U.S. Federal Academies, showcasing both his strategic leadership and thinking.

Focused on tangible outcomes and applied expertise, Yavor pursued specialized training at the Washington International Diplomatic Academy and Harvard Business School Online's Business Negotiation Program during his bachelor's studies. He earned his Master's degree in Behavioral Economics with highest honors from The Chicago School of Professional Psychology in 2024. His thesis focused on enhancing clarity and objectivity in organizational decision-making processes through a step-by-step model facilitating the process.

As creator of the theoretical-practical concept of the Loyalty Quotient to Loyalty®, introduced initially as a diagnostic tool by The Aleksiev Group in 2019, Yavor uniquely merges strategic insight with actionable methodologies, detailed comprehensively in Loyalty by Design. His consulting practice as an apprentice to his father spans diverse industries, including logistics and distribution, B2B, B2C, online sales, manufacturing, defense, cybersecurity and IT, road construction, investment construction and real estate, online casinos, etc., delivering targeted solutions and results on strategic, tactical, and operational levels. Furthermore,

Yavor leads the development of ArtaPava, an advanced web platform offering access to the diagnostic tools provided by The Aleksiev Group.

IVAYLO ALEKSIEV, FOUNDER OF THE Aleksiev Group, possesses more than three decades of extensive management consulting experience. A former Major First Class with combat experience, Ivaylo's military background is complemented by his expertise as a PhD in mental crises in combat scenarios, head of the Center for Psychological Provision for the National Military Academy, and associate professor in Management. His hands-on approach to refining the management consultingpracticess and creating new concepts —including the diagnostic instruments Loyalty Quotient to Loyalty®, the Team Intelligence Model®, Leadership Self-Awareness®, and Feedback Reflection Mastery® —enables teams and leaders to effectively and efficiently manage real-world organizational and personal challenges.

Together, Yavor and Ivaylo Aleksiev offer a distinctive blend of family values, psychological acuity, and strategic insight, empowering leaders to build cultures of reciprocal loyalty characterized by profound trust, sustained dedication and quantifiable results.

www.ingramcontent.com/pod-product-compliance
Lightning Source LLC
Chambersburg PA
CBHW021919190326
41519CB00009B/839